STRIVING
FOR BEAUTY

D1258418

STRIVING
FOR BEAUTY

A Memoir
of the Christensen Brothers'
San Francisco Ballet

Sally Bailey

To order additional copies of this book, contact:
Xlibris Corporation
1-888-795-4274
www.Xlibris.com
Orders@Xlibris.com
17049

CONTENTS

To Snoopy, as he blissfully flaps across his comic strip saying, "To live is to dance. To dance is to live."

Acknowledgments

Because of the help and encouragement from a number of people, this book finally came to fruition. I would like to thank them all. First there is my brother-in-law, Michael Jasperson, who for many years was in the English Department at the U.S. Naval Academy at Annapolis. He read every page of my first draft, which was much longer than this version. At the same time, my old friend—originally from Salt Lake City and now teaching English in San Francisco—Lyn Cosgriff Isbell also offered to read it and help me edit it. We all decided it needed re-writing. At this point, a friend and colleague of my brother-in-law's from the Naval Academy, Molly Tinsley, offered to give me some direction in the re-writing. With her help I produced a second version. Then, as I was looking for a publisher, my old friend Renée Renouf, who was working as an editor for a publisher, offered to read it and came up with many good suggestions. I rewrote it again. And finally, my manuscript sparked enough interest in Lindy Hough, publisher of North Atlantic Books, that she read the whole thing. Though she couldn't afford to take the project on, she encouraged me to go ahead and publish it with Xlibris. And so did my husband and son, who for ten years put up with late dinners. They said I'd better do something with it.

And so, with my thanks to all these people, here is my memoir of the Christensen Brothers' San Francisco Ballet.

The Christensen Brothers

THE THREE CHRISTENSEN BROTHERS—WILLAM, HAROLD AND Lew—danced most of their lives.

Their grandfather, Lars Christensen, a musician in his native Denmark, converted to Mormonism and immigrated to the United States in 1854. Settling in Salt Lake City, Utah, he taught folk and ballroom dancing, music and etiquette, and also sponsored popular public dances. Four of his sons followed in his footsteps.

Lars's fourth son, Peter, stayed with his father's school in Salt Lake City.

The third son, Moses, established academies in Boise, Idaho and Portland, Oregon. He brought the Italian tradition of classical ballet into the family schools. On a visit to New York he saw his first ballet performance and was so impressed that he decided to begin studying with the Italian *maestro*, Stefano Mascagno, who, like the Diaghilev Ballet's *Maestro* Enrico Cecchetti, had been a student of the early ballet master Giovanni Lepri. He convinced his brothers to study with Mascagno, as well.

Frederick, Lars's second son, became a cellist in the Seattle Symphony and also taught ballet and ballroom dancing there.

Christian, the eldest son, established an academy in Brigham City, Utah. He was the father of Willam, Harold and Lew.

Christian's three boys took dance classes in the family schools and all learned to play musical instruments. Willam—known as Bill to his associates—was the oldest, born in 1902. He was out-going and resourceful, and loved performing. He became the showman. Harold was born two years later on Christmas day, 1904. He was reserved, somewhat moody, and studious. He became the teacher. Lew wasn't born until 1909. He was the baby, the fair-haired child, the family's Adonis. He became the artist.

Growing up, the boys helped run the various family businesses, doing whatever was needed; teaching in the schools, playing in the orchestra. Harold disliked doing these things, though. He thought they were "sissy". He called the dancing "fancy dancing". Instead, he earned himself a congressional appointment to the Military Academy at West Point. He went for only one year, though, before leaving.

Years later, after Harold's death, I questioned Bill about this. Bill said Harold had rebelled against the hazing and the discipline, and was homesick. Lew's wife, Gisella, said there was something about a girlfriend in Ogden. In a transcript of an interview (9/22/87) with Debra Sowell, author of **The Christensen Brothers—an American Dance Epic,** Harold mentioned that his girlfriend in Ogden became ill and died. He couldn't continue at West Point because he'd failed English. No one at home made him feel that he could go back and take the course over again, and then continue. His parents, in fact, weren't impressed with the military.

So there was Harold, back home, unhappy with himself, discouraged, and feeling that he had no choice but to go into the family business. He always felt that West Point was the best school in the world—it had been his dream to go there—and that a college education was the best thing to have. In another interview with Debra Sowell (this one on 9/25/87), Harold mentioned that when his second daughter, Stephanie, was a student at U.C. Santa Barbara and wanted to return to ballet—she'd quit in discouragement in her mid-teens and now found herself crying whenever she attended a ballet performance—Harold felt he had to dissuade her. "God, what could I do?" Harold anguished, "I wanted to go to a university and she wanted to study ballet!"

Yet what military training Harold received in that one year at the academy lasted the rest of his life. At the San Francisco Ballet School we all thought of him as "The Commanding Officer". He was tall and stern, always stood straight as a ramrod, and commanded absolute discipline from us all.

Harold first started teaching ballroom dancing in the Seattle school of his Uncle Fred; the school Bill was supposed to be running. Bill, however, preferred performing and was at the time busily putting together a vaudeville act for himself and Lew, who was then barely eighteen. As Harold became more familiar with ballet, he started teaching it, too. Luckily for him, he showed a marked aptitude for it. He began teaching it in the family schools in Ogden and Brigham City, as well, quickly gaining recognition for being one of the finest ballet instructors—teaching "The Mascagno Method"—in the country.

By 1927 Bill was ready to take his vaudeville act on the road. He, Lew, and two girls from the family schools—Mignon Lee and Wiora Stoney—billed themselves as *Le Christ Review: European Dance Novelty*. If they called themselves ballet dancers, no one would come to see them. Their advertisements called them interpretive, expressive dancers. The men wore trousers, shirts and cummerbunds, and the girls wore attractive, brief, flowing costumes. The only obvious ties to classical ballet were the ballet shoes on the men's feet and the toe shoes on the women's—and, of course, their dance technique.

The boys' father, Christian, traveled with them to conduct the orchestra. They started out with one-night stands. Bill drove the car into which they piled themselves and all their gear. Soon they graduated to split week engagements, then full week engagements. They switched to traveling by train with three big trunks; one for the backdrop, one for the hotel, and one for the theater. They went from one show a day to two, then three, then four. They became one of a five-act bill that included big bands, singers, Jack Benny, and Bob Hope. Before long they were picked up by R.K.O. [Radio-Keith-Orpheum], the organization that controlled seventy-five percent of the country's vaudeville houses. Their appeal was their all-dancing format, presented in an unaffected, straightforward manner.

They came under the management of Mascagno, and were billed as *The Mascagno Four; Dancers Extraordinaire*. They trained under him as well, though not exclusively. As they traveled, they took every opportunity to study with such teachers as Laurent Novikoff in Chicago, who had been one of Anna Pavlova's partners, and in New York with both Luigi Albertieri, Ballet Master of the NY Metropolitan Opera whose students included Fred Astaire and Albertina Rasch, and Michel Fokine, Serge Diaghilev's choreographer when Diaghilev's *Ballet Russes* made such a hit in Paris in 1909.

One night, while performing in New England, Mignon Lee—who was by now married to Bill—fainted on stage. Lew picked her up and carried her offstage. She was soon diagnosed as having multiple sclerosis, but she continued to dance because they were already contracted for another big tour. When that tour was over, however, Bill felt they should leave the group because of her health. Since the death of their Uncle Moses, their Aunt Carrie had been running the Portland school by herself. She asked Bill and Mignon to come help her. It was at this time, in 1930, that Harold stopped teaching in order to replace Bill in *The Mascagno Four*.

The Mascagno Four continued touring on the vaudeville

circuit, but by now the effects of the Depression were being felt, as was the competition from radio and sound films. Many huge auditoriums built during vaudeville's heyday stood dark, and many performers switched to careers in film. *The Mascagno Four* thought they'd better switch to something else, too. In 1934, Lew, Harold, and Ruby Asquith—a young dancer who joined them from the family school in Portland—ended up on Broadway in **the Great Waltz.** During this engagement they began taking classes from George Balanchine at his new American Ballet Studio on 59th Street.

Balanchine, who had been choreographer for the *Ballet Russes* at the time of Diaghilev's death, was brought to New York from Europe two years before by Lincoln Kirstein, a wealthy, young Bostonian who loved ballet and dreamt of establishing a ballet school and company in America. Balanchine was now, with Kirstein's help, building the school, as well as a small performing group. Lew, Harold and Ruby wanted to join him, but he had no money to pay them. They couldn't afford to leave **The Great Waltz.**

Soon after this, however, Balanchine obtained a contract from the Metropolitan Opera Company to provide the dances for its operas. Balanchine now had his official American Ballet Company and could offer his dancers six months of steady employment. The year was 1935. Lew, Harold, and Ruby joined right away.

Among the members of Balanchine's group was a young dancer named Gisella Caccialanza. Lew noticed her right away and soon started dating her. Gisella was one of the first dancers to join Balanchine's company. She came to him via Italy, via the great *Maestro* Cecchetti, himself. Though born in San Diego, California, Gisella trained in Italy under Enrico Cecchetti, who was at the time director of the Ballet School of Milan's *Teatro alla Scala.* While there, Gisella became not only one of his prize pupils, but his goddaughter, as well. One time Cecchetti invited her to have tea at his apartment with Diaghilev and Serge Lifar, Diaghilev's last *premier danseur*. The two were passing through Milan and wanted to pay their respects to their old Maestro.

After Gisella returned to America, there being no ballet companies to dance with, she joined the Albertina Rasch Girls—first in New York, then later in Hollywood—and danced in her *corps de ballet*, one of the "live" acts presented between the films in the big movie houses. Gisella was part of the *corps de ballet* when the Radio City Music Hall opened in 1932. She was still there, dancing five shows a day, when Lifar brought his own small dance group to America in 1933. When Lifar heard what she was doing, he had a fit. He told her, "With your background, you can't just dance in the Music Hall. You are a disgrace to your old teacher and to us all. I have a good friend, George Balanchine, who is starting up a ballet company. I'll give you a letter of introduction. You must go to him and audition, say that I, Lifar, sent you. Join his company, and stay there, period."

In April 1937 the American Ballet participated in a Stravinsky Festival at the Metropolitan Opera House. The festival consisted of two gala performances with Igor Stravinsky conducting his ballets, **Le Baiser de la Fée**, **Apollon Musagète**, and **The Card Party**. Gisella danced the lead role of *the bride* in **Baiser**, and Lew danced the title role in **Apollon**, a role Balanchine had originally created for Lifar in 1928 while both were still in Paris with Diaghilev. This role helped establish Lew as the first true American *danseur noble*.

Of Lew's performance in *Apollo*, Lincoln Kirstein wrote in his book, *Thirty Years: Lincoln Kirstein's the New York City Ballet*, "In the thirties, he danced the best **Apollo** both Balanchine and I have ever seen. His luminous clarity in life and on stage, his apparent separation from mundane consideration—indeed his sober naiveté—gave a luster to his performance, which was, in the lost accuracy of the word, 'divine' . . ."

Though Kirstein included Balanchine in this opinion, it

may have been more his than Balanchine's. Interestingly, in Bernard Taper's book, *Balanchine, a Biography,* Taper quotes Balanchine as saying Lifar was the most impressive Apollo of all those who ever danced the role.

After the American Ballet's first Opera Season with the Met, some of the dancers—including Lew, Gisella, Harold and Ruby—formed a small touring group of their own to tide themselves over the Opera's six-month layoff. They called themselves The Ballet Caravan. Lincoln helped them form their new group; Balanchine did not involve himself with it. The dancers built their own *repertoire.* It was at this time that Lew first started to choreograph.

Lew's **Filling Station**, choreographed in 1938, is considered to be the first truly American Ballet; an American story set in an everyday American setting with commonplace American characters. An American composer, Virgil Thompson, wrote the music, and Lincoln Kirstein wrote the *libretto,* using a gas station for his setting. The ballet is about *Mac,* a gas station attendant, and some of the characters he encounters while on duty. Lew danced the role of *Mac* and Harold that of the henpecked *Motorist.*

Shortly before the ballet's premiere, Kirstein published a passionate diatribe against "the enemies of American dance—those people who stubbornly believe that 'true' ballet can only be created by Russians." **Filling Station** was his and Lew's answer to them. It was the first popular hit produced by Ballet Caravan.

Other than Eugene Loring's **Billy the Kid,** also choreographed in 1938—and also, today, considered an American classic—none of the other ballets were popular. Audiences stayed away, and money was always scarce.

This same year, 1938, Balanchine's many disagreements with the Metropolitan Opera management came to a head. They had been arguing from the beginning over what sort of position the ballet should hold in an opera company. Unlike the European opera houses that even presented special "Ballet Evenings", the Met considered the ballet little more than moving scenery. When the Met finally relented and gave the ballet some prominence, as it did in Gluck's **Orpheo ed Eurydice** and in the presentation of the Stravinsky Festival, the management hated what it saw. It let Balanchine and his American Ballet go. Unfortunately, the company could not survive without this contract and had to fold.

Balanchine went off in a rage. This show of emotion was rare for him. He was noted for remaining calm under all provocation. But he felt they, of all people, should have understood his work. They should have known better than to do this. He would never have anything to do with opera again. He preferred to set dances for shows on Broadway, films in Hollywood, even a number for baby elephants with the Ringling Brothers Circus.

Ballet Caravan struggled on by itself for a while, but by 1940 it had only one engagement for the year, an appearance at the New York World's Fair in a piece commissioned by the Ford Motor Company, *A Thousand Times Neigh!*, which depicted the horse being ousted by the automobile. After this, Ballet Caravan also gave up and disbanded.

In 1941 an opportunity arose to make a goodwill tour to South America under the auspices of the U.S. Office for Coordination of Commercial and Cultural Relations between the American Republics. Balanchine, Kirstein, and dancers from both the American Ballet and Ballet Caravan decided to regroup, merge their repertoires, and call themselves the American Ballet Caravan. They took off for South America in May. Lew and Gisella married just before leaving. The Company returned in November. In December the United States declared war on Japan.

That was it for the future plans of the American Ballet Caravan. Lew, who was then thirty-two years old, probably nearing the peak of his performing years, gaining recognition for both his dancing and his choreography, was drafted into the Army. But before he left, he had the opportunity to choreograph one more ballet for the newly formed group, Dance Players. He set his moody circus ballet *Jinx* to the haunting music of Benjamin Britten. It, also, has lasted through the years.

In the meantime, after leaving *The Mascagno Four,* Bill busied himself in Portland with expanding his uncle's school and developing his own Willam F. Christensen Ballet Company. When Serge Oukrainsky invited him to come to San Francisco in 1937 as *premier danseur* for the Opera's Fall Season, he was excited. San Francisco was "big time" compared to Portland. In recent years the San Francisco Opera Ballet had been having spectacular successes. The Opera Company's founder and General Director, Gaetano Merola, seemed—unlike the Met—committed to the idea of having a fine, strong ballet as part of his Opera Company. By now the Opera Ballet had grown to fifty-two dancers; sometimes performing independently of the Opera.

When Bill arrived in San Francisco, however, he discovered that the Opera Ballet's future, rather than being bright, was actually quite uncertain. For some reason Bolm's three-year contract had not been renewed. Serge Oukrainsky, who had been Ballet Master prior to Bolm, was brought back just for this one season. The only dancing spot scheduled for a soloist this fall was in *La Traviata.*

Bill decided, rather than letting this dubious situation get him down, to turn it to his advantage. Merola might still be looking for a new Ballet Master. Bill immediately brought nine of his dancers down from Portland and scheduled an all-dance concert at the Oakland Women's City Club in early September, before the Opera's opening. Bill asked Lew and Harold to come from New York to dance with him on this one program as guest artists. In November, after Opera

Season had ended, Bill—not Oukrainsky—organized a series of out-of-town performances for the Opera Ballet. When the series ended, Merola hired Bill as Director of the San Francisco Opera Ballet.

Bill had big plans right from the start. By March of the next year, his new company was performing with the Sacramento Municipal Orchestra in the state capital's Civic Auditorium. There followed a performance in San Francisco, a summer West Coast tour, then Opera Season and another tour through the Pacific Northwest in late fall.

The following year, 1939, Bill decided to create America's first full-length production of *Coppelia,* a ballet he'd been drawn to ever since seeing Anna Pavlova's condensed version of it. *Coppelia* was premiered during Opera Season and it scored a major success. Bill took it on a second Pacific Northwest tour right after Opera Season. Lew again joined him for this, to dance the role of *Franz.*

Because of the Company's increasing tour schedule, Bill once again needed help running the School, and once again turned to Harold. Not much was going on in New York at the time so Harold agreed and brought Ruby with him. The two believed they were coming out West for just the three months of Bill's tour, but then they stayed on. They decided not to return to New York when the American Ballet Caravan reorganized for the South American tour. They married in August of 1940 and decided to remain with Bill while he concentrated on his next big project, the mounting of Tchaikovsky's complete *Swan Lake.*

Bill had never seen the complete *Swan Lake* before—it also had never been produced in the U.S.—but many of his friends in San Francisco's White Russian community had. Some of them knew it quite well. So Bill went about picking their brains. He premiered his version of the complete *Swan Lake* at the War Memorial Opera House in September of 1940. The Tchaikovsky Centennial Committee, headed by Prince and Princess Vasili Romanoff, sponsored the first performance. This full-length production was also a major artistic success, but, unfortunately, not such a popular one. Some of the ballet audience preferred to wait for the annual visit of the Ballet Russe de Monte Carlo, with its long list of "stars".

Bill took both ballets on successful tours, however, and by 1941 had enough community support to expand the company even further. A preliminary meeting to form a Civic Ballet Association was set for Sunday afternoon, December 7, 1941—the day the U.S. declared war on Japan.

All plans came to an abrupt halt. All arts organizations were put on hold for the duration. Their main concern was how to even survive. Everyone had to cut way back. The Opera could no longer afford to underwrite its Ballet, so they offered the School and Company to Bill and Harold for $900. With that purchase, the name of the organization officially became the San Francisco Ballet, with Willam as Director of the Company and Harold as Director of the School.

Soon afterward, the two asked Gisella to come to San Francisco from New York to sit out the war with them. With Lew in the Army, and the American Ballet Caravan disbanded, she was lonely and having trouble finding a dance job in New York. She could teach for Harold in the School and dance for Bill in the Company.

With the combined efforts of Bill, Harold, Ruby and Gisella, the new organization managed to stay afloat. The School continued to have its supply of students, which gave them an adequate income, but for a while the Company was a reality in Bill's mind, only. First, as with all groups, the men left to go off to war. This discouraged some of the women, who then left, as well. If it hadn't been for Mrs. Julliard McDonald, a civic leader who was determined to keep the Company alive, the group would certainly have gone under. Mrs. McDonald kept at the community until it went ahead and formed the San Francisco Ballet Guild, war or no. The new Guild presented a series of one-hour performances in the Garden Court of the Palace Hotel at 5:30 PM, allowing audiences to return home before the wartime "dim-outs".

Luckily, the Opera still had a season of sorts in the fall and still employed the Ballet. For the Christmas Holiday, Bill put together an original adaptation of Humperdinck's **Hansel and Gretel**, a ballet-pantomime with vocal accompaniment. This was Bill's third full-length work in five years. His dancers were mostly the School's advanced students, the taller girls often taking the roles of the boys.

In spite of the war, by the spring of 1944, Bill's plans for the Company were again ambitious. The largest and most publicized work was Bill's "patriotic tribute to America", **Triumph of Hope**, a four-scene ballet set to music of Cesar Franck. It was written and designed by Jean de Botton, a noted French muralist who had his mural, *America at War,* at San Francisco's Legion of Honor museum. The ballet was timed to coincide with the unveiling of the mural. Bill pulled together sixty dancers and used Ruby in the lead role of *Woman.* Everything about the production was grandiose except its success. It was criticized for being naïve and old-fashioned. A muscular *Atlas* lugged a big globe around on his shoulders, and *Hope* and *Satan* made their entrances and exits on aerial wires.

Bill didn't allow this failure to slow him down any, though. He went right ahead with his summer engagements, the fall Opera Season, then what turned out to be one of his most important undertakings of all—a full-length **Nutcracker** for the Holiday Season.

Though *divertissements* from **The Nutcracker** had been presented as a "Suite", the complete version of this Tchaikovsky classic, like **Swan Lake,** had never before been produced by an American company. The only place Bill could find the complete orchestral score was in the Library of Congress. At this point Bill had a stroke of luck; the Ballet Russe was passing through town with Alexandra Danilova as one of its ballerinas and Balanchine as temporary Ballet

Master. Both of them, as children, had danced in **The Nutcracker** at the Maryinsky Theater in St. Petersburg, Russia. Bill invited them to his apartment after one of their performances, along with his own conductor, Fritz Behrens. They talked through most of that night, going over the entire score, remembering the different parts of the Maryinsky production. They spoke of the Party Scene, the tree that grows, the fight between the *King of the Mice* and the *Nutcracker*, the Snow Scene, *Mother Buffoon* and the children who emerge from under her huge hoop skirt. Every now and then Danilova would remember some of the steps and get up to demonstrate them, but Balanchine would say, "No, no, *Shura*, don't give him the steps. Let him choreograph his own. Let's just give him the idea of what happens." And with their wealth of memories, Bill went to work.

Willam's San Francisco Ballet

1: I Enter the San Francisco Ballet

IN SPITE OF ALL THE WARTIME SHORTAGES, BILL GOT HIS *NUTCRACKER* production on and it was a success. The Opera House was packed every performance, and I was in the audience for one of them; a long-legged, spindly, twelve-year-old who had just recently come to the San Francisco Ballet School. This was the second ballet performance I'd ever seen. My first, in 1942, was when my parents took me to see Alexandra Danilova in *Giselle* with the Ballet Russes de Monte Carlo. I remember both that time and this, preferring the big numbers when lots of people were dancing—I was somewhat bored when only one or two people danced— but I was impressed with Gisella. I thought she was beautiful and she did some hard steps. She danced the *Grand Pas de Deux* with Bill. I felt I sort of knew them both. Though Harold was my regular teacher, I'd also had some classes with Bill, and Gisella taught the class one level above mine. I knew three girls in her class; Nancy Johnson, Janet Sassoon and Jane Bowen were only a year older than I, and were friendly to me in the dressing room. They were *Pages* in the performance and I recognized them on stage.

If at this point I already assumed I would one day be up on stage with them, it's hard to say. I'm not exactly sure when I decided to be a ballet dancer; it wasn't from seeing a certain performance, or a particular dancer. It was more just something I liked to do and kept on doing. As my ballet lessons came into conflict with other activities, and I had to choose between them, I always chose the ballet lessons. I realized I was separating myself from my friends, but I also somehow understood that if I missed a class—let up in any way—I would not be able to dance as well as I knew I could.

I took my first ballet lessons from Merle Marston Garthwaite. She lived in my family's neighborhood in Berkeley, across the bay from San Francisco. She had studied ballet in Europe before marrying and was now starting up a class for girls my age. I was about nine. She asked me if I'd like to join. My mother said "yes", so I began with one class a week.

Until now, I'd been doing what most children in our area did; ride bicycles and horses, play hopscotch and jacks, climb trees, hike in the hills, join the Brownie Scouts. I also played the clarinet in my grammar school orchestra and sang in the Episcopal Sunday school choir. I particularly liked the singing. I remember my older sister, Cheyney, and I each earned a hymnal after learning all the verses to twenty hymns. We had to sing each hymn all the way through by ourselves, standing next to the organist while she played for us in the empty church.

My sister and I sang together a lot, often in two-part harmony. We knew many songs from scouts and school, as well as Sunday school. It kept us from fighting while we did the dishes, and on car trips, too. Our mother and father used to join in on the car trips. It's funny, but for a long time I assumed everyone could sing. It hadn't occurred to me that some people couldn't carry a tune.

I found I especially loved the dancing, though. Before long, I wanted to take a second ballet class a week. That would mean giving up the weekly ice-skating lesson Cheyney and I also took, but that was all right with me. I knew that two lessons a week for each of us—my sister's other lesson was piano, which she took from our Sunday school organist—

was the financial limit for my parents. I remember always needing to be careful with money. We had some, but were always a little short before the end of the month. My mother was good at portioning out our money, which was lucky, because my father wasn't. He loved beautiful things. He instinctively liked the finest of whatever it was that interested him at the time. He liked acquiring it. He never seemed to worry about how it would be paid for. I remember he had a beautiful shotgun with a barrel of satin-smooth wood. He never used it. He no longer liked to hunt. The eyes of the deer bothered him. He got so he didn't even like to hunt duck. But he loved to spend hours oiling and polishing the barrel of that gun.

Around this time my teacher asked if I'd like to demonstrate for one of her other classes. This would give me a third class a week. Then she also offered to give me private lessons in exchange for washing her dishes and ironing. She started me on toe. She was the one who, after two years, sent me to the San Francisco Ballet School. She said I'd reached the point in my training where I needed more than she could offer. She must have phoned the Ballet School and told them what level I was at because I didn't even audition. I just went one day and started taking Harold's Intermediate 2 class.

Luckily, my parents didn't object. I knew it would be an additional expense for them and much more of a hassle. I could no longer walk to my ballet classes. I would have to commute to San Francisco. I was only eleven. But they allowed me to go ahead and do it.

For my parents, Sidney and Bill Bailey, the idea of following an interest in the arts was not foreign. My mother's mother, Elizabeth Wall Cheyney, had been a concert pianist. Though born and raised in Oakland, California, she graduated from the High School of Music in Berlin, Germany. Her graduation exercise was a solo appearance with the symphony orchestra. I remember her telling me she was so nervous that she played faster and faster, until by the end she was going much too fast. She intimated that her nervousness—which she could never quite control—probably limited her career. She played Brahms particularly well. Johannes Brahms was a teacher at the conservatory while she was there. He was elderly by then, and she was young, but he liked the way she interpreted his music. She understood it. He corresponded with her for some time after she left. I remember seeing a packet of letters from him tied up with dark cord in the bottom drawer of her secretary. I don't know whatever happened to those letters.

Interestingly, out of all my family, it was Grammy who was most against my dancing. To her, even though she performed on stage, herself, ladies didn't dance. Women danced on stage for their living after going through the divorce courts. Music was entirely different, however. Music was an Art. Shortly before she died, and after she'd had cataracts removed from her eyes, she came to see me perform at the Opera House. She finally acknowledged that my feeling for dance was much like hers for music.

My father's mother, Ruth Atterbury Bailey—whom Cheyney and I called "Gram Ruthie", to differentiate between my mother's mother, whom we called "Grammy"—on the other hand, was very much in favor of my dancing. She loved the dance. She grew up on a *rancho* in Santa Rosa, California, among the Old Spanish families there. Her father, William Atterbury, received one of the last Mexican land grants before California became a state. To stem the Russians' approach from Fort Ross to the north, General Vallejo was offering land to anyone who would settle. Though of English descent, my grandmother danced in the Spanish fiestas each year. My father remembered seeing her dance. He said she was beautiful.

Gram Ruthie never had the opportunity to study ballet, but she went to every ballet performance that came to the Bay Area. My father remembered her taking him to the Oakland Auditorium as a boy to see Anna Pavlova dance. My mother had sat through many a concert of Grammy's, but never saw a ballet until after she married my father. Gram Ruthie used to give them tickets to the *Ballet Russes* each January for my father's birthday.

My father was particularly pleased when I showed an interest in ballet. I think, secretly, he would love to have been a ballet dancer. He was an engineer and built bridges, instead. He'd been working on the San Francisco/Oakland Bay Bridge until shortly before I was born. This was in the depth of the depression, 1932; construction on the bridge had recently come to a halt. My poor father; I couldn't have come at a worse time for him. He, my mother and my sister were living with Grammy. My grandmother's address is on my birth certificate. My father was mostly doing odd jobs for her friends—painting garage doors, gardening, anything. He liked the gardening. One of my grandmother's friends, Sally Spens Black, had a large estate with gardens in the Berkeley hills. All went smoothly until Aunt Sally felt she should ask Dad to join her for lunch on her terrace. That didn't go over too well with the other gardeners.

At any rate, over and over again throughout my life, I have heard this story about my arrival, always told with much mirth. My father said they might as well laugh. Crying wouldn't do any good. I was in the last batch of babies born in Oakland's old Fabiola Hospital before it was torn down. All the babies in that last batch were boys except me. My parents wanted a boy, too. I was long and skinny, my head was lopsided, and my eyes slanted upward. My father said I also had pointy ears and was covered with peach fuzz. I looked like a little monkey. The nurses used to come into my mother's room in gales of laughter, saying, "Here's your funny baby." They said I already had personality.

When my father brought Cheyney—who had been a beautiful baby—to see me, she tried hard to be brave. She fought back the tears of disappointment and stammered, "I . . . I guess she's cute."

It was my father's turn to name the baby. My mother named my sister after her family's surname, Cheyney. She wanted to name her Sally—she loved the name Sally—but my father exclaimed, "My God, with a name like Sally Bailey, she'll end up in vaudeville." So when my father now said, "Let's call her Sally," my mother thought he was kidding. But he continued, "At this point we could probably use someone in vaudeville, or the circus, or something."

I was named Sally, for Aunt Sally Black, and I always knew, from the time I first arrived, that I delighted my father.

Willam's San Francisco Ballet

2: The Young Technicians

THE WAR WAS OVER IN 1945; THE MEN STARTED COMING HOME. Some of those men used their GI Bill to study ballet—a boon for ballet. The new supply of male dancers was indeed welcome. Lew arrived in San Francisco by the end of the year to pick up Gisella and return to New York, but before leaving, he wanted to get back into some kind of shape. Four years of marching in the infantry had ruined his muscles. He started taking classes, and I remember watching him in one of those classes.

We students were allowed to watch as long as we sat quietly on the floor. I remember sitting as inconspicuously as possible between the studio's one heater and the set of *barres* that ran along that wall. Lew was the first person in line at the *barre* and was standing practically on top of me. He was a large man—large head, large feet, large all over— but perfectly proportioned. To me he looked like a Greek god. I didn't think he looked like either Bill or Harold. Harold was about as tall, but much thinner, and had darker hair. Bill's hair was about the same color, but he was shorter and had a rounder head. He was also starting to go bald. Lew was wearing a navy blue shirt, black tights, black shoes and white socks. But what I remember most were these big feet in black ballet shoes in perfect *fifth position.*

Before leaving San Francisco, Lew occasionally taught some of Gisella's classes. One class he particularly enjoyed teaching was the one I had recently been promoted to; the one that Nancy Johnson, Janet Sassoon and Jane Bowen were in. We were all in our early teens. Lew started choreographing little pieces for us. He called us his Junior Ballet.

One day Lew gave us an *adagio* in class that included a *promenade en arabesque.* I was struggling to keep my balance in *arabesque* while slowly revolving on one leg. Lew began yelling at me, "Get your hip down, Sal. Get your hip down!" Suddenly he strode over to me and struck my hip with such force that I crumpled to the floor.

I don't remember being bothered by this incident. I think I just accepted it as Lew's way of telling me to get my hip down. In fact, I'd completely forgotten about it until Lew reminded me of it years later. He said he never forgot it.

"Sal, I felt awful." He still looked bothered. "I didn't mean to hit you that hard. I was just trying to get your hip down."

Then he continued, "You didn't say a word as you picked yourself up off the floor, but that look on your face. Yeesh! It gave me the creeps. It as much as said, 'O.K. for you, you bastard.' I hadn't seen that kind of look on many faces before, much less that of a thirteen-year-old."

I suspect it was that look as much as the hit that bothered Lew. Though I don't remember making it, the counter-challenge it revealed was always part of our working relationship. He was always challenging me to do things, and I was always challenging his domination. I remember him once fretting, "Sally, why do you always fight me?"

This sparring went on for twenty-two years, but in spite of it all—or maybe because of it—Lew ended up teaching me a great deal and helping me to achieve a great deal. What's more, I ended up agreeing with him entirely on his concept of ballet. His values made absolute sense to me. I knew what he was after, and he knew that I knew. That is probably why we put up with each other for so long.

After Lew and Gisella left for New York, Bill set a piece for us "Junior Ballet" dancers, too. We performed his **Bach Suite** at a recital the following spring at the Marine's Memorial Theater. We were even billed as The Junior Ballet. The older Company girls began calling us "the young technicians", which inferred that, though we could execute difficult dance steps, we weren't necessarily good performers. They didn't like us much; they kept their dressing room separate from ours.

Bill didn't mind that Lew and Gisella wanted to return to New York rather than stay with him. He'd always known they wanted to continue working with Balanchine. He, however, had never wanted to work with him. His idea of what American ballet should be was quite different from Balanchine's. Bill preferred to choreograph within the classical convention—though he felt he added his own American touch—and he liked reproducing the European classics on his American bred and trained dancers. He wanted them to be recognized as being as good as, if not better than, their European counterparts.

Though Bill never said anything against Balanchine, he told this anecdote with great glee to a group gathered in his honor at the new San Francisco Ballet building years later. "My group was touring the West Coast with **Bourgeois Gentilhomme** at the same time Balanchine and his Met dancers (including Lew and Harold) were touring. We ran into each other in Portland. Balanchine suggested we work together; I had the booking for the theater in Portland. I said, 'If you are free, you can super.'"

In the spring of 1946, with the war now over, the San Francisco Civic Ballet Association swung into full gear. It set goals for itself that included using internationally famous choreographers, composers, designers and dancers who would lend stature to the performances and help sell tickets. The Association adopted a three-year plan that could build the group into one of America's leading ballet companies.

By the fall of 1947, the Civic Ballet had its first gala season using international stars. Alicia Markova and Anton Dolin were featured as guest artists in Dolin's staging of *Giselle*. Bill and Jocelyn Vollmar, a promising young soloist who was to be *Myrtha, Queen of the Wilis,* flew to Mexico City to learn the ballet from them, then teach it to us upon their return.

This was my first year in the *corps de ballet*. I had just turned fifteen, but still looked about twelve. I was the last girl in the last row. Bill told me to keep out of sight if someone enforcing the child labor laws should come around. I didn't realize I was supposed to have a work permit until I was already sixteen and no longer needed one.

Adolph Bolm, the San Francisco Opera Ballet's first Director—who now lived in Hollywood—created a new ballet, *Mephisto*, for the Civic Ballet's debut. He used San Francisco dancers in all the principal roles. Many of the rehearsals took place in Hollywood while we were dancing with the Opera in Los Angeles.

Bill's contribution was a lavish "carnival" ballet, *Parranda*, set to Morton Gould's *Latin American Symphonette*. Morton Gould conducted the orchestra for the premiere.

The season was so well received, and the reviews were so enthusiastic, that a four-performance season was planned for the coming February. *SF Chronicle* critic Alfred Frankenstein was the only one to add a rather foreboding paragraph to his review, " . . . It will be interesting to see where we go from here. The Civic Ballet got a magnificent break when Hurok sent no big company on tour this year. If he has one next year, it is by no means unlikely that the Art Commission [who sponsored the Civic Ballet performances this year] will suddenly discover that the local group, to use a favorite Art Commission epithet, is composed of amateurs."

Bill revived his *Coppelia* for the second season with guest stars Tamara Toumanova as *Swanilda*, Michael Panaieff as *Franz* and Simon Semenoff as *Dr. Coppelius.* John Taras came from New York to restage Fokine's *Les Sylphides* for us, and to choreograph a new ballet, *Persephone*, for Jocelyn.

I had by now grown taller and was being used in more ballets. Not all of the *corps* was chosen to be in *Persephone,* but I was. I was thrilled. I began to rehearse long and hard. I only went to school in the mornings. I had both afternoon and evening rehearsals, with my ballet class sandwiched in between. By now, my family had moved from Berkeley to Marin County and I was commuting by bus over the Golden Gate Bridge. I didn't get home until midnight and had to rise at 6:00 AM to get to high school on time. I remember my father coming into my bedroom, pulling my hair in exasperation, trying to wake me up. I would lie there thinking, "If I had just one wish in the world, it would be to stay in bed."

This is when I first experienced a sensation that would become so familiar to me; my body felt so tired and heavy by the time I finally got into bed that I felt as if it would drop through the mattress.

Our second season was also an artistic success, especially for Jocelyn, who was singled out as the Company's rising young ballerina. Financially, however, it was a disaster. The Civic Ballet Association could not meet expenses and had to declare bankruptcy. The organization was dissolved. It was only through the personal generosity of Mrs. McDonald that the dancers got paid.

This failure was a terrible blow to Bill. He'd had such high hopes for his Civic Ballet and now there was nothing. He stayed on in San Francisco, trying to keep the Company going, perhaps because he could think of nothing else to do. There were a few performances scheduled for the summer, and there was still Opera Season in the fall, but that was about it. A number of dancers, including Jocelyn, left to join other groups. Bill's operations were stripped to bare essentials. There was no holiday season this year.

In January of the New Year, 1949, Lew and Gisella returned to San Francisco to help Bill out. They had been working for the past two years with Balanchine and Kirstein in New York, helping to build Ballet Society. [Ballet Society came after American Ballet Caravan and before New York City Ballet.] Lew ended up dancing little. His muscles never did get back into top shape. He functioned as the group's Ballet Master, instead, and contributed some choreography to the repertoire.

Lew didn't seem to mind his dancing years being cut short. He was amazingly philosophical about it. I remember him once sort of shrugging and saying, "I'm more interested in choreography, anyway."

I think his war experience had something to do with it. He never talked about it, but I think it always haunted him. I knew that one of his duties was to pick up the bodies of American soldiers killed on the battlefield. But I didn't learn about another worse duty until after Lew's death; neither did Gisella. Their son, Chris, tried to keep it from her. I read about it in one of Debra Sowell's transcripts from an interview with her on 9/30/87.

Shortly after Lew's death in 1984, while sorting through some of his papers, Gisella and Chris came across a journal Lew had written while in Germany in the liberating forces. In it he described the horror of what he saw when he came upon Buchenwald.

Gisella said, "It was the little camp. I don't think it was Dachau. He went in and found bones and people all over."

They also found a dossier on a man who had been a

prisoner there, which Lew kept. It described the man's days in the camp. Gisella said she could find neither the journal nor the dossier, again. She thinks Chris must have hidden them.

But in 1948, while Lew and Gisella were still in New York with Balanchine, Gisella slipped and tore her Achilles tendon one afternoon during a rehearsal of **Symphony in C**. Balanchine was resetting her variation in the third movement, taking advantage of her exceptional ability to jump. The doctors said she might never walk again, let alone dance. Under the circumstances, they thought it a good time to return to San Francisco. While Gisella's injury was healing, Lew could be of help to Bill.

As soon as Lew returned to San Francisco he picked right up where he'd left off with the Junior Ballet. He separated us from the older company dancers and started training us in a class of our own. I can still see him standing there lecturing us, "Living is too easy in California. The weather makes you soft. You're all lazy. You don't know how to work. You'd be better off if you had it a little tougher."

He began to work us hard. He started choreographing regular ballets for us. One ballet was **Vivaldi Concerto,** set to a piano concerto of Antonio Vivaldi. Nancy Johnson, Janet Sassoon and Jane Bowen were the three girl soloists. Alton Basuino was the one boy. Ten of us were in the *corps*. We premiered it at "Two Evenings at the Ballet", given at Commerce High School in April 1949—our spring season for that year. Two pianos were our accompaniment.

Bill premiered a new work as well, **Danza Brillante,** set to Mendelssohn's *Piano Concerto No. 1*. He used the regular company for this ballet. Celena Cummings danced the lead, backed by four soloist couples and a small *corps*.

Les Sylphides and a restaging of Lew's **Jinx** were also presented during this short season. Dancers from both the junior and senior ballets were used in these. I was used in the *corps* for **Sylphides**, but I wasn't cast in **Jinx**. I understudied everything, though.

During the summer, we had one engagement at Hollywood Bowl. The program was **Les Sylphides, Danza Brillante**, and **Parranda**. Lew was going to be in St. Louis for the summer, choreographing for "summer stock", so Bill was in charge of this performance. Since our spring season, some of the dancers had left the company and there was now a spot open for a soloist girl in **Danza**. Much to the amazement of us all, Bill gave the part to me. I was still sixteen.

I remember that suddenly no one liked me—neither the *senior* group nor the *junior* group. No one wanted to eat with me. This is when I decided to like eating by myself. Maybe I wasn't popular, but I was certainly excited.

Balanchine saw that performance at Hollywood Bowl. He came up to Bill afterwards and asked, "Can she come to New York and study with me?"

Bill answered something like, "Not now. She's too young. She's still in school."

Bill never told me this, but he told my parents.

By fall Lew was listed, along with Bill, as Associate Director of the San Francisco Ballet. He went back east to stage **Jinx** for the New York City Ballet while Bill did Opera Season, but came back in time to help Bill restage **The Nutcracker** for the Holidays. It hadn't been performed since 1944, but starting with this Christmas Season of 1949, it has been presented every year since.

I think the staying power of **The Nutcracker** surprised everyone involved in that first production of Bill's. Gisella once told this delightful anecdote about Russell Hartley, who had designed the costumes for it. [Hartley, who continued to design costumes and sets for the Company for years, also later founded the San Francisco Performing Arts Library and Museum.]

"Russell asked me if I had an old pair of toe shoes I might autograph for him.

"I said, 'Yes, I have some.'

"Then Russell remarked, 'It's too bad it's for *Nutcracker*, though. The ballet will probably never be performed again.'"

The following spring we had a second series of "Evenings at the Ballet"—this year five performances instead of two—given at Commerce High, plus one final gala performance at the Opera House. Bill added his *Swan Lake Act II, Sonata Pathetique*, and *Romeo and Juliet* to our current repertoire. Jocelyn, who had been dancing with Ballet Theatre for a couple of years, rejoined us for this season. I remember I was a Montague servant boy in *Romeo and Juliet* and had to learn to fight with a sword. I also got to be one of the soloists in *Vivaldi Concerto* and a bareback rider in *Jinx*.

While rehearsing the bareback riders' part in *Jinx* one afternoon, my fellow rider, Carolyn George, fell through the floor. Two of the unfinished, wood floorboards in the center of the studio broke and she fell into the hole, up to her shins. We were dancing around in a circle, moving fast. I was right behind her and couldn't stop in time. I fell right on top of her. Luckily she wasn't hurt.

I don't remember any of us being particularly upset by this accident. We just avoided the hole in the middle of the floor for the rest of rehearsal. We put masking tape around it as a reminder. We were all used to bad floors. That's just how they were. Keeping a third eye out for rough spots, cracks, and splinters was second nature to us. The Opera House stage was the worst. Sections of it could be raised, lowered, or pulled apart hydraulically for special effects. Sometimes they weren't drawn back together quite all the way and big cracks remained in between. The corners of each section also had pieces of metal hardware on them. We executed our diagonal turns on that stage, even so. We also darned the satin toes of our *pointe* shoes with crocheting cotton to keep them from ripping apart so quickly.

For this second series of "Evenings at the Ballet", Lew revived **Charades**, a frothy ballet about a debutante's coming out party. He'd originally done this ballet for Ballet Caravan in 1939. Gisella, whose Achilles tendon was healing better than expected, danced her original role of *Trixie,* the younger sister; Harold took on his original role of the father.

Bill also choreographed a new ballet this year; **Nothing Doing Bar,** using Darius Milhaud's *Le Boeuf sur le Toit* for the music. The ballet turned out to be the hit of the season. It was about a speakeasy during prohibition. All the stock characters were there—the bartender, a rich couple slumming, a flapper, Weasel the bookie, a punch-drunk boxer, Shady Sadie with her long cigarette holder— including a shuffling doorman named *Yo-Yo,* who was played in blackface. Poor *Yo-Yo,* though he was based on well-established theater tradition, he caused the company some trouble. A special meeting was held with representatives from the National Association for the Advancement of Colored People (NAACP). They had taken offense at *Yo-Yo.* They said he was racist. They threatened to picket our Opera House performance if he wasn't changed.

He was changed, and *Yo-Yo* has been played whiteface ever since.

CHAPTER ONE

Willam's San Francisco Ballet

3: High School—A Contest of Wills

WITH A BIG SIGH OF RELIEF, AFTER OUR SECOND SEASON OF "Evenings at the Ballet" in 1950, I graduated from Tamalpais Union High School in Mill Valley. Even at commencement time I wasn't sure I was going to get my diploma. My problems with the school principal—which began in my junior year when he discovered exceptions were being made for me because of my ballet—never got better. Though I made up all my work, I did miss a lot of school. He didn't approve of any student getting special treatment.

The first year was fine because I attended school full-time; only my after-school activities were curtailed because I took 5:30 class every afternoon in San Francisco. Even so, I did make the effort to go to the Ross Assemblies—dances held for Marin County's young social set—each month. It was hard. My mother had to drive over to San Francisco with my dress and a thermos of soup. I'd take a quick shower, change my clothes, drink my soup in the car, and barely get there on time. Once I got there, I had a good time, though. I've always liked ballroom dancing and I enjoyed my friends. However, my friends' mothers became increasingly critical of me. Part of each Assembly was "the little dinner party" beforehand. I, of course, could never go. They didn't understand that. They criticized my mother for allowing me to be so headstrong and rude.

My parents were being criticized on my account by others, as well. They were allowing me to put them to great inconvenience. They met my bus at the highway at all hours, which, I agree, must have been a real chore. One of them sometimes left in the middle of a party to pick me up

I remember being at a picnic once when one of my father's friends came over to him and asked, "Bill, you're not going to allow her to continue doing this, are you?"

I remember thinking, "*allow?*" I liked the term "*assist*" better.

My father just looked at him and answered loftily, "She can create. She doesn't have to procreate."

I always adored my father for this.

I felt fortunate to have the parents I did. They never pushed me to dance, but they never tried to stop me, either. They probably would have been glad if I stopped, but felt as long as I was so determined, they might as well help.

My second year of high school, the year I started to dance with the Company, was actually fine, too. Each day I was excused after lunch in order to make rehearsals on time. I took my four required subjects in the morning, then instead of taking Physical Education in the afternoon, I wrote essays comparing ballet technique to swimming or whatever—one essay for each quarter missed—and was given my grade and credits in exchange. I studied on the bus and on the floor during rehearsals. I developed great power of concentration, as well as the ability to sense bus stops and musical cues. I kept my grades up. The arrangement worked well.

But then, during my junior year, the Principal found out what I was doing. At that time, California State Law required every able-bodied child to take Physical Education. To be excused, one needed a written excuse from a doctor. My doctor was willing to write one, stating that five hours of dancing a day was enough exercise for me; I probably shouldn't have more. The Principal didn't agree. He felt that if I could dance five hours a day, I was able-bodied. He would not excuse me.

My psychology teacher tended to agree with him in that I was doing something outside the norm of my peers. That might not be good. However, I felt if I got all my work done and kept my grades up, why should anyone complain?

At any rate, my parents, being upset, went over the principal's head straight to the State Board of Education in Sacramento. All they managed to accomplish was to infuriate the principal.

Now that I was sixteen and no longer required by law to go to school full time, or take PE if I went only half time, I had three choices; attend half time and be shy one unit each semester, quit entirely and try to take an entrance exam to get into college, move to San Francisco and enroll in high school, there.

At that time the schools in San Francisco had a "4/4 Plan" whereby students could work four hours and go to school four hours. Some of the girls who lived in the City were on that plan. Dance classes and rehearsals counted as work. I was out of the district, however, and couldn't transfer unless I moved.

I was tempted to quit entirely and try for college, but fearing I'd never finish college, I decided I'd better just continue half time. Because I maintained good grades, many of the teachers were behind me. I later found out many of them were also warring with the Principal; not an entirely good situation for me. My counselor managed to convince the Principal to accept one course from U.C. Extension for each semester I went half time so that I could graduate with my class.

Some unexpected good things came from all this. The studios were at the time located in an old building across the street and down half a block from the Opera House. Now that I was through school every day at noon and didn't always have rehearsal, I could go Friday afternoons to the Opera House and listen to the Symphony's matinee performances. Because my sister, Cheyney, was now a music major at U.C. Berkeley, she could get ushering tickets through the music department, and got them for me, too. Grammy was particularly pleased that we were both going to concerts. And that is how I became familiar with most of the San Francisco Symphony's repertoire.

Other free afternoons, I went down the street to the Main Library or to the Museum of Modern Art, which was housed in the Veteran's Building next door to the Opera House. I remember the Museum once offered a film series called *Art in Action*. It was on Wednesday evenings. Several of us dancers subscribed to it and went each Wednesday after class.

One other thing I learned to do; whether I had rehearsal in the afternoon or not, I gave myself a good, thorough *barre* first thing upon arriving at the studio. I found that if I didn't do this, my muscles would feel so stiff, logy, and unresponsive by 5:30 that I'd have a bad class. If I took an extra *barre*, I had a better class. Everything was easier. I danced better.

I found this to be true throughout my whole career. This, ultimately, may have been what made the difference for me. I always danced better if I took an extra *barre*, so I always took an extra *barre*. Not all dancers' bodies require this, but my muscles were tightly knit and needed the extra conditioning. The good side of having a tight-knit body was that I didn't tire as easily as dancers with looser, more flexible bodies. Also, I bounced back faster when I did tire.

Things at school went along smoothly enough for a while, but then, in the fall semester of my senior year, I missed two weeks of school because of the Opera's Los Angeles Season. If this absence remained on my record, I would lose five citizenship points; enough to keep me from graduating.

One day I was called into the Principal's office. As I approached it, the Vice-Principal met me outside in the hallway. He warned, "Don't go in there. He wants to expel you."

"But he's sent for me. How can I not go in?"

"Pretend you never got the message. We'll fix your attendance record for you. We'll have you quit school the day you left for Los Angeles and then re-enroll you the day you returned. You won't lose citizenship points that way."

I finished my fourth correspondence course by the end of the school year, did well in my regular classes, avoided the Principal, and graduated in a cap and gown with my class one hot June afternoon. Even as I shook the Principal's hand while he gave me my diploma cover—both of us smiling big, fake smiles—I wasn't sure my diploma was inside. My father swore he saw me lift one corner of the cover to peek inside as I walked off stage. The diploma was there.

Willam's San Francisco Ballet

4: Realities and Changes

WHILE I WAS BUSY GRADUATING FROM HIGH SCHOOL, THE COMPANY launched a comprehensive fundraising and audience-building campaign. Lecture/demonstrations were presented throughout the Bay Area. A branch of the Ballet Guild was formed on the Peninsula. Glowing editorials about the Company were written. Everyone seemed in agreement with Bill; to be a functioning ballet company, it had to function all year. Dancers had to dance if they were to stay in top form. All that was lacking, now, was public support at the box office.

This fundraising and awareness effort couldn't have come at a better time for me. I was now out of high school and needed to be concerned not only with my dancing, but also with earning a living. Perhaps I could do both right here in San Francisco.

In the fall we did Opera Season with Bill while Lew and Gisella once again returned to the New York City Ballet, this time for that company's first European tour. Lew was Ballet Master for the tour, and Gisella just went along for the ride. Though she was back dancing with us, she never tried to dance for Balanchine again.

For the duration of the 1950 Opera Season, I moved into my first apartment; a single bedroom with a bath and kitchen that my two roommates, Carolyn George and Joan

Vickers, and I shared with roomers down the hall. Both Carrie and Joanie were older than I, and had been soloists longer than I, but they didn't mind squeezing me in because I had one important asset—a car. Our apartment was out in the Avenues in the Sunset District, quite some distance from the studio and the Opera House.

For some of the dancers, Opera Season was just a paycheck. For me, it was not only a paycheck, but also a source of education and adventure. Coming from my wholesome background, it was like an intriguing, decadent, melodramatic free-for-all. Rehearsals were certainly different. For one thing, the Opera had no respect for ballet dancers. The only people lower than us were the "supers". They dressed in the basement underneath the stage, alongside the big wheels of machinery that moved the overhead sections of the flooring around, next to where the musicians left their instrument cases. We dressed way up on the fourth floor in a dressing room next to the Music Room, where the chorus practiced. Single practice rooms for the soloists were on the floors below us. We could hear them warming up, or practicing with some conductor.

I always felt the Paris Opera's Nineteenth Century term for their *corps de ballet,* "*Les Petits Rats*", was quite apt for us, too. I felt like a little rat; often underfoot, hanging around for hours, snacking on food, and then suddenly having to scurry into place on stage. We could never understand what was going on because everyone was spouting a foreign language. We might rehearse only ten minutes out of a whole evening's rehearsal, yet we had to be there the whole time in case our scene was repeated. All of us—the stars, chorus, orchestra and ballet—had learned our parts in separate, daytime rehearsals. These evening rehearsals were for pulling the production together.

During all this waiting around, I began to listen to the singers. I got so I recognized the melodies, the operas they came from, and the composers who composed them. I got so I could even recognize some of the singers' voices, and what registers they sang in.

Other times I would sit out past the footlights, on the front edge of the stage and watch the orchestra. I was right above them. It was easy to see how they took their cues from the conductor. I was fascinated by the intensity in everyone's glances as they darted from music to conductor then back again, the amount of communicating going on, the amount of concentration.

Different conductors had different styles of conducting. Some were stern and precise and barked out their instructions. Others were dramatic and seemed to physically pull emotion out of the orchestra. Some almost danced themselves off the podium, while others moved with relative restraint. Whatever their style, there was no question that they ran the show.

Everyone had to "see" the conductor. The prompter in his prompter's box, down in the middle of the footlights, placed a rearview mirror on the stage floor beside him so he could always see the conductor. The chorus, of course, had to see the conductor. They were rude to us if we blocked their view. All those assistant conductors milling around backstage, clutching their musical scores and flashlights, had to see the conductor, too. Sometimes one would be up on a ladder peering through a hole in the scenery, watching the conductor, following the beat with his flashlight, while another conductor watched him, waiting for his cue that he would then pass on to someone else. The wings were always full of assistant conductors. We'd been warned about them. "Don't stand too close; you might find someone's hand on your fanny." Some considered us fair game.

I can remember two incidents when I was considered fair game. The first one was during my first year with the Opera. I was just fifteen. This particular year the Opera, besides going to Los Angeles, also went to Portland and Seattle for a week. We went on the train, overnight. I felt terribly grown up wearing my first suit, hat, stockings and high heels. Even dressed up, I still looked twelve. On the homeward trip, not arriving until midnight, everyone dawdled over dinner. Groups of us were seated at various tables set with crisp white linen, silver service, and fresh flowers. The famous *basso*, Ezio Pinza—one of the stars that year—was seated at the table next to ours. After dinner he came over to our table and joined us, I guess to pass part of a long, boring evening. After much animated talk with us all, he took a pencil from his pocket and started sketching my head on the tablecloth. He looked amused. Different singers and musicians wandered by, watched us for a little, then laughed and passed on. Pinza continued drawing my portrait. Everyone seemed to be enjoying themselves immensely. I wasn't exactly sure why, but I sensed that it was at my expense. I remember being uncomfortable.

The second incident happened several years later, during the tavern scene in **Carmen**. Some of us were gypsies. We danced on tabletops and flirted with the soldiers. One of the lead singers, an officer in this scene, began singing his *aria*. I was standing nearby so he grabbed me—which was within his character—then proceeded to put one of his hands on my breast. This may still have been within his character, but I thought he'd stepped over the line. I didn't like it.

I turned my head away from the audience and hissed, "Take your hand off me."

And he did, right then, without so much as changing expression or missing a note. The following performance I noticed he steered clear of me.

Much of the time our dancing in the Opera consisted of adding movement to group scenes. An automatic response to a sung "Gloria" was a raised right arm. We did lots of street scenes. I became adept at "milling around". We also danced minuets, gavottes, waltzes, tarantellas, flamenco dances,

German polkas, polonaises, fandangos—you name it. In a season, we were generally given several regular ballet scenes to perform, where we took over the stage action, as well. We thought they never gave us enough room. If the chorus had to sing during our dance, they'd crowd us even more—to see the conductor, they'd say. We swore they stuck their feet out on purpose to try and trip us, especially if the audience responded enthusiastically to our dancing, as they did the year we performed *Dance of the Hours* in **La Gioconda**. We stopped the show.

Other times we were little better than moving scenery. We'd be paid five dollars extra per performance if we supered. Some super parts required more response to musical cues than others. We were trained for that. Regular supers weren't. One time we were, literally, moving scenery. We made waves in Wagner's **The Flying Dutchman** in the storm scene near the climax of the opera. With sticks in hand, we crawled under a canvas that was spread out on sawhorses across the stage. The boat was nearby. On musical cue— given by an assistant conductor with flashlight in hand—we poked the canvas with our sticks, making it go up and down. The stage director yelled at us, "Ballet, make waves, make waves." A stagehand rocked the boat. Lights overhead flashed like lightning. The music pounded on. With our combined efforts, we made a wonderful storm.

One season we were short of boys. I think we only had six or seven and most operas called for at least ten. The tallest of us girls were enlisted—by then I'd grown to be five feet eight inches. We did our best to be dashing partners for our girlfriends, but I think we were in hysterics most of the time.

In particular, I remember being a boy in **Boris Godounoff.** I was Carrie's partner in the *Polonaise* in *Marina's Garden.* The girls were supposed to wear little white Russian boots with their ball gowns. The boots were actually boot-shaped canvas covers that went on over a pair of high heels. I don't remember why, but for some reason Carrie wore her canvas covers without the heels inside. Maybe the covers were too tight for her shoes; maybe she thought she'd be too tall for me. In any case, she stuffed the heels of the canvas boots with Kleenex, and then struggled through the whole polonaise on half toe. She needed support, and I tried my best, but I think we both ended up teetering through that court dance, mostly trying to stifle our laughter.

This whole season was odd for me. Not only was I a boy in most of the operas, I also found out that I appealed to lesbians. I was familiar with homosexuals. I'd been growing up with them in ballet. In the Arts there has always been openness about one's sexual preference. It's not what counts. What counts is whether you're good at your art. But I was not so familiar with lesbians. I was unaware of them in ballet, but I was finding them quite prevalent in opera. At any rate, the Opera Company's pianist, who used to play for our daytime rehearsals, had a girlfriend that often accompanied her, to turn her music pages. I would notice the girlfriend watching me during rehearsals in a way that made me self-conscious. The homosexual fellows, who had delighted in coaching us girls on how to look "butch", picked up on this right away and thought it was hilarious. They teased me no end about my "girlfriend".

During one of our many long waits backstage, I was sitting in the hallway in conversation with one of my homosexual friends, both of us in our boys' costumes. The hallways were long and narrow, with many closed dressing room doors along the wall away from the stage. Suddenly my "girlfriend" came out of one of the dressing rooms down at the far end and headed towards us. I then realized my friend and I were the only other people in the hallway.

My friend started laughing. "Here comes your girlfriend, Sally."

I was sure he was going to leave. I remember pleading, "Stick with me, please, stick with me." And he did.

Actually, if he hadn't stayed with me, I'm sure I would have been just fine. Homosexuals and lesbians don't like being rejected any more than anyone else. Since I didn't respond to their overtures, I found they never proceeded with advances.

One day, after this incident, my friend tried to explain to me what it was like to be homosexual. He said, "There you were, Sally, dressed in a man's costume, feeling the way you do. I feel more like you, but I'm stuck in a man's body. I can't just go and take it off."

In the spring of 1951, after New York City Ballet's European Tour, Lew and Gisella returned to San Francisco in time for our scheduled performances at Commerce High. They brought with them a friend, James Graham-Lujan, who was an associate of Kirstein and Balanchine's and who had gone with them on the South American tour. He was not a dancer. He was a writer. For our up-coming season—this year renamed "Ballet Premieres"—he wrote the librettos for Bill's new ballet *Les Maitresses de Lord Byron* and for Lew's new ballet *Le Gourmand*.

Our series at Commerce High was again followed by a Ballet Gala at the Opera House. At the end of the Gala we were called on stage to hear some announcements: An exchange policy with the New York City Ballet was being established—the two companies would be exchanging soloists and repertoire; Bill would be leaving the Company to accept a professorship at the University of Utah in Salt Lake City; Lew would assume full Directorship of the San Francisco Ballet Company; James Graham-Lujan—by now, known to us all as "Néné"—would be Artistic Director; Harold would remain as Director of the School.

CHAPTER TWO

The SFB/NYCB Exchange

1: A Guest Artist Perhaps by Default

FOR THE PAST TWO SUMMERS BILL HAD BEEN GOING TO SALT LAKE City to choreograph for the University of Utah's Summer Festival. Last year he took some of the older Company girls with him as soloists. This summer he was again to choreograph for the Festival, then set up his own new ballet program in the fall. None of the older girls were going with him this year, however. They were staying in San Francisco with Lew. The SF Ballet had gotten a contract with the Summer Civic Light Opera, which gave performances in both Los Angeles and San Francisco. Lew was to choreograph for it. Everyone would be spending the summer commuting back and forth between the two cities; everyone, that is, except me.

For some reason, I was the one chosen to go with Bill as his "guest ballerina" this year. Why, I've never been sure. Maybe it was because no one else wanted to go; I'd been doing solos for two years, but I hadn't yet begun dancing ballerina roles. Whatever the reason, it turned out to be the beginning of something very nice between Salt Lake City and me. For the next nine years I made guest appearances once, twice, and sometimes three times a year—so many appearances that a lot of people assumed I was from there.

During this time I made lifelong friendships. One such friendship was with the Cosgriff family. Enid Cosgriff was Bill's first Ballet Society president. Her husband Walter was

President of Continental Bank. They and their two daughters Lyn and Trix adopted me into their family. I met them the second summer I came to Utah. They had just returned from Washington D.C. where Walter was on business for several years. Enid, as a teenager, had been one of Uncle Pete's students in Salt Lake City. She remembered the "boys" coming to the studio whenever passing through town, and all of them standing around, gawking in awe. I stayed with the Cosgriffs every time I came to Salt Lake City after that.

At the beginning of that summer of 1951, I drove off with Bill and his family across the desert of Nevada to Utah. I'd never seen such strange country before. What I remember most was vast expanses of nothingness with mountain ranges stretched in between; mirages making their ends lift up off the desert floor. The family car was a big yellow Packard. Their son, Lee—who was exactly my age, eighteen—had an old, pale blue, Model T Ford of his own, so there were the two cars to drive. Lee allowed me to drive his Model T some of the time. His younger sister Roxanne wasn't even allowed in it. It was a convertible, with the top down. I remember sitting up high in that car, the sun beating down on both of us, the wind buffeting us as we drove those long, straight stretches of highway through the desert and past the salt flats.

Bill and Mignon had already rented a professor's house for the summer. I was to stay with them. I could help Mignon with the cooking and shopping and have transportation back and forth to rehearsals with Bill. Three or four fellows from the evening classes at the SF Ballet School—who had not gotten contracts for the light opera—also came to Utah as "soloists" for the Summer Festival. Leon Kalimos, who later became Managing Director of the SF Ballet, was one of these fellows. He was at this time taking ballet classes in the evenings, working during the day, and dating one of the older Company girls, Wana Williams, whom he later married. The fellows stayed at one of the fraternity houses near the campus in order to have meals and be within walking distance of Kingsbury Hall, where we rehearsed, and the football stadium, where we performed.

The principal male dancer, Barton Mumaw, was from New York. He was a modern dancer, one of Ted Shawn's protégés. [Ted Shawn was considered the first American male dancer, a modern dancer in the tradition of Isadora Duncan and Ruth St. Denis, whom he married. During the early 1900's the two formed the *Denishawn Dance Group* and toured both in and out of the U.S. for nearly two decades. Shawn later formed the *Shawn's Men's Group*. Barton joined him at this time.] Barton had been in both the Broadway production and the touring company of **Annie Get Your Gun**. I saw him in that show in San Francisco. He danced a spectacular Indian number to the song "I'm An Indian, Too, A Sioux" in just a loincloth and feather headdress. I remembered distinctly. Barton was now nearing the end of his career and I was just beginning mine. He was surprisingly sweet to me. He taught me my first modern dance class. He and I used to alternate teaching daily class—he a modern class, me a ballet class—for the dancers before rehearsals when Bill had meetings.

This year's Summer Festival was the third put on by the University of Utah. The directors for all three were Dr. C. Lowell Lees, head of the University's Theater Department, Maurice Abravanel, conductor for the Utah Symphony, and Bill, who would now be forming a Dance Department for the University. Gail Plummer, Kingsbury Hall's theater manager, was business manager. The format for each Summer Festival was the same; one light opera and one grand opera. This year the choices were **The Merry Widow** and **Tales of Hoffman**. The movie, **Tales of Hoffman**, starring Robert Rounseville as *Hoffman* and ballerina Moira Shearer as the actress *Stella*, was just out. The Festival had managed to contract Rounseville to sing the role of Hoffman; a real *coup* for the Festival. I was to be Stella, in this production a short vision scene in the first act. Other than the leading roles, the cast was made up of local talent, chosen by open audition.

Bill held his dancers' audition the day after we arrived. There were no formal dance groups in Salt Lake City at the time, but there were lots of ballet schools. Students from most of those schools came to take class with Bill that day. After class he chose the dancers he wanted to use. They were not professionals, but by the time he got through with them, they looked polished and put on a darn good show. I always felt this was Bill's special talent; to take nothing and make it look like something. Now, as I write this, I wonder. Was this the reason I'd been chosen to go with Bill? Lew wanted to use me, and I needed polishing.

Bill never let on how he felt about his return to Salt Lake City, whether he looked upon it as coming full circle or as ending up right back where he started. He was cheerful, we started right off working hard, and he seemed to enjoy renewing friendships with his old friends. Being with his family, I was included in many of these reunions. I remember meeting the oldest Christensen brother, Guy— we'd never heard much about him because he was older and had never gotten involved with ballet—and thinking, with some surprise, "Lew looks just like Guy." They were both the same height and build and both had that same "largeness" about them.

One afternoon, on the way home between rehearsals, Bill and I stopped off at the moving/storage warehouse where he and Mignon were temporarily keeping most of their belongings. We had to find some sheets for Mignon. We were both tired from rehearsing all afternoon in the heat, and now had to shove boxes around and search through them. Bill stopped for a moment, then looked directly at me and said, "You know, Sally, they pushed me out"

He never said anything like that, again. In fact, when I

talked to him on his 90th birthday, and reminded him of it, he wouldn't admit to having said it then. He said, "Oh no, what I was discouraged about was the failure of the Civic Ballet. And then, of course, there was Mignon's health." He told me several universities had approached him; the University of California at Berkeley, Stanford University, and the University of Utah. He thought a dance department would be something good to build—he had always been building something. Dance at U.C. Berkeley would be in the PE Department, at Stanford it would be in the Music Department, and at the University of Utah it would be in the Theater Department. The Theater Department was by far the best place to start.

Bill ended up not only establishing a Dance Department for the University of Utah, but also building a ballet company that evolved into Ballet West. But still, when he saw Lew—with the backing of Balanchine and Kirstein—moving his San Francisco Ballet in a direction in which he wouldn't fit, he felt pushed out. At least that is how he felt that one hot afternoon when he was tired and had to rummage through his family's belongings in the warehouse for some linens for Mignon.

I had a wonderful time that summer. No one was mad at me for dancing the solos. In fact, the dancers seemed to like me for it. That was the whole reason I was there. Everyone was so friendly and hospitable. I was included in swimming parties after rehearsals, picnics in the canyon, tours to see the sights of the city. The only thing they kept questioning me about was why, at my age, I wasn't married, or at least engaged.

I remember going to Gail Plummer's house for breakfast one Sunday morning. A creek ran through his garden that watered the most delicious raspberries I have ever tasted. He let me pick a basket-full to take home. It was my job to make the fruit salad for supper each evening. Mignon would buy one of each kind of fruit in the store that day and I would cut up the selection and put it into a bowl. Gail's berries made a wonderful addition. After that Sunday, he'd stop by rehearsal every so often with another basket-full.

Doc Lees—everyone called him "Doc"—and Maurice Abravanel were nice to me, too. Each evening during the run of **The Merry Widow**, Abravanel would give me a big smile from his conductor's podium as I made my entrance down the steep staircase at center stage for the *Grand Waltz*. Abravanel said that with each performance he could see me gain a little more confidence, a little more command.

After the closing show of **Merry Widow**, Doc Lees gave a terrific cast party at his house. Though we all knew we would have to be back on stage the following day for **Hoffman** rehearsals—we had only four days to pull the opera together—this night we felt like celebrating. Salt Lake City, being a Mormon town, was assumed to be alcohol, coffee, tea, and tobacco-free, but some of the best parties I've ever been to have been there. Doc's was one of them. Somewhere around 1:00 AM, after "official" people had gone home, someone brought out a bottle of Irish whiskey. I knew Bourbon from home and had tasted Scotch before, but never Irish whiskey. Those of us remaining thoroughly enjoyed it.

At one point, some of us—we were all dancers—decided it would be fun to go swimming in the Great Salt Lake at sunrise. Barton was in the group, and so was Leon. There was another girl besides me. She had the car. At any rate, we all drove out to the lake and arrived just as the sun was rising. We went swimming in our underwear and had a wonderful time.

On the way home, after stopping for breakfast, I was the first to be dropped off. It suddenly occurred to me that the door to Bill's house would be locked and I didn't have a key. I would not be able to get in without waking someone up—

probably Bill. Barton started laughing at me. I decided I would not go to that door by myself; Barton had to come with me.

"But Sally," he protested, "it will look worse if I come."

But I wasn't going if he wasn't coming with me.

When we got to the door, Bill answered it. He didn't say a word, but he had this funny, quizzical expression on his face. Barton looked sheepish.

Bill's son, Lee, saw me later that day and said, "God, Sally. Are you ever lucky! If that had been me, my dad would have killed me."

Well, in his own way, Bill did kill both Barton and me. The first staging rehearsal of *Tales of Hoffman* was scheduled for 5:00 PM that evening. In that our scene, the "vision" scene, was at the end of the first act, we thought we'd be through early. The staging of it was a little tricky—it was to be performed on a platform behind a scrim—but all seemed to go smoothly.

As expected, we finished Act I quite early. Bill felt that Barton and I should practice the staging of our vision scene once more, however. This meant at the end of rehearsal, who knew at what hour. Barton and I knew what he was doing. The three of us just sat there. The wind started whistling down from the canyon into the stadium. We got colder and colder and more and more tired, but neither of us would complain.

Finally everyone went home—Doc, Abravanel, all the singers, musicians, dancers and stage crew—except one electrician who kept the lights on for us. Then, frozen and exhausted, Barton and I staggered through our vision scene one more time. Bill looked on with amusement and satisfaction.

The SFB/NYCB Exchange

2: The Standard Hour to the Rescue

WHEN I GOT BACK FROM SALT LAKE CITY, THE SAN FRANCISCO Ballet had to move. Our building was to be torn down and replaced by an insurance company. We hated to leave. This location was so perfect. However, we were able to rent space from the Theater Arts Colony, a theater group occupying a one-time church converted into a theater with two floors of studio space. The building was some distance from the Opera House, but at least the neighborhood was better. The upstairs studio, where the congregation originally sat, was where the audience now sat during theater performances. The present stage was where the altar had been. The room was beautiful. It had a high, vaulted, beamed ceiling, high windows that the sun slanted through in the afternoons, wood-paneled walls, and a hardwood floor. The downstairs studio also had a hardwood floor, but it was laid on concrete, which was hard on our muscles. That didn't stop us from holding classes and rehearsals there, though. One plus for the lower studio; it opened out onto a patio and lovely gardens. Two tiny studios, which we seldom used, were tucked around in back. Though all these spaces were shared, everyone seemed to have enough room.

An opportunity arose for us to make a TV pilot film for *The Standard Hour,* a long-time popular radio show featuring classical music, sponsored by Standard Oil (later to become

Chevron). They wanted to expand into TV, a relatively new medium then. KGO was producing the film. If accepted, we would be involved in a twelve-program series. At one program a month, that would mean a source of income for a whole year.

How we managed to make this pilot film around our fall opera season schedule, I don't quite recall, but I do remember camping out in the Richmond Auditorium—across the bay from San Francisco, near Standard Oil's headquarters—for four days of filming.

One of the numbers we filmed was *Waltz of the Flowers* from **The Nutcracker**. I was the soloist and made my entrance weaving in and out of three arches on the set. I did this while the harpist played her series of *arpeggios*. For an added artistic touch, the director wanted the camera to follow me through the harp's strings. This shot turned out to be a challenge for us all. It took all afternoon. The flooring, with patterns painted on it, was of masonite, wrong side up—the rough side—so we wouldn't slip. I'm sure I ran two miles that afternoon, wearing holes in my point shoes before I even went on toe once.

During the making of this pilot film, we all knew that its acceptance would be good for us, but none of us realized just how good. What it actually did was enable Lew to keep a group of dancers together long enough to start building his company.

For this year's **Nutcracker**, Lew decided to rechoreograph parts of it. He kept Bill's *Act I*, but changed the *Snow Scene* and the *Act II Variations*, including the *Grand Pas de Deux*. He cast Nancy Johnson in the role of *Sugar Plum Fairy* and me as *Snow Queen*. There were still plenty of solos to go around, but the older girls were not pleased that the two top spots went to Nancy and me.

At the end of the year, most of the older dancers left,

including my two roommates, Carrie and Joan. They went off to New York. I had actually been thinking of going to New York, too. I had been gaining experience, with some degree of success, and was tempted to try my wings. One thing that held me back, though; I had no definite prospects of a paycheck when I got there. I had no idea when someone would hire me. I hadn't yet learned of Balanchine's interest in me and felt I could starve more easily in New York than in San Francisco. Another thing, Lew was really beginning to work with me; he was starting to choreograph special things for me that highlighted whatever qualities I might have. In the long run, I might gain more by staying in San Francisco. Most of the older dancers did not feel this way. They felt, with Bill now gone and Lew and Néné taking off in a new direction, this was no longer the company for them.

For those of us who stayed in San Francisco, 1952 turned out to be a great year. In January we heard that our pilot film was accepted. We would be making twelve units for the Standard Hour TV series. We were elated. We'd have money coming in all year, plus Lew was convinced that TV would become one of the biggest audience-builders ever.

In February, we also received the first of our exchanges with New York City Ballet. Balanchine gave us **Serenade**. His ballet mistress, Vida Brown, came out from New York for two weeks to teach the ballet to us. Nancy and I shared the lead parts, which were divided among four girls in NYC Ballet's version. I remember looking forward to rehearsal every day. I loved learning that ballet. The steps "moved" so.

Nancy and I both learned the role of *Odette* in Bill's version of **Swan Lake, Act II,** as well. This was certainly my biggest challenge to date. The only *pas de deux* I had danced prior to this was in Lew's **Snow Scene** in **Nutcracker** barely two months before. A *pas de deux* takes much more stamina than a ballet in which you alternate your solos with the ensemble. It's not that the steps are so much harder; it's just that you have to do them one on top of the other without a break. You lose your breath—your oxygen supply and therefore your strength—for the ending, where all your *virtuoso* steps are, and if you flub them, you've lost the whole thing.

If it hadn't been for our ballet master, Aaron Girard, I probably wouldn't have made it through *Swan Lake.* We all complained bitterly to Lew about Aaron, "He makes us do every single exercise at the *barre* sixteen times." That was twice as many times as usual. "He's killing us." But each day for the three months prior to our two Opera House performances, whether we had other rehearsals or not, Aaron took the time to run my partner, Roland Vazquez, and me through the *adagio* and our *variations.*

The French word for rehearsal is *répétition,* and it is indeed repetition that makes the difference. Not only do you build strength through repetition, but you also become so familiar with each musical phrase, each step, each gesture, that you can do with it exactly as you wish. You keep refining and refining until every part feels just right.

To help give our season some glamour, Alexandra Danilova agreed to be our guest star for the opening performance. Danilova's *Swan Queen* was legendary, but she was now nearing retirement and preferred to dance one of the leading parts in *Serenade,* instead.

One week before our opening, I found out I was the one to be dancing *Swan Lake.* Evidently there had been some question right up until the end. In fact, Nancy's name was printed on the program for opening night; mine for the second performance. To assume that Nancy would be dancing the first performance was easy enough. She had always been ahead of me. She was in the class ahead of me when I first came to the SF Ballet School, she was usually cast ahead of me in ballets—exceptions being *Danza Brillante* at Hollywood Bowl and going with Bill to Utah—and she had been Lew's *Sugar Plum Fairy* at Christmas. However, in that it turned out to be me dancing opening night, I was mad. Here I was, doing my first **Swan Lake**, and my name wasn't even on the program.

My anger may actually have helped me; by taking the edge off my nerves. In the long run it didn't even matter. An announcement was made in front of the curtain and I received full credit.

By now, Nancy and I had grown accustomed to being pitted against each other. Harold often did it in class. Competition was supposed to be good for us, to make us work harder. Often Nancy came out ahead, but sometimes I did. Whichever, unlike the stereotype duels between dancers of ballet lore, we tried not to take it out on each other.

Danilova, who practically owned the role of *Swan Queen*, couldn't have been more gracious or kind to me. She sensed exactly how I was feeling about **Swan Lake** and was supportive in so many thoughtful ways. After watching one of my rehearsals, she offered, "Let my secretary sew your shoes for you."

I, of course, declined. Most dancers insist on sewing their own toe shoes. Each one has her own special way of making sure her shoes won't fall off. That is one of the biggest insecurities; *pointe* shoes always feel as if they're going to slip off your heels. I'm sure Danilova understood my refusal, but this was one way she could show me her support.

The night of the performance finally arrived. Russell Hartley had designed and executed a beautiful tutu for me. I knew I looked as good as possible. I also knew I was as well rehearsed as possible, thanks to Aaron. I don't think I was scared-nervous, but I remember being keyed-up. My mother was so nervous she couldn't eat all day. My father was sure I'd fall down. I was mainly worried about running out of breath. I think Lew was worried about the choice he'd made, the chance he was taking. He had no way of knowing whether I'd crack under the responsibility or rise to the challenge.

About 6:30 PM I was by myself on stage, carefully pacing through every movement I would be making, and then staring out at the empty seats. Lew walked out on stage and just stood there watching me for a while. Finally he came over to me and said, "Well, Sally, there isn't a thing I can do to help you now. It's up to you."

Curtain time; the performance began. The opening strains of Tchaikovsky's emotional *Overture* started to swell. I was already standing in the wings in my beautiful costume, waiting for my musical cue. The next thing I knew, I was on stage going through each movement exactly as I had rehearsed it every day for the last three months. The familiarity of it all gave me confidence. The auditorium, however, didn't feel anything like it had during rehearsal. It was now alive. I couldn't see the people sitting in their seats except for the first few rows—the lights were all on me—but I could certainly feel them. I could tell they were responding to me.

Then suddenly it was over. My shoes hadn't slipped off. I hadn't run out of breath. I hadn't fallen down. There were lots of applause, excitement, people clamoring around me, compliments.

I guess I rose to the challenge.

One compliment I still remember came from a director at Theater Arts Colony, Les Abbott. I had been taking drama classes from him. He was always after me about my voice, which was naturally high-pitched and "distinctive", if nothing else. He said it improved greatly when I placed it down in my diaphragm where it belonged. However, it was down there only during drama class. The rest of the time it was up in my throat. He could hear me all day long during ballet rehearsals and it drove him crazy. One day he came to me and said I was at the point with my acting where I should start putting more time into it. But he came backstage that night and said, "Sally, when you can dance like this; forget about your voice."

I don't remember Lew saying anything, but I remember him looking relieved.

Then Néné came up to me and gave me a big hug, saying, "Sally, you were beautiful. You were a success and you have your parents to thank for it. They've given you the right genes." And I sensed the unspoken, "Time will tell how you use them."

I also sensed some changes in attitudes towards me; suddenly the directors expected a lot more of me, the dancers no longer considered me one of their group. Russell, who also designed our costumes for the Standard Hour TV series, plus helped with our makeup, spelled this out for me one day while we were in Richmond filming a unit. He was busy gluing feathers on my face. I was once again a chicken; I'd already been a plucked chicken in Lew's ballet, **Le Gourmand**, where I'd worn a big chicken head and ankle, elbow and tail feathers sewn on beige all-over tights. In this episode we were a *Commedia dell' Arte* troupe of traveling players, putting on a show with the stock characters *Harlequin, Columbine, Pantalone, El Commandante* and—for some reason— a chicken. He said, "Sally, since **Swan Lake**, do you realize you're alone from here on?" Then he continued, "You've left the others behind, and they're not going to consider you one of them anymore."

CHAPTER TWO

The SFB/NYCB Exchange

3: A Fluke Appearance in New York

VIDA BROWN CAME OUT FROM NEW YORK AGAIN THE FOLLOWING spring, this time with three more Balanchine ballets; **Concerto Barocco, A la Francaix** and Balanchine's version of **Swan Lake, Act II**. I learned them all. That was a lot of learning. I don't think I had ever worked so hard before, but I don't think I'd ever been happier, either. I loved dancing Balanchine's ballets. The style came easily to me, and the musical phrasing of his steps made dancing them so satisfying.

The exchange between the two companies was genuinely reciprocal at this time. Lew, who was also Administrative Director of the New York City Ballet, went back east to set **Filling Station** for them while Vida set Balanchine's additional ballets for us. While with us, Vida also rehearsed **Serenade**, to see how the ballet had fared since last year.

I went through my entrances for her, confident of my memory. I'd always been good at remembering ballets. Suddenly she stopped me and asked, "Sally, why are you doing those steps that way?"

I answered, "Why, that's the way I've always done them. That's the way you showed me."

"No, it's not," she retorted, then started to demonstrate, "You pull away from *this* corner, like *this*."

I tried the steps her way and could have sworn I'd never done them like that. But later, when I saw NYC Ballet perform **Serenade**, those steps did indeed go as Vida said. This was a good lesson for me about one's memory. It is possible to remember wrong.

As soon as Lew returned from New York, he began setting his new ballet, **Con Amore**, for us. He chose three Rossini overtures for the music. Néné wrote the libretto; a comedy in *opera buffa* style. James Bodrero, an artist who married our Guild President, Geraldine McDonald, designed the sets and costumes, the ideas for which came from nineteenth century lithographs.

Leon Danielian, a well-known star with the Ballet Russe de Monte Carlo, came to San Francisco as our guest artist this season. He helped us premier **Con Amore**. He was *the Bandit* who broke into an encampment of Amazons in the first scene. I was *the Amazon Captain* who took a fancy to him, but ordered him shot when he didn't respond to my advances. We were just about to shoot him when the scene ended. In the second scene, Nancy was *the Married Lady* who entertained a series of men, none of whom got out the door before the next one arrived. At the end of this scene *the Husband* returned to discover them all. The third scene resolved the first two by introducing *Cupid*, who shot arrows into everyone and mixed everything up. *The Husband* ended up with *the Amazon Captain*, *the Bandit* ended up with *the Wife*, the soldiers turned into sylphs, and everyone lived happily ever after.

Unlike many guest stars, Leon Danielian also worked into several ballets in our repertoire. Besides **Con Amore**, he danced **Don Quixote Pas de Deux** with Nancy, *the Tennis Player* in **A la Francaix** with Harold's wife, Ruby—in that ballet I was *the sylph* who floated in and out of the tennis game— and a new version of the **Pas de Trois** from **Swan Lake, Act I** that Lew set for Leon, Gordon Paxman—a GI Bill student who was now one of our first dancers—and me.

The *adagio* movement of the **Pas de Trois**, which I danced with Gordon, was one of the most difficult things I'd ever been given to do. At this point Lew was giving me technical challenges to execute on stage, movements I was having trouble with. I had to correct my technique or fall flat on my face. He gave me a lot of help, though. He would devise exercises in class that helped me accomplish those movements. He often yelled at me—anything that came into his head—as long as it got the desired result. He was hard on me, but I understood what he was doing.

One evening, after an extra class of his that I'd taken, he felt he'd gone too far. He came up to me and apologized, "Sal, I'm sorry. I said some terrible things to you in class this evening. Please don't take them personally. I was just trying to get the right reaction out of you."

I answered, "I know that, Lew. There's no need to apologize. I can't even remember what you said."

But I could tell he still felt badly. Here, once again, was Lew being bothered by something he'd done that I hardly even noticed.

Leon Kalimos, who was still taking evening classes, was there this particular night. I remember him coming up to me afterwards saying, "Sally, you're as strong as steel; finely spun steel wire. You bend, but you don't break."

This year, 1953, our Spring Season was at the Veterans' Auditorium, a much smaller theater next door to the Opera House, in the same building as the Museum of Modern Art. We performed these new ballets there, plus **Le Gourmand**, a repeat of **Serenade**, and a reworked version of Lew's **Vivaldi Concerto**, now called **Balletino**. This was an ambitious undertaking financially as well as artistically. I'm not sure where all the money came from—I know the Ballet Guild was constantly trying to raise money—but I think that sometimes it came out of the pockets of individuals on the Board.

I remember years later, at a gathering at the new San Francisco Ballet Building, Anna Logan Upton—one of our long-time Directors—telling about the time she got a phone call in the middle of a pre-performance dinner party she was hosting; she had to bring a deposit check to the theater right then or we wouldn't be allowed to perform that evening.

We dancers were paid only by the performance; union minimum, which was about twenty-five dollars a performance. I don't remember if we yet received rehearsal pay. At some point we started getting two week's rehearsal pay prior to a season, which had nothing to do with how long we rehearsed. We rehearsed all the time. For each TV unit we made, we received the goodly amount of $100. This covered all rehearsals, plus the four days of filming required. We made about one unit a month.

One day, after filming a particular unit, I happened to see a copy of the budget sent to Standard Oil. Nancy and I, as soloists, were budgeted for a larger salary, but actually received the same pay as everyone else. I confronted Lew with this.

He gave me what to him was a perfectly logical answer, "But Sal, we needed the money for costumes."

I persisted, "Then why didn't you budget it under costumes? Costumes are on the list."

I never got an entirely satisfactory answer, but I don't believe the money went into anyone's pocket. I think there was just never enough to go around. "Rob Peter to pay Paul"; this practice was used frequently by the Company throughout my dancing career. At any rate, Lew, Néné and Harold decided to shut me up by teasing me. For quite a while after this I was known as "Salary" Bailey.

It must have been around this time that the Guild decided to give Nancy and me a small stipend of eighty dollars a month on the condition that we stay with the company for the year. The agreement was to be renewed each year. It definitely made a difference. We didn't have unemployment in those days, but with the classes Harold gave me to teach, our TV series and scattered performance dates, I could now—just barely—support myself. I was determined not to be dependent upon my family.

Regardless of the company's financial situation, and the smaller auditorium, our Spring Season was a success. All the new ballets were well received, and *Con Amore,* in particular, received rave reviews. The ballet was even written up in *TIME* Magazine. There was some discussion about Lew giving it to the New York City Ballet. There was even a rumor that Nancy and I might go to premiere it, but that seemed mostly like wishful thinking.

In the meantime, as soon as our season was over, Nancy, Leon Danielian, Gordon Paxman and I flew to Salt Lake City to appear in Bill's first Spring Season of the University of Utah's Theater Ballet. We performed at Kingsbury Hall for five nights. Gordon and I danced *Swan Lake*—Bill's version—with his group, and Leon and Nancy danced *Don Quixote Pas de Deux*. The season was successful, and we were treated royally. Nancy and I stayed with the Cosgriffs, Enid put the fellows up at her club, and we were given a car to drive.

One more performance was scheduled for the San Francisco Ballet—in Reno, Nevada—before Danielian had to return to New York. After that, our busy season ended. Gordon and I would be returning to Salt Lake City for the Summer Festival—this year *Naughty Marietta* and *La Traviata*—but right now we had the chance to rest.

At this time my father was building houses in Las Vegas. He wasn't yet sure for how long, so he was living in one of the downtown hotels along the "strip", which was still small. I flew from Reno to Las Vegas to visit him for a few days. He then planned to drive me back to California to my Aunt's house outside of Taft—an oil town near Bakersfield—where my mother would meet us.

One morning in Las Vegas Dad told me to get up early, about 5:30 AM. An atomic bomb was going to be tested out in the desert about seventy-five miles away. We would be able to see it from the roof of the hotel. Up we went onto the roof at sunrise. Suddenly the whole sky flashed bright as the sun, and a moment later we felt the pressure of the explosion push hard against us. I remember my skirt swinging backwards. Then a mushroom-shaped cloud began to form. We just stood there watching it, with awe more than anything else—not fear. At that time no one was aware of radiation danger. It was eerie. Everything was a strange color. After a while, the wind gradually blew the mushroom cloud away from us.

A couple of days later, Dad drove me back to my aunt's house through the Mojave Desert and over the southern Sierra Mountains. The following morning my mother woke me up. Western Union was on the phone. Néné had sent me a telegram.

"Dear Salary, Lew wants you in New York by Monday, May 25. Love, Néné."

Nancy and I were to dance our original roles in **Con Amore** for New York City Ballet's June season. I could hardly believe it. I jumped out of bed, shrieking with joy. Those rumors were more than wishful thinking after all.

I rushed back home and Nancy and I flew to New York that Sunday. I was terribly excited. I had never been farther east than Salt Lake City. I don't think Nancy had, either. Our flight to New York turned out to be unusually rough and bumpy. Because of electrical storms over the Rocky Mountains, we were rerouted south over the desert, with its accompanying heat waves and air pockets. These were the days of prop planes, which couldn't fly high enough to rise above the turbulence. We just had to go through it. Almost everyone on the flight got sick except Nancy and me. The stewardesses looked on us with relief each time they ran up the aisle past our seats. We finally went to sleep out of self-defense. This rough, bumpy flight set the tone for our whole New York visit. Nancy and I not only survived it, we went through it with flying colors—so did Lew.

Even our arrival in New York, being six hours late, caused a problem. Lew was supposed to meet us at our hotel after NYC Ballet's performance that evening. We had arranged to take the limousine from the airport to the terminal in Manhattan, then go straight to our hotel and wait for him there. Now he would be there before us, and we weren't able to let him know.

Nancy and I finally arrived at the Henry Hudson Hotel on West 57th Street around midnight. We were starved by then. Our flight attendants had been too busy tending airsick people to serve us anything to eat, and we hadn't wanted to take the time to eat at the airport in Kansas City. So we checked in and went in search of some food.

We were wandering down West 57th Street when a cab drove by and stopped. Lew and Carrie, my old roommate who had joined New York City Ballet shortly after she arrived in New York, were in it. They had been driving aimlessly around the streets of New York, not knowing where to find us. They had come by the hotel after the performance, but we hadn't checked in. There were no messages. At any rate, we were relieved and happy to see one another and went off to Lew's subleased apartment for a stiff drink and something to eat. We talked late into the night.

It seemed not all the company was delighted we were coming; especially not Balanchine. Lincoln Kirstein and Betty Cage, the company's manager, were for the idea. They thought the novelty of it could help increase sales for an otherwise sluggish June season. Lew had been getting raves for his revival of ***Filling Station,*** and so had Jacques D'Amboise, the young up-and-coming dancer, in Lew's original role of *Mac* the gas station attendant. Another ballet by Lew, with Jacques in a leading role, might generate additional excitement. Nancy and I—Lew's soloists from San Francisco—appearing in our original roles, could add extra interest. And we were cheap. We would dance for a modest sum per performance, a pair of toe shoes and tights, and free classes at the School of American Ballet. I think the two of them overruled Balanchine.

The following day was Monday, the company's free day—they had eight shows in six days each week—so Carrie took Nancy and me on a sightseeing tour of New York City. After a ferry boat trip around Manhattan, we went to the top of the Empire State Building, past Rockefeller Center, the Radio City Music Hall, and Central Park. We ate a cream-cheese-and-walnut sandwich at Chock Full O'Nuts and ice cream at Schraft's. Carrie also showed us the way from our hotel to the School of American Ballet on Broadway and West 59th Street, and to the stage door of the City Center Theater on West 56th. We could walk to both places from our hotel, and Lew's apartment was on the way to the school. Lew nicely offered us the use of his kitchen so that we could cook breakfast each morning and save money. Unlike many theater people, he was an early riser and long gone by the time we arrived.

The next day we began working with the company. We started with 10:00 AM class at the school. It was the Advanced Class, taught alternately by Pierre Vladimirov, Felia Doubrovska, and Muriel Stuart. Company Class was taught before the performance each night on stage in the theater. Most of the company members only took that class, but I noticed that both Maria Tallchief and Tanaquil LeClercq—Balanchine's ballerinas and one the former, and the other the current Mrs. Balanchine—were usually in the morning class as well, and sometimes Melissa Hayden.

Rehearsals were in the afternoon in a windowless practice room in City Center. That first afternoon Lew began with *The Amazons and the Bandit* scene. More people were involved, and it would take longer to learn than *The Husband's Return.* Vida Brown was there to learn the ballet, too. She would be rehearsing us once Lew had everything set. Jacques D'Amboise was there, and what I remember most about him was his wide, ready smile. I think he was still only nineteen and rather like a big, bouncy, lovable puppy. He was open and friendly and fun to work with. Patricia Wilde was there, too—to learn my part. She would be dancing it once I left. Carrie was cast as one of my two lieutenants. Everyone seemed cordial enough and went right to work learning their parts. In general, not just in this instance, any big explosions over casting usually occur when cast lists first go up. Once they're up for a few days, and nothing looks as if it's going to change, dancers accept the decisions and get on with their work. The rehearsal went well.

Nancy and I were given backstage passes to the theater so that we could come and go as we liked, and we were each assigned a place to use in the large dressing room on the second floor. If we were there during performances, we could get passes to go out front and watch. Lew thought this would be a good thing for us to do. Having little money and not much else to do in New York, I think I went to all eight performances each week. Nancy didn't always come. She didn't quite have the tolerance for performances that I had. Often, for dancers, *doing* is great but *watching* is boring. I began to know the repertoire and the different dancers quite well.

Maria Tallchief, often partnered by Andre Eglevsky, usually danced **Swan Lake, Firebird, Scotch Symphony**, the first movement of **Four Temperaments** and *Eurydice* in **Orpheus**; all

Balanchine works. She did not have the typical "Balanchine look"; long, thin arms and legs, long neck and small head. She was shorter, more compact, and not rangy at all, though still slim. And she was gorgeous. Her technique was so clean and perfect. The way she used her feet; I remember hearing they were naturally long and flat, but by the time I saw her dance, she had trained them—painstakingly, I'm sure—to work just like hands. They were so supple and shaped so beautifully, with muscle tone right down to the very ends of her toes.

Tanaquil LeClercq, on the other hand, was the epitome of the "Balanchine look". She was thin and long-stemmed. She was about my height, but I think her legs were a little longer and her waist a little shorter than mine. She was gorgeous, too, but in a different way. She was like a rarefied, exotic creature. This quality was especially apparent in Balanchine's *Metamorphoses*—the "bug" ballet, as the dancers used to call it. She looked like a magical dragonfly. She also had a marvelous, zany sense of humor that was utilized in such ballets as Balanchine's *Bourrée Fantasque* and Jerry Robbins's *Pied Piper*.

Both Maria and Tanny—what everyone called Tanaquil— were nice to Nancy and me, and as far as I could tell, nice to each other, too. The fact that one had recently divorced, and the other recently married, the same man didn't seem to cause tension between them. Again, the stereotype of ballerinas dueling to the death didn't seem to apply. I remember the other dancers joking that Tanny had made a bet with Maria that she would outlive Balanchine as Mrs. Balanchine.

I later read in Moira Shearer's book, *Balletmaster* that Balanchine said all his wives left him; he didn't leave any of them. He also mentioned they all remained loyal to him. He didn't think of himself as being a particularly good husband. Once he said of himself, quoting the Russian poet Mayakovsky, "I am not a man, but a cloud in trousers". He mostly lived his life through his ballets.

Tanny was stricken with polio just three years later while on tour in Denmark. My sister happened to see her dance in Copenhagen the night she became ill, her last performance. Tanny became permanently paralyzed from the waist down. Though Balanchine was devoted to her, and for years did everything in his power to care for her, in the end Tanny lost the bet. They were divorced, and this time Balanchine did the divorcing.

For a slow June season, the company danced a lot of ballets. To have this many ballets in performing condition and perform eight shows a week was almost too much for the dancers. There were injuries and illnesses, with the accompanying cast changes and substitutions.

I remember Carrie telling Vida at supper between shows one evening, "I don't care how much overtime you pay me, I can't do any more ballets." Then Vida's glance rested briefly on Nancy and me sitting there healthy, uninjured, and in condition. She was sorely tempted to use us, but she knew she'd better not. Not only Balanchine, but also half the company would be up in arms.

And that's pretty much how it went. We were around a lot, and everyone was friendly enough, except Balanchine, to whom we still hadn't been introduced. When we ran into him, he just sort of glared. But we were definitely kept on the outside. Poor Carrie was caught in the middle. She and I still felt we were good friends, but now I was also a liability. One evening Carrie came right out and said, "Sally, you can't come with me every night for a snack after the show."

I once again "preferred" to go by myself, unless I was specifically invited.

As our premiere approached, the costumes and sets arrived from San Francisco and it was time for a costume parade in front of Balanchine and Kirstein. Lincoln, in contrast to Balanchine, was always darling to Nancy and me. He gave us a big hug every time he saw us. This time was no exception. He seemed interested in all the costumes and made frequent comments and suggestions to Lew. Balanchine, on the other hand, remained aloof and silent. He looked displeased with everything. He had a way of sniffing and wiggling his nose—rather like a rabbit—when he was displeased. He still didn't speak to us. He thought the costumes were terrible. But this was what we had, and what we were going to use.

The day of our premiere was one of those miserably hot, humid, June days. I think the temperature was something like 98 degrees, with 100 percent humidity. We had tech rehearsal all afternoon. I remember the large doors at the back of the stage being open, hoping to let some movement of air in, but it was as still, hot, and wet outside as it was inside. My toe shoes squished. I was dripping wet. Rehearsal seemed to go on forever.

Jacques was surprisingly cheerful. He did his best to keep both of us in good spirits. I had learned there was more than one reason for his friendliness towards me. He had a crush on Carrie, and at that time Carrie wasn't the least bit interested in him. By being nice to me, he could be a little closer to her.

I guess there was a dinner break. I know Nancy and I were expected to take class on stage with the rest of the company this evening and each evening we were scheduled to dance. I forget who taught. It wasn't Balanchine. We were nervous even though the ballet wasn't technically difficult for either of us. We were both definitely "on the spot". Some of the dancers empathized with us and were touchingly sweet. Little good luck mementos appeared at our dressing places. One said, "Small, but mine own tribute, Bill." That was Bill Inglis, who danced the role of *A Student* in Nancy's scene. Another one said, "Good Luck, John." That was John

Mandia, who was the *Man About Town*, also in Nancy's scene. A bouquet arrived with a card pinned to it that said, "Best wishes from the Ballet Kids." I think Carrie probably organized that one. Another card accompanying some flowers said, "Best of luck for tonight, Tanaquil LeClercq." That was Tanny, Balanchine's wife.

As I put on my makeup, I hummed the tune of Edith Piaf's song, **Chant du Pirate**, to myself over and over again. I loved that song. It somehow caught exactly the right amount of *bravado* needed for my *Amazon Captain*. It helped me get into the mood to swagger down the stairs and onto the stage.

By the end of the ballet, everyone—audience and dancers alike—was having a wonderful time. Everyone was laughing in the right spots, responding exactly as they should. We got enthusiastic curtain calls. We felt high with excitement. But whether or not we were going to get good reviews was another thing.

There was no particular celebration that night. Everyone backstage just did what he or she always did after a show. I remember an older cousin of my mother's, Cousin Cheyney Smith, came on the train from Philadelphia to New York to see me dance. I met him after the performance. He took me to Schraft's for ice cream before catching the train back to Philadelphia. I at least wore a new blouse I had bought.

The first thing Nancy and I did the following morning was rush to the newsstands, half with eagerness and half with trepidation. By the end of the day we had collected reviews from all four papers. They were all good. They all liked us, they all liked Jacques, and they all liked Lew's ballet. They said Nancy and I were assets to the production. They were glad to have the opportunity to see us dance. They commented on our beautiful training and said Lew had another hit on his hands.

The New York Daily News said we were "corking young dancers", adding, "It would be a pleasure to have them move their dancing shoes eastward and stay with us forever."

Lincoln, Betty Cage and many of the dancers seemed genuinely pleased and congratulated us. Balanchine appeared even less pleased than before, and still didn't say anything to us. He now seemed displeased with Lew, too. It began to dawn on me that Balanchine's problem was really with Lew—not us—especially now that Lew had a second success on his hands.

This feeling was reinforced when Jacques asked me to take Adagio Class with him one Saturday. I remember being pleased that he had asked me. We enjoyed working together. We were a good height for each other and we worked easily together. Vladimirov taught the class. Balanchine came to watch. Jacques and I went through each exercise; the slow, controlled movements, the balances, the turns, the lifts. Every time I looked at Balanchine out of the corner of my eye, I saw he was watching us. I pretended I didn't notice, but I don't think he ever took his eyes off us. And he still didn't say a word.

The evening of our last performance came and went, the season ended, and Nancy and I were officially through with the New York City Ballet. I bumped into Balanchine in the elevator before leaving the theater that last night. No one else was in the elevator with us. We still had never spoken. I remember thinking, "This is ridiculous. I have to say something." I was, after all, brought up to be polite. One always thanked one's host before leaving. He had been my host—even if unwillingly.

So I said something like, "Mr. Balanchine, thank you for having me as a guest in your company." He again wiggled his nose and sniffed—and didn't say anything.

The SFB/NYCB Exchange

4: The Exchange Continues—One-Way

AT THE END OF THE SEASON CRITIC JOHN MARTIN WROTE IN *THE New York Times*, "The New York City Ballet should circle the genial brow of Lew Christensen with a laurel, for his two new works are both great fun and unquestionable hits, adding a definite brightness to the season."

Lew wasn't asked to give another ballet to New York City Ballet until 1982, twenty-nine years later, when Balanchine requested his *Four Norwegian Moods* for the Stravinsky Centennial Festival. None of our dancers again danced with Balanchine's company as guests, either, though some of them did join his company. For all those years in between, however, Lew and Balanchine kept up their exchange of ideas, and the San Francisco Ballet continued to receive Balanchine's ballets and occasionally his principal dancers as guests.

Bill returned to San Francisco in the fall for Opera Season while Lew, who still held his position as Administrative Director of the NYC Ballet, remained in New York. For the first time in many years the Opera asked us to present a full-length ballet. Bill choreographed Beethoven's *Creatures of Prometheus*. We were delighted with our new status; the Opera was finally beginning to appreciate us.

Lew returned from New York in time for *Nutcracker* and for the birth of his only son, Chris. Somehow, Lew had never seemed child oriented, nor family oriented either, for that matter. I remember Gisella once saying, "I think the Company means more to Lew than his family." But I think Lew was touchingly pleased with Chris. One day I went to their house to see the baby—he was still in his crib—and Lew told me, "Sal, when your own baby puts his little arms around your neck and hugs you . . . There's nothing like it." Years later, when my own baby toddled over to me for an "uppy", then once settled on my hip, put his little arms around my neck and hugged, I remembered what Lew said.

After *Nutcracker* there was no more work for us until a late Spring Season in May. There were no more TV units to film, no single performances scheduled. How we managed financially I don't remember, except that I had my eighty dollars a month, now lived back home, and Harold gave me the evening adult class to teach all the time. Once our 1954 Spring Season finally came, however, it was a good one. Maria Tallchief and Andre Eglevsky came out from New York to be our guest stars for the season. They danced *Swan Lake* in our production and Balanchine's *Sylvia Pas de Deux.*

Immediately following our season, Eglevsky came with Nancy, Gordon, and me to Salt Lake City to dance in Bill's second Spring Season. Maria didn't come with us for this. She returned directly to New York. Nancy, Gordon and I shared solo roles in *Les Sylphides* with Barbara Barrie, an English dancer on Bill's teaching staff who had at one time danced in Fokine's company and had been coached by him in the *Prelude* from *Les Sylphides*. She came down to San Francisco during our season to teach us our parts. Though Nancy and I had both been in the *corps* of *Les Sylphides* when Bill was still in San Francisco, we were glad to have the chance to learn and perform the solos. Lew would not allow such a

"Romantic Era re-hash" in our current repertoire. Nancy and I also danced with Andre Eglevsky in Balanchine's **Minkus Pas de Trois**, which he and Maria taught us while we were all still in San Francisco.

In the fall, Bill once again returned to San Francisco for Opera Season, but this year Lew stayed on, too. The two of them shared choreographic duties. One of the assignments Lew took on was an 18th Century period-piece ballet that conductor Pierre Monteux put back into Massenet's **Manon**. This ballet interlude was seldom performed, but I guess Monteux wanted it in. It made a nice spot for us. Monteux could well have been partial to the ballet. He conducted for Diaghilev's *Ballets Russes* in the early 1900's and conducted the premiere of Nijinsky's **Le Sacre du Printemp**, when it caused such a scandal in Paris in 1913.

Lew choreographed the *Cours La Reine* scene in proper 18th Century style. However, he used our current ballet technique and threw me another "challenge". I had to hold several long balances. I alternated this role with Nancy, who could hold the balances quite easily. Moving, no matter how fast, was never a problem for me—whether turning, jumping, beating, whatever—but when I had to stop and hold my balance; that was something else. I always worried about the balances.

Another production given this year was **Joan of Arc at the Stake** by Arthur Honegger. I guess it was an opera. There was singing in it, but the main characters spoke, and the ballet carried all the action. Bill did the choreography for this. The Hollywood actress, Dorothy McGuire, took the role of *Joan of Arc*, she was tied to the stake the whole time. The actor, Lee Marvin, played *Friar Dominic*. We dancers mimed the roles of all the other characters. The chorus wore monks' robes and sat on the sidelines.

I was given the role of *Death*. I wore black all-over tights and a voluminous black cape, had my face made up like a skull, and played a violin. I had seen the ballet **Paganini** as a child—on the same program with my first ballet, *Giselle*—and the image of a violinist playing wildly, leading people to their death, had always stuck in my mind. I played my characterization of *Death* the same way, standing on top of a high platform, controlling all the action on stage below me with my violin playing.

This same Opera Season I also became aware of a tall, dark, good-looking young *basso* who hadn't been in the chorus before. His name was John Flynn, a classic "dark Irish" man with round face, round brown eyes that twinkled when he smiled, and dark brown curly hair. He told me he was working his way through graduate school at U.C. Berkeley in biophysics. We saw a lot of each other during the season. For once rehearsals and performances helped rather than hindered a budding relationship. By the time we got to Los Angeles, we were dating regularly. This didn't mean we were sleeping together, however. In those days, girls—even in the performing arts—usually waited for marriage. Whether fellows did or not, we never asked. But I remember one of the older men in the chorus telling John, "You be good to her. She's a nice girl."

When the season ended, John and I decided we should stop seeing each other, just go our separate ways. He had lots of studying to do, and I would be busy with my dancing. We soon discovered, however, that neither of us really wanted to stop seeing the other. We couldn't do much because neither of us had any money, but I had continued going to the Symphony each week—now on Saturday nights—unless we had performances. I usually met my friend and fellow dancer, Patricia Johnston, there. She had been a boy along with me during that weird Opera Season. She was one of the Company beauties; tall, willowy, elegant. She looked like a fashion model. She was married to a clarinetist in the Symphony, Frealon Bibbins, whom everyone called Bud.

Neither of us had to usher these days. All the doormen and head ushers knew us and just let us in. Now they were sweet and let John in, too. So John and I spent much of what turned out to be our courtship meeting on Saturday afternoons after my rehearsal, doing whatever was free in San Francisco until dinnertime, having a cheap dinner in North Beach, then walking into the Opera House and listening to the concert with Pat.

The following spring we had even less work than the spring before. Things in San Francisco were indeed looking bleak. Lew must have been discouraged. I know I was. I was also growing more concerned about my relationship with John. I wasn't sure we were headed toward marriage, but if we were, he might expect me to stop dancing. I knew I wasn't ready for that. If I were ever going to leave San Francisco, this might be the time.

By now I'd learned of Balanchine's early interest in me, and I remembered how he'd watched Jacques and me during that adagio class in New York. I also remembered Nancy, at the time, commenting, "This would be a good time for you to stay in New York, if you're thinking of staying." and me wondering if Lew had put her up to discussing this, then thinking, "How could I do that to Lew? That would be really dirty."

So now I decided to write and ask Balanchine if he could use me in his company. I waited in great anticipation for his answer. Before long, I got a carefully worded reply from Vida—not Balanchine. I don't remember exactly what she said, but I do remember thinking, "She's saying a lot between the lines." The gist of it was that Balanchine probably wouldn't use me if I came.

I have always wondered about this. I was sure he had been interested in me. I knew I had the "look" he wanted. He'd probably wanted me to stay on in New York after dancing with his company. So why wasn't he interested in me, now? One answer could be honor, like not taking another man's wife. I was Lew's dancer. Lew was developing me. He wouldn't touch me unless I left Lew first.

In 1978 Lincoln Kirstein wrote the book, *Thirty Years— the New York City Ballet,* for that company's thirtieth anniversary. In speaking about the Ford Foundation Grant's intention to raise the national level "of practice and performance", he wrote of some inherent problems. " . . . Suppose that an ambitious girl or boy, educated on the Pacific Coast and given good basic training there, joins a local company. How much does the dancer owe to the company which grants him a start or even an early reputation? Is he condemned by loyalty to remain forever where he commenced by circumstance?"

Lincoln then goes on to ask what the feelings of directors of regional companies might be when they find their dancers leaving for the glamour of New York. Then he continues, "As for the New York City Ballet, we can satisfy conscience that we never approach any individual who is under contract to another company, nor do we discuss contracts with dancers who have not already terminated a previous association."

In the end, did I regret not working with Balanchine? I certainly danced many of his ballets. I always loved dancing them. I always felt "right" in them. But for me, maybe working with him indirectly was best. If I clashed with Lew about domination, what would I have done with Balanchine?

Many times during this empty spring of 1955 we had only daily class and no rehearsals. This wasn't enough to keep us in performing condition. Therefore, in order to stay in shape, and also to help keep our spirits up, Nancy, Gordon, Conrad Ludlow—one of our younger talented dancers who had begun to work into top roles—and I decided to practice *pas de deuxs* on our own each afternoon.

The four of us coached one another. The fellows and I helped each other by "doing", by smoothing out each rough spot as we came to it. Nancy, on the other hand, had a particularly good, analytical eye. She could just look at something, pinpoint exactly where it was wrong, and then explain what to do about it. Her body was a natural for *adagio* work. It practically fell into place. Mine didn't. Mine was long and rangy and looked right, but it was tight and resilient rather than loose and supple. The slow movements did not come easily for me. I loved doing them, but I had to work at them.

These daily practices turned out to be a surprisingly good idea. Not only did we stay in shape, we got stronger and better. Before long the four of us were in condition to do a *pas de deux* anytime anyone wanted to pay us, and these one-shot opportunities did come up from time to time, often because of the connection our Character Class teacher, Anatol Joukowsky, had with the White Russian Community. We often danced for their various balls.

The best and most lucrative opportunity, however, came up just for me; a *solo*, not a *pas de deux*. It came out of the blue as a result of the Standard Hour TV series that had aired two years before. I was invited to dance Anna Pavlova's famous solo, **The Dying Swan** on Liberace's TV show. When Liberace thought he might like to use Camille Saint-Saens's *The Swan* for one of his telecasts, a Hollywood agent remembered seeing me in the **White Swan Pas de Deux** on the Standard Hour and recommended me. I did not know **The Dying Swan**. In fact, I hadn't even seen it. I knew about it, of course, because Pavlova's interpretation was legendary, but that was about all. Luckily, a choreographer in Hollywood had been in either Fokine's or Pavlova's company at one time and remembered it. I flew to Los Angeles a couple of days early to learn it from him.

Liberace and his TV show were extremely popular in 1955. His audience was estimated to be around 30,000,000. I did not consider myself one of the 30,000,000. My general impression of Liberace was that he over-dressed, over-smiled, played the piano quite well, and made thousands of women swoon. The first evening I arrived at his studio—he was still filming that day's segment—my driver for the duration said, "Look, there's Lee."

I looked at Liberace, then back at my driver and said something like, "Yeah."

I think he was disappointed. He had expected me to be impressed. But I wasn't—yet.

I was indeed impressed with Liberace before we were through, however. Underneath all that superficial glitter was a hard-working, even-tempered, cooperative, dedicated perfectionist; a true craftsman and artist. I say that after seeing the man work for twelve hours straight. The day we were filming, things were running late. He and I were still filming at 9:00 PM. I hadn't been working the whole time since 9:00 AM, but he had. He was in every scene. I didn't see him once lose his temper, become impatient with any of his crew, or let down on the quality of his playing. That was impressive.

In May of this year Bill invited the whole Company—not just us four "guest artists"—to be in his Spring Festival. This was the Company's first work since **Nutcracker**. Lew choreographed a new short ballet, **Mozartiana**, for this occasion. We inserted it, along with **Con Amore**, into Bill's program. And this year Enid Cosgriff put all of us up—not just me or us soloists—and fed us all, too; and introduced us to "Ballet Society Punch".

After Salt Lake City we had a short Spring Opera House Season, then an appearance at the Ojai Stravinsky Festival where Stravinsky was conducting. Balanchine gave us two more of his ballets; Stravinsky's **Renard (The Fox)** and **Apollo**.

Lew taught his role of *Apollo* to Conrad, and—a stroke of luck—Maria Tallchief happened to be in town with the Ballet Russe de Monte Carlo. She had taken a leave of absence from the NYC Ballet and was currently touring with Ballet Russe. She could teach us *Muses* our parts. Nancy was *Terpsichore*, Muse of Dance; Christine Bering was *Calliope*, Muse of Poetry; and I was *Polyhymnia,* Muse of Mime. While watching Lew during these rehearsals with Maria, we got a glimpse of what he must have looked like as the young *Apollo*.

Soon after this, Conrad and I returned to Salt Lake City for the Summer Festival—another example of being ready for opportunity because of practicing *pas de deuxs*. This year's Festival choices were **South Pacific** and **La Bohème**. Neither production offered much dancing. In order to give the ballet something to do, Bill assembled a suite of dances from Tchaikovsky ballets that could be presented along with **La Bohème**. Our well-rehearsed **Black Swan Pas de Deux** fit in nicely here.

This appearance turned out to be my most demanding ever in Salt Lake City. For one thing, Conrad and I were performing Bill's version of the *adagio*, which had more dancing and less walking around and posing than the original Petipa version. It took more stamina. Being at an altitude of 4,400 feet, after coming from sea level, we were winded, anyway. The surface of the stage had been improved somewhat—pieces of plywood had been taped together and placed over the padded canvas flooring—but it was still pretty makeshift. I worried about executing my thirty-two *fouettés* on it. I also worried about the spotlights following me from the top of the stadium. They were so bright that they blinded me, and made me so dizzy when I turned that I couldn't tell where "up" was. Dancing this *pas de deux* here was not fun. I spent most of my time working and worrying. I don't remember socializing much this trip.

By the time the Summer Festival was over, however, I

had figured out what I was going to do. I would take a leave of absence from the Company for the fall, skip Opera Season—which John was still doing—and go to Europe to study for three months. I would be back in time for *Nutcracker*. Bill and the Utah Ballet were also planning a *Nutcracker* production this year, and they invited Conrad and me to be their *Cavalier* and *Sugar Plum Fairy*. San Francisco's *Nutcracker* would finish two days before Bill's started. It should work out fine.

In the meantime, during my leave, I would have the opportunity to learn how I fit into the larger dance world. Whether Balanchine wanted me or not, I already knew how I compared to his dancers—and how the critics felt about me dancing with them—but I wasn't so sure how I compared with European dancers. In any case, this trip would be a marvelous, broadening experience for me. With the extra dancing engagements, teaching for Harold, Liberace's TV show, and a small educational fund given to me by my grandmother's friend, Aunt Sally, I could just afford it.

Once I saw this trip actually working, I became excited. I began to gather as many names of dance teachers, friends of friends, and contacts as possible. Through the *Oakland Tribune*'s TV columnist, James Abbe—his daughter, Tilly, was beginning to work with the company—I got letters of introduction to cultural attachés in each European capital I was to visit. The family of U.S. Senator William Knowland owned the *Oakland Tribune*; Senator Knowland, himself, wrote those letters for me.

Things started falling into place. I had a good idea of where and from whom I wanted to study, I had lists of things I wanted to see and do, and I had tons of reading material and maps. I made a loose itinerary, got my passport and my small pox vaccination, said good-by to John, and told him I would write.

Then I was off.

CHAPTER THREE

Self-Determination

THERE HAD ALWAYS BEEN THIS FEELING AMONG SAN FRANCISCO dancers that if you left the Company, you wouldn't be welcomed back. I didn't think this applied to me, though, because I wasn't leaving. I was just taking a leave of absence to expand my knowledge. Then I'd be back. I'd already made commitments for after my return. I thought this growth experience of mine would be an asset to us all.

What I didn't realize; the problem wasn't the leaving and coming back, it was the exposure to new ideas while I was away. Lew had been developing me his way, to be his dancer. If I went into the broader world of dance, I could be changed.

Unaware of such a perception at the time, I happily set off in the middle of August, off-season, when tickets were cheapest. I took a tourist ship from New York to London, celebrating my twenty-third birthday on board. The only hotel reservation I made ahead of time was in London, my first stop. After that I found little *pensions* as I went. Sometimes friends recommended places. Sometimes the tourist booth in the train station did. In Edinburgh, even at the height of the Festival, I found a room to rent in someone's home. I traveled third class on the trains, usually at night, to save hotel costs. I bought fruit, cheese and bread from the markets. I spent the money I saved on lessons, theater tickets, and sightseeing.

I found definite advantages to traveling by myself. I could do what I wanted when I wanted. I didn't have to wait around—either for people, or for decisions to be made. I met people in a different way, too. If I had been with a friend, strangers would probably not have approached me. They would have felt they were intruding. But this way, it was easy for them to just come up and start a friendly conversation. I was also at the perfect age for all this. I was old enough to take care of myself, yet young enough to accept help without feeling obligated.

I made friends as I went. I had the names of the teachers I wanted to study with in London, Copenhagen, Vienna, and Paris. I also had friends of family friends to contact in each of these cities, plus all those official letters of introduction.

The teachers were not hard to contact. I was used to doing that. I usually did that as soon as I arrived; I wanted to get my classes lined up before making any other plans. I tried to get in a class each day. This was not so easy in London because I arrived in August, when everyone was on holiday. I hadn't known about this. Many schools and businesses were closed, including the School for the Sadler's Wells Ballet [forerunner of the British Royal Ballet]. The Company, however, was performing at the Royal Opera House in Covent Garden, so I was at least able to see them perform and contact some of their people. Two instructors, Harold Turner and Harjis Plusis, offered to give me private lessons. Harold Turner also allowed me to watch some of Company Class before one of my lessons with him. He was encouraging to me and wanted me to stay and study in London for a while.

As far as calling up people who were strangers to me, however, and saying, "Hi, I'm a friend of so-and-so's. I'm here and I'd love to meet you if you're free."—that was a different matter. I felt uncomfortable. I felt even more uncomfortable going to the U.S. Embassy to deliver my letter of introduction to the Cultural Attaché, then asking, "What can you tell me about ballet in this city? Who are the best teachers? What performances are going on? Who can you introduce me to?"

I had to keep telling myself over and over again, "You haven't come all this way to chicken out." Each time I went to the phone to make a contact, I'd get nervous. I had to sort of give myself a kick from behind, then just go ahead and dial—fast—without thinking. I kept reminding myself the worst thing that could happen would be they'd hang up on me, or say, "No. Sorry I can't help you."

The more I made these contacts, the easier it became, and they did make a difference. Because of contacting the U.S. Embassy in Rome, I was able to observe a class at the *Scuola di Danse* for the Rome Opera. The Embassy in Paris arranged for me to meet Serge Lifar, who was then Director of the Paris Opera Ballet. Lifar met me backstage at the Opera House and allowed me to watch him teach a class to the stars of the company. It was held in a practice studio on an upper floor of the theater that had a "raked" floor, just like the stage. [A "rake" means the floor is slanted at an angle. Stages were built higher at the back, and then slanted down toward the front, originally to give a production perspective.] After class, Lifar took me on a backstage tour of the Opera House. I didn't mention Gisella to him because, at the time, I didn't know of their connection, but he couldn't have been nicer to me.

Each Embassy helped me to the extent it could, even if it was just to get a ticket to some event. In any case, the staff always found someone for me to talk to. Sometimes I was even included in social events. I remember being included in a party given for some Fulbright students in Copenhagen.

In Copenhagen, however, the Embassy was not able to help me professionally. They said it was almost impossible to get inside the Royal Danish Theater. The Danes were extremely reticent about having visitors come inside their theater. But by the time I talked to the Embassy people, I had already gone to the theater and had contacted both Vera Volkova, who was now Director of the Ballet School, and Neils Bjorn Larsen, Ballet Master of the Company. Barbara Barrie, from Salt Lake City, had told me I must try to study with Volkova. She had been Margot Fonteyn's coach in *The Sleeping Beauty* in London.

The Embassy was correct, though. Both Volkova and Larsen were cordial to me, but were not at all interested in having me see Company classes or rehearsals. Mr. Larsen did, however, tell me all about the School and the Company. He gave me a tour of their facilities inside the theater and finally said I could watch some of the stage rehearsals. Volkova then agreed to teach me a few private classes in one of the theater classrooms. The Cultural Attaché was impressed I'd gotten that far.

The following afternoon I met Madame Volkova backstage at the Royal Theater for the first of my private lessons. She was a petite, middle-aged woman with dark, short hair and a pleasant, lively face. She was originally from St. Petersburg, from the Maryinsky Imperial Ballet School, as were so many of ballet's great dancers—as well as Balanchine. Because of poor health, she hadn't had much of a dancing career, but she had become a marvelous teacher.

She showed me to her dressing room, saying, "You may change your clothes here, if you like." It was a private dressing room, much like the other stars' dressing rooms, I imagined. It was about the same size as our stars' dressing rooms at home in the San Francisco Opera House, though much more ornate. There were carpets on the floor, a dressing table, a comfortable chaise lounge, a *chiffonier* in which to hang clothes, and a huge mirror standing in a heavy, carved gold frame.

After changing, I followed Volkova down one of the many hallways to a high-ceilinged studio. Tall, narrow, inset windows lined one wall. *Barres* ran across them and along two of the other three walls. The fourth "front" wall was paneled with mirrors. The floor was of unfinished hardwood. A pianist was waiting to accompany us.

The lesson went well. I think both of us enjoyed it. I wrote in my journal, " . . . *Volkova's work is surprisingly like Lew's."* I remember Volkova being interested in how I did certain exercises, especially to the rear. Under Balanchine's influence, the American technique was taking on a new look. He was utilizing our innate athleticism. Everything was becoming more extreme; bigger, higher, faster, slower. *Arabesques,* in particular, were beginning to have a different look. They were much freer and higher than their European counterparts—"incorrect" by some standards. During *barre work,* Volkova would occasionally stop me mid-exercise and ask, "What exercises do you do for *fondu* . . . for *rond de jambe* . . . for *frappé* . . . for *developpé?"*

Things were now pretty well set for the remainder of my stay in Copenhagen. Each afternoon I was to come to the theater for class.

The following Monday the Company began rehearsals for **Giselle,** with Alicia Markova in the title role of *Giselle* and Erik Bruhn dancing *Albrecht* opposite her. Because Volkova wanted to attend rehearsals, she was unable to work with me. She told me to give myself class each day, anyway, and arranged for the pianist to be there. I had never before— nor have I since, for that matter—given myself a warm-up with my own personal accompanist.

After several days of watching rehearsals, Volkova squeezed in a short class for me. After class, Mr. Larsen dropped by to visit, and then made arrangements for me to watch some children's classes in the School and some Company rehearsals on stage. He also saw that I got tickets to see the three Russians from Moscow's Bolshoi Theater who were making a guest appearance with them in a few days.

The following morning I was in the theater by 9:00 AM to watch the boys' class. I remember a line of small, blond boys standing along one of the *barres*. They were all about ten or eleven years old and dressed in white shirts, black tights, white socks and white shoes. They were executing simple exercises—perfectly. I particularly remember their feet flexing and pointing fully, always in proper position, with their knees pressed hard to the side. I was impressed. They were so cute, so intent on what they were doing, working so hard.

After the boys' class, I prepared for my own lesson, but the Russians were rehearsing, so I spent most of the afternoon waiting in the hall with John, the pianist. It proved not to be a waste, though, because I met Inge Sand, the ballerina I would see the following evening in *Coppelia,* and Erik Bruhn, and my old friend Ray Barra—whom I'd known as Barallobre—from San Francisco. Ray and I had always had fun together. He was one of my "butch" coaches in **Boris Godounoff.** He left the SF Ballet several years before, had been dancing with the Opera in Bremen, Germany, and was now studying in Copenhagen until December.

When I came for class the following day, I found Volkova had asked Ray and Erik to join us. It was fun and stimulating to have their companionship. I think we all, including Volkova, had a good time working together. Volkova stayed after class for a while and worked with me on my arms.

That evening I went to my first of the Royal Danish Ballet performances. Besides *Coppelia* with Inge Sand, I saw Balanchine's *Symphony in "C".* Vida had taught it to them a couple of years before. The dancer I particularly remember in that ballet was Mona Vangsaa. She danced the *Second Movement,* the *adagio* movement, Tanaquil LeClercq's movement, the movement I had always liked best and would be dancing, myself, about six years down the line.

Though I didn't realize it at the time, I think Mona Vangsaa's dancing probably influenced mine more than any other dancer's, and I don't think I even met her. I just remember seeing her dance several ballets, and loving her in every one. I saw her doing things—mostly with her head—that other dancers just didn't do, and I thought it made all the difference.

Later, in reflecting on her performances, I could analyze exactly what it was that she did. It was as simple as keeping eye contact with her partner as often, and for as long, as possible. Also, she followed through—a little delayed—with her head almost every line she made with her arms and hands. I determined to do these things in my dancing, too.

In the years that followed, people would come up to me and say, "Oh, you were so romantic! I just loved it." That's how I felt in watching Mona Vangsaa's performances.

For my next lesson, Volkova also asked one of the young Company girls, Kirsten Simone, to join Erik, Ray and me. Kirsten was about my age, blonde and petite. I think all the female dancers were short compared to me. I was even tall for an American dancer. I got by, as far as partners were concerned, because I was also naturally quite thin and therefore didn't look "bigger" than they did, even when I was taller on point. Kirsten was friendly, spoke good English, and was a good technician. She made a nice addition to our class. The four of us took Volkova's class together several more times before I left.

This same afternoon I was also able to watch the Russians rehearse; two men and a girl. They were soloists from the Bolshoi and spectacular dancers. However, their style seemed to me exaggerated, overdone, melodramatic. It was quite different from what I was used to seeing. The adagios were full of mad lifts—all done by one of the men who was thick, clumpish, muscular and tall. The male variations had huge jumps, many flashy tours and pirouettes—all done by the other man who was also muscular, but more agile, less chunky, and shorter. The girl looked like anything but a dancer— exactly like a Rubens painting, all pink and round—but as soon as she was in motion, she was extremely light on her feet, and had a beautiful, plastique line.

The girl and I shared Volkova's dressing room; one of us changing into, the other out of, our practice clothes. We were probably close in age. She seemed pleasant, if a little shy. I guess I was a little shy, too. I didn't speak Russian and she didn't speak English, but haltingly we tried French—and gestures. The combination worked fine. Soon we were comparing toe shoes, styles and fabrics of practice clothes, and I'm sure—though silently—our body types.

The next evening I saw the three perform the pieces I'd watched them rehearse, selections from popular ballets in their repertoire—*Flames of Paris* and *Fountain of Bakhchisarai* among them. I found out the girl's name was Raissa Struchkova, that the large man was her husband, Alexander Lapauri, and the smaller man, who did most of the virtuoso dancing, was Georgi Farmanyantz. Their performance style was even more florid than in rehearsal. To me it was outlandish.

I saw their second performance, too, and this time they were much more subdued, more like in their rehearsal, and really quite nice. It doesn't take dancers long to sense when they aren't pleasing their audience.

Interestingly, when I saw the Bolshoi Ballet in the United States several years later, all the dancers had trimmed down to about our size, including Struchkova. In fact, she looked downright slight and small. Their style of dancing was no longer particularly overdone, either.

During one of my classes with Volkova, Mr. Larsen came in to watch. The next day the press came to take some photos of Volkova and me together. That night I met one of the critics. Then a paragraph and picture about me appeared in the newspaper.

When the night of Erik Bruhn's opening *Giselle* with

Alicia Markova arrived, I went home with Volkova after class for a drink and met her husband, Mr. Williams, who was an artist—a painter, I think. They were both so warm and friendly. We talked of many things, but I remember in particular that Volkova explained to me why the Danes didn't usually allow visitors in classes or rehearsals. They were unsure of themselves and afraid of showing their weaknesses. They didn't want to leave themselves open to criticism. I had been shown only what they were most proud of. She was glad I was planning to study elsewhere, too.

After our drinks, I went off with Mr. Williams to the theater. He had gotten me a seat along with his. The performance was beautiful. Though Markova couldn't do as much as she used to, her jumps were still extremely light and her characterization was as excellent as ever. Erik was marvelous. He looked perfect for the part—so blond, so noble, and his dancing was flawless—no mannerisms at all.

And then it was time for me to leave Denmark.

My next stop was Vienna. I was charmed by that city. It had an ambiance all its own. I remember waking up the first morning I was there—after sleeping the night between the top and bottom puffs of a real feather bed—to the strains of an organ grinder floating up through my open window from the street below. To me, the tune sounded distinctly oriental. I could hardly wait to start my wanderings. The small *pension* where I was staying was some distance from the center of the city. I was anxious to walk to the *Staatsoper,* the State Opera House, which was inside the *Ringstrasse,* the wide, tree-lined boulevard that surrounded what had once been the old city.

I had a letter of introduction to Gordon Hamilton, the current Ballet Master at the Vienna Staatsoper. He was there, and I did meet him. He recommended that I study with Willi Franzl, who had a studio nearby. Some of the dancers from the Opera also studied with him. I phoned Mr. Franzl right away, but he couldn't understand me, so I just showed up the following day. All ballet terms are French, so once you're in class, you can get by without speaking another common language. I took a class from him each afternoon after that.

I found out from Gordon Hamilton that the Opera House, along with many other buildings, was virtually destroyed by the end of World War II. The Viennese Government, which had just gotten back its sovereignty in May [for ten years after World War II, Vienna was partitioned and occupied by the French, British, Soviet and U.S. Allied Forces], gutted what was left of the Opera House, leaving just the exterior walls standing, and was now completely rebuilding the interior. It was almost finished; just some final touches on the auditorium were needed. Hamilton gave me a tour of the facilities. It was the most beautifully equipped theater I had ever seen. The auditorium, in spite of our having to climb over large rolls of red plush carpeting, was the most elegant I had ever seen. Everything was painted a cream color and trimmed in gold leaf. The carpets and seats were of scarlet plush. The crystal chandeliers were simple in design, yet opulent, and to me just gorgeous.

The Opera House was scheduled to reopen in just three weeks. The whole city was polishing itself up for this grand occasion. The exhilaration of finally getting their independence, the pride taken in rebuilding their city, the excitement in anticipation of the Opera opening—all these things contributed to the euphoric mood of Vienna's citizens, a heady mood that was catching. Everybody loved everybody.

One day I ran into a harpist visiting from San Francisco whom I knew. She played with the Symphony back home. She had some friends in Vienna who kindly included me in their group when she introduced me to them. We had a wonderful time together; dinner parties, nightspots after concerts, excursions. A fellow in our group—a tall, blond

Swiss about my age—made particular friends with me. He took me out dancing. He took me for *Sacher torte* at the Sacher Hotel, Viennese coffee at a coffeehouse, to a fancy cocktail party, to a nightclub where I met his cousin and his cousin's ex-wife. And for my last day, after lunch at his *pension*, he took me for a ride on the huge Ferris wheel in Vienna's famous amusement park, the *Prater*. Strains of a string quartet came floating out over the loud speaker. Then after the Ferris wheel, we went for a ride on the *Lilliputbahn*, a miniature train that wound through the Vienna Woods. Autumn was just coming; the trees were turning a beautiful golden color. He wanted me to return for the opening of the Opera in three weeks. I was sorely tempted.

But, instead, I went on.

My plan was to take the next two weeks off from ballet and travel through Italy. At that time, Italian ballet wasn't doing much, so I hadn't planned to take any lessons, but I wanted to see as much as I could of everything else. I knew I would be out of shape by the time I got to Paris, but it would be worth it. In Paris there were many good teachers to study with. Many of the Russian "greats" had ended up there. I could get back into shape with them before returning home. These two weeks in Italy were for absorbing; before they were over, I was saturated.

I had only two personal contacts to make; one in Rome and one in Milan. Otherwise, I was by myself. I usually never minded being by myself. I didn't really mind now, either, except that I found myself feeling lonely each evening as the sun went down—a feeling I hadn't experienced since I was a child at scout camp. Part of me wanted to return to Vienna.

I arrived first in Venice, a fairy tale sort of place. With its canals, arched bridges and gondolas, its narrow winding streets that were more like walkways, wide *piazzas*, sinking *palazzos,* and the Byzantine splendor of the Doge's Palace, it seemed more like a stage set from Opera Season than a real city. I couldn't imagine everyday life going on here; people getting up to go to ordinary jobs, mothers sending children off to school, doing laundry and housework. I remember one afternoon walking by a theater that seemed unusually small to me. I looked at the posters outside the entrance, read the list of coming attractions, and wondered how any "live" performance could possibly fit in there.

In Rome I was awed by the remnants of the Imperial City. I had never before seen anything so old. These structures were all 2000 years old. In the United States, the oldest buildings were 200 years was old. I spent one whole afternoon wandering among these ancient ruins; Capitoline Hill, the Forum, the Arch of Constantine, and the Coliseum. I remember pausing for a rest in an ancient garden on Palatine Hill, sitting on a bench in the warmth of the afternoon sun, trying to grasp the fact that the ancient history I had studied in school had actually occurred right here on this ground. At the same time I realized I was sensing something familiar. Then it occurred to me—the trees and plants and warm soil—they smelled like California.

I spent most of another day trying to see as much as I could of Vatican City. I arrived at the Galleries just as they opened. There was a piece of classical sculpture—one of Apollo—that I particularly wanted to see. I had seen its photo in my guidebook and it looked so alive. It was on the second floor, which turned out to be huge. There were many rooms, and I didn't know which one contained the statue. I ran from one room to the next searching for it. Everything began to look alike. I must have gone right past Apollo, because I ended up back where I'd started without seeing him. I finally asked a guard where he was, and then found him, at last.

I'm not sure how long I remained in front of that beautiful statue. I just stood there staring up at him, expecting him to move, or talk, or something. I remember thinking "This is Lew—the youthful, noble dancer—the Lew I'd gotten a glimpse of during those *Apollo* rehearsals. This is what he must have looked like when he was dancing *Apollo*."

I also spent time in the Sistine Chapel looking up at Michelangelo's amazing paintings on the ceiling. They seemed almost three-dimensional. I was particularly impressed with Adam; his dark hair, his broad and muscular shoulders, his outstretched finger just barely touching God's as God imparted life to him. By the time I left the chapel, I had a stiff neck.

And by the time I reached *La Scala* in Milan—my last stop in Italy—I was bleary-eyed from so much looking. Though I remember the concert in that lovely theater, and the beautifully dressed and jeweled women in the audience, I was having a hard time remembering what I'd seen where. I was also anxious to get to Paris to start my classes, again, and see my childhood friend, Jackie. Our mothers were best friends and we had grown up together. He was like a brother to me. He was at the time living in Paris and was finding me a place to stay.

Jackie was at the train station to meet me when I arrived. I knew everyone now called him *John,* but I couldn't. I had grown up with him as *Jackie,* I'd always called him *Jackie,* and besides, *John* was my boyfriend back home with whom I wondered if I was still in love. Jackie and I had coffee and croissants at the station, caught up on each other's news, then took my bags to the small hotel near *Place Pigalle* where Jackie was living in an attic room. He'd reserved a room for me on the fourth floor. I later found out that rooms on the first two floors could be rented out by the hour. I didn't even unpack before going off down the street to ballet class from a Mme. Nora in *Salle Wacker,* a building with several floors of studio space.

Jackie lined up teachers, their class schedules, and the locations of their studios for me. He knew quite a bit about the local ballet scene because he had only recently stopped taking lessons, himself. The reason he'd started in the first place was probably my fault. I had seen him the summer before his senior year in college. I had just returned from my first guest appearance in Salt Lake City and, naturally, couldn't talk about anything other than ballet. He told his parents that if I could see that much in it, maybe he should take a look. Nothing they said could change his mind. What's more, he insisted on studying in England with the Sadler's Wells. No place else would do. He studied in London for some time, met a lot of dancers, and eventually came to Paris. He was tall and strong and became a fairly good partner, but had a harder time with the technique. He felt, at best, he would be only a mediocre dancer, so decided to give it up. I also suspect he got tired of dealing with the homosexual contingent. He wasn't attracted to men. He was now studying Chinese at the Sorbonne, unsure of what to do next. I think his family hoped I would convince him to come home.

I took classes from all the teachers Jackie recommended, one a day. Three of them taught in *Salle Wacker.* Mme. Nora, Mme. Rosanne and Mme. Preobrajenska. Olga Preobrajenska had been one of the Maryinsky's great ballerinas in the early 1900's. She was now in her nineties, but still taught every day. I took two classes from her. A man dressed in a suit stood at the front of class to translate from Russian into French. I thought her classes were excellent for line, expression, and a study of the Romantic style; technique was secondary, though. One day her class lasted two-and-a-half hours. A standard class is an hour and a half. She couldn't remember what she'd already given, or what she would give next, but she was amazingly alert about what she was doing at the moment.

I also took several classes from Lubov Egorova, another Maryinsky favorite, whose studio was in a different part of Paris. I had never been so cold in my life. Her studio was heated by one wood burning stove. The pianist wore knitted gloves on her hands while she played.

I was having a wonderful time; I was getting back into shape, plus I had someone to "do" Paris with. And because of all the cooking Jackie and I were doing on an alcohol burner in his room, I was able to save enough money to exchange my boat ticket for a plane ticket, stay an extra week in Paris, and have a last night splurge on the town.

Another thing that happened while I was in Paris; I received a letter from John suggesting that, if we continued to see each other after I returned, we should consider getting married. I didn't say anything about this to Jackie, but I became terribly excited. Now there was no longer any question about what I wanted to do. I wanted to return to San Francisco, dance with Lew, and marry John.

This decision was based on more than just wanting to get married. After taking so many wonderful classes from so many first-rate teachers—all of whom were encouraging to me, I came to the conclusion that I was an American dancer. I looked like one and I thought like one. Though the background of ballet was European, and ballet was still very much alive in Europe, my life and my work should be in America.

Chapter Four

A Rude Awakening

As my plane circled to land in San Francisco, the City looked so good to me. Even after experiencing the grandeur of all those time-honored European capitals, it still compared. I was proud to be a part of it. I was glad to be back. I was anxious to see John and I wanted to start working, again. While I was away, the San Francisco Ballet had moved to new quarters out on 18th Avenue, north of Golden Gate Park. I was eager to see the new facilities. On my first day back I was full of enthusiasm; for seeing everyone, again, for the adventures I had just had, for what lay ahead.

I loved the new building. Our struggling but dedicated Ballet Guild, now under the leadership of our new President, Bettine Bayless, leased an old two-story garage, then completely renovated it. The second floor contained three large studios. The ground floor accommodated the offices, dressing rooms, and a huge storage area where both costumes and equipment could be kept. Until now, they had been stored in various warehouses around town. Many new plans were in the making.

The first thing Lew said to me in class was, "You're fat and out of shape."

I was completely taken aback. I had been so looking forward to seeing him, again, and I thought he would be glad to see me. He wasn't at all. The part about being fat was true enough. I had gained some weight—eight pounds to be exact. All those *baguettes* and cream cheese I had eaten were not only delicious and cheap, they were also fattening. I was the heaviest I'd ever been. However, I was sure I would have the weight off within a month. But I certainly didn't feel I was out of shape. In fact, I'd been anxious to show Lew some of the new things I'd learned.

He wasn't the least bit interested. He would hardly even look at me.

I found my friend, Christine Bering, cast in my role of *Snow Queen* in **The Nutcracker**. I wasn't cast in it at all until way down the line, for one matinee, though this time as *Sugar Plum Fairy*, and with Conrad Ludlow as my *Cavalier*. I might not have been cast in it at all if Conrad and I weren't dancing this for Bill in Salt Lake City. I suppose Lew felt, for Bill's sake if not for mine, that he couldn't send me if I hadn't performed the role at least once.

A new souvenir program was produced for this year, one that told the story of **Nutcracker**. Photos were taken of all the soloists in their various costumes, and the pictures were inserted into the text at the appropriate places. I didn't yet have a costume, let alone a photo of me in it. Néné snuck in a photo of me in my *Black Swan* tutu. Otherwise, I wouldn't have been in the souvenir program at all.

No one other than Lew seemed mad at me. Sweet Mrs. "A"—Eloise Arnold, our wardrobe mistress and grandmother of one of our dancers, Béné Arnold—took the time to make me a *Sugar Plum* tutu of my own so that I wouldn't have to share Nancy's. Sharing costumes was not unusual. A surprising thing about dancers' sizes; though lengths in legs and torsos might differ, the girth is often similar. Costume adjustments are relatively easy to make.

Lew, however, was obviously angry with me and was punishing me for having taken the leave of absence. If he'd known that John and I were planning to marry, as well, he would probably have given up on me entirely. Not only might my priorities change, I might also become pregnant, which would certainly disrupt things. Luckily, we weren't getting married for a while, so there would be time enough to tell Lew later. John wanted the second year of graduate school, with all its tests, out of the way first. He thought we could marry before his orals, however, and his research and dissertation, and on . . . and on . . . He would be so busy that I thought I could safely plan on dancing another seven years or so, at least until I was thirty. I thought he'd be glad I had something other than him to take up my time.

Over the years, I gradually came to understand Lew's feelings, his point of view. He had spent a lot of time and effort training me to dance exactly as he envisioned for his ballets. I was one of the tools of his craft. He used me for the expression of his ideas. Other artists expected to have control over the tools of their chosen mediums, to have them remain the same from one use to the next. Was it wrong of Lew to expect the same? A pianist could expect his piano to stay basically the same. It might get out of tune, but that was about all. A painter could expect his canvas, brush and paints—the picture he was painting—to remain the same. A sculptor certainly expected the stone he was shaping to remain as he left it. A writer had no fear that the words he was writing would go jumble themselves up while he was off doing something else. But the material of a choreographer is different. It can change unless kept tightly under control. I'd been gone only three months, and here I was, looking and dancing quite differently than what Lew had so painstakingly been developing. I probably made him sick. I was no longer of any use to him unless—and until—I once again became what he envisioned. At this point he wasn't convinced I ever would.

I didn't want him to give up on me. I knew I could still dance as he wished. In fact, during my trip, that is what I decided I wanted to do most. Though I gained some ideas of my own, the ones concerning ballet still meshed exactly with his. I felt he could probably develop me more fully than anyone else and I wanted him to keep on doing so. I liked being one of his tools.

There is one glaring flaw with this idea of being someone's tool. The flaw isn't present in other art forms. The fact that the tool is completely willing doesn't matter. In dance, the tool for both choreographer and dancer is the dancer's body. Inside that body is a human being. What happens to that human being when it allows itself to be used by another, manipulated if you will—even to produce a beautiful work of art, is not good. At the least, it is stunting.

But in ballet there is no other way.

CHAPTER FIVE

The Break That Made The Difference

PLANS FOR THE SAN FRANCISCO BALLET'S EXPANSION WERE MOVING ahead nicely, but one more element was needed if the Company was ever to gain more than regional recognition. Someone had to go out and "sell" it. Leon Kalimos, who had by now married Wana Williams and was running a dance studio with her in San Jose, believed he could be that someone. He offered his services to Lew. When Lew accepted them, the course of the San Francisco Ballet changed for good.

Leon started right off by booking five spring engagements for us up and down the West Coast. By summer, he had lined up a small tour on the East Coast. We spent a week at the Corning Glass Works in Elmira, New York, three weeks at Jacob's Pillow in the Berkshire Mountains of Massachusetts, a couple of dates in Kennebunkport, Maine, and single ones in Denver and at Red Rocks in Colorado.

Jacob's Pillow was an important engagement for us. Ted Shawn, its founder and director, had transformed an 18th Century farm into an international summer showcase for dance, and he was noted for discovering up-and-coming dance groups. The New York critics frequently attended these performances, and major tours often followed in their wake.

Lew and Néné—with some background maneuvering by our resourceful Ballet Guild President, Bettine Bayless—

laid the groundwork for this engagement. They knew the "players" and were in communication with them. Bettine arranged a San Francisco visit for Anatol Chujoy, editor of *Dance News*. From this visit came a nice write-up about us in his publication, plus the suggestion to Ted Shawn that he engage us at Jacob's Pillow.

Walter Terry, dance critic for the *New York Herald Tribune*, wrote a nice article about us, too. It was headlined, "A Ballet Grows Up Out West." He wrote about the Christensen brothers' background, about our new quarters, about the school and the company. He also wrote a nice piece about us in the April 1956 issue of the magazine, *Etude*. He started out with, "Almost anyone with ambition and theatrical talent heads for New York. This is understandable, for New York is the center (always in quantity, often in quality) of America's theater . . . Other cities in the nation's various regions deserve the best in theater but often their home-grown artists slip away to New York for their futures, and the few who remain are those afraid of New York's competition, those whose talents are limited, and those who possess a genuine pioneering spirit. This last category may be small but it includes those who stay in or come to an American city with the belief that that city can and will support a first-rate art enterprise . . . Among the best of the regional groups in the field of dance is the San Francisco Ballet."

The East was primed, but if it hadn't been for Leon's crustiness and persistence—as well as his undying faith in us—our eastern debut would never have taken place. Leon went east in the spring, making the rounds of agents and talking to anyone who would listen to him.

I remember Lew telling us, "Every time Leon came in to see an agent, saying, 'We're the San Francisco Ballet,' the agent would answer, 'So, who are you?' then kick him out the door and down the stairs. Leon would pick himself up, brush himself off, and come right back in, again, saying, 'But listen, you should see us first before you go kicking me downstairs.' They finally took us on just to get rid of Leon."

Nancy and I had already faced some of this "who are you?" attitude in New York, but the others learned to face it soon enough. We were repeatedly confronted with "who are you?" Lew, Néné and Leon instilled in us the response, "give us a chance and we'll show you." We became a feisty bunch. We had to. We had to keep proving ourselves. And it paid off.

Generally, people were at first surprised by the quality of our dancing; then they would begin raving about us. It was kind of funny. Here was Leon saying, "You're wonderful. You're the best. Believe that, no matter what", while Lew was admonishing, "Don't let it go to your head. Don't start believing the write-ups. That's the beginning of the end."

We were a success wherever we went, including Jacob's Pillow. Many people were now curious about us. Some came from quite a distance to see us. Leon even convinced the people from ANTA (American National Theater and Academy—the U.S. Government's Cultural Exchange Program) to come up from Washington D.C. to take a look at us.

For our repertoire we brought eight ballets; six of Lew's and two of Balanchine's. Of Lew's ballets we brought *Jinx, Con Amore, Le Gourmand, The Dryad, A Masque of Beauty and the Shepherd* and *Tarot*. Balanchine's two ballets were **Concerto Barocco** and **Apollo**.

All spring I felt that Lew used me only when he had to. For days on end I would not be involved in rehearsals. When he expanded **Mozartiana** into **Tarot**, he choreographed me out of it, though I was cast in the part he choreographed for Nancy most of this tour. I had a hard time keeping up my morale. John kept asking me why I didn't start taking some college courses, or *something*. But now that we were performing, again, I was feeling better. Also, Lew was using me more, if grudgingly.

All the reviews were good, though some critics picked at Lew's ballets and at our decor and costumes. Walter Terry, however, wrote that Lew's creative style, though generally along Balanchine lines, was distinct from any other choreographer's, and he was glad for the opportunity to savor more of Lew's works.

All the critics liked us dancers. We were "fresh with the spirit of youth", beautifully disciplined to "an admirable peak of exactitude", our artistic taste was high, and we were good looking. Selma Jeanne Cohen wrote in a special report for the *New York Times* that we "proved to be a happy addition to Mr. Shawn's roster of imported groups." Doris Hering, in her summary of our season in the September 1956 issue of *Dance Magazine*, said we "wore the classic tradition like an easy mantle."

Dance News, in its September 1956 issue, carried a full-page article by Anatol Chujoy headlined, "San Francisco Ballet Dances at Jacob's Pillow and Wins". He stated that this engagement was a milestone in our development. It was the longest trip we had ever made and it was the longest season we had ever worked. He described us as "a young, ebullient, well trained troupe, with a good deal of skill, a fair amount of talent, and little experience." And he felt we would find our place "in the scheme of American ballet."

Newsweek Magazine wrote about Ted Shawn stepping to the front of the stage "with the air of a man on the verge of a momentous event", telling the audience that Jacob's Pillow had once again worked its magic and had another "first". An important tour would be following our engagement. We had been chosen by the U.S. State Department to tour eleven Asian countries under the auspices of their International Exchange Program beginning the following January.

We were all euphoric. The world was ours. We, of course, thought we had gotten this tour because we were such talented, wonderful dancers, but what really sold the State Department on us was our fresh youthfulness. We were a perfect example of "the flower of American youth", young people devoting our lives to beauty. We had nothing to do with money or political influence, the two things by which so much of the world knew America, the things that had earned some of our countrymen the title, "The Ugly Americans". Showing us off could do a great deal to counter this image.

Sally Bailey, May '52, in her first *Swan Lake*.
Photo by Romaine, S.F.

Lew Christensen and James Graham-Luhan,
Summer '52- a break before an outdoor performance

Commedia dell' Arte sequence, the Standard Hour TV
series, 1952- Left to right; Roland Vasquez as *Harlequin,*
Leo Duggan as *Pantalone,* Sally Bailey as a chicken,
Nancy Johnson as *Columbine,* and Gordon Paxman as
El *Commandante.*

Sally Bailey as the *Amazon Captain* in **Con Amore**, 1953.
Photo by Walter E. Owen, N.Y.

Sally Bailey as the *Amazon Captain* in **Con Amore**.
(This photo may have been taken later in S.F.)

Sally Bailey and Gordon Paxman in the opera,
La Traviata, for the University of Utah's Summer Festival,
1953. Photo by Boyart, S.L.C.

Sally Bailey as the *Black Swan*, 1955. Photo by Romaine, S.F.

The S.F. Ballet at Jacob's Pillow, Summer 1956.

The State Department Tours

1: The Orient—High Adventure

OUR DEPARTURE DATE FOR THE FAR EAST WAS SET. WE WERE TO leave January 6, 1957, which meant we barely had six months to prepare for this tour. We had both Opera Season and *Nutcracker* to do before then, and right after our *Nutcracker*, Conrad and I were again going to Salt Lake City for Bill's second *Nutcracker*. The two of us would return home on New Year's Day, exactly six days before taking off.

Poor John, in the middle of all this, he and I decided to make our engagement official. For Christmas he gave me a beautiful diamond ring, and Christmas night I left for Salt Lake City. We planned for our wedding to be in June. We would set the exact date after I got home from the Orient. In the meantime, my mother could start the wedding machinery rolling, and I could buy clothes and furniture in Hong Kong.

We dancers may have been caught up in a whirlwind of activity, but compared to what Lew and Leon had to accomplish, we were coasting. I don't think we had any idea of the details they had to wade through, the problems they had to solve, the frustrations they faced, the hurdles they climbed over—or crawled under. All we knew was that when it was time to go, everything was ready, and off we went.

Our repertoire was not a problem. We took the same ballets we'd taken east with us, except *Apollo*, and added the *Divertissements* from **Nutcracker, Act II**, and **Black Swan** and **Don Quixote Pas de Deuxs**. No new ballets were needed, which saved us time. As it turned out, both **Con Amore** and **The Dryad** were particularly good choices for the Orient. The broad humor of **Con Amore** was much like Eastern traditional comedy and some countries related directly to the story of **The Dryad**; they, too, had spirits—knats—that lived in their banyan trees and lured men to their deaths.

Stage equipment was another matter; nothing standard would do the job. We were going to many places that had no conventional theater and we'd be mounting our performances "from scratch", which meant "from nothing". This is when Leo Diner entered the life of the San Francisco Ballet.

Leo was a film man. He'd started *Leo Diner Films* in a loft on Golden Gate Avenue in the late 1940's. He made newsreels, TV commercials, documentary films, and kinescope recordings. When he couldn't find a piece of equipment to do what he wanted to do, he'd just invent it. He was used to making tools and processes for whatever he dreamed up. How he and Lew first got together, I'm not sure; it was probably during our Standard Hour TV days. In any case, Lew was able to interest Leo in what we were trying to do, and Leo had some ideas. His first idea was to build mobile, all-purpose stage equipment that could be easily set up, torn down, packed, and unpacked. It needed to be lightweight because we were flying most of the time. These were still the days of "prop" planes, when total weight was critical. The towers for our lights were made of aluminum poles that could be clamped together in different shapes and sizes like giant Tinker Toys. Not only our lights, but also our black drops could be hung from them. They could be set up anywhere. All that was needed was a space.

Another problem, neatly solved, was *what* to pack our gear in. Cases for all the electrical equipment, including a transformer, were made to size out of aluminum. A wooden case for our makeup kits was specially designed so that the kits—metal tackle boxes we were requisitioned, like the Army—fit neatly into it. We each wrote our name on adhesive tape with indelible ink and stuck it to the end that was "up" in the case. We also each received two muslin bags; one for tights and one for shoes. We printed our names in indelible ink on them, too. They, along with our costumes and our supply of toe shoes—the toe shoes took up a whole crate by themselves—were to go in huge wicker baskets that were lined with unbleached muslin. In these, our things could survive the tropical heat and humidity. Even if they didn't dry all the way, they could at least breathe. I think my *Nutcracker* tutu, which I danced in at least once a day, never did dry the whole trip. I remember Mrs. "A" hanging it in front of an electric fan every chance she had. It finally started to turn green inside from mildew. I used to laugh and say, "I have to dance fast to stay ahead of the smell".

One other piece of equipment Leo devised was a sound system for our music. This doesn't sound unusual today—many groups perform with recorded music—but in those days, recorded music meant "records". Tapes weren't on the commercial market, yet. Tape machines were big, clumsy things, with each reel about eight inches across. Music for performances was generally "live". For both of our recent tours, because we couldn't afford an orchestra, we'd used duo-pianists. All our musical scores had been transcribed for two pianos.

To solve our music problem, Lew bought some of the finest tape recording equipment available and started recording all our music from records onto tapes. This was no small task, considering the cuts, repeats, and tempo changes needed for each ballet, not to mention the permissions and royalties required for doing this at all. I remember Lew, by the hour, recording in his private office in the back room, tucked between the costumes and the equipment. If anyone asked, "Where's Lew?" you were likely to be correct if you answered, "In the back room recording."

We went to Jacob's Pillow with eighteen dancers, two pianists, Lew, Néné, and Leon as front man. For this tour we needed more staff and a few more dancers. We picked up two dancers for our *corps* from Bill's group in Salt Lake City. The younger girls who were still in school made special arrangements with their teachers to bring their studies along with them. Those of us who were over twenty-one each took a "child" for a roommate and became their "mother". Paula Tracy was my child.

To add weight to the top of our roster, Leon Danielian and Jocelyn Vollmar came with us as guest artists. Leon was free to come because Ballet Russe de Monte Carlo was not active at this time, and Jocelyn, who for the past three years was a ballerina with the Borovansky Ballet in Australia, recently left that group and returned home.

Besides Lew as Director and Leon Kalimos as Managing Director—Néné didn't come with us on this trip—our expanded staff now included Gordon Paxman as *Maitre de Ballet*, Leo Diner as Sound Engineer, George Vogel as Stage Manager, and Bruce Kelly as Assistant Stage Manager. I'm not sure where George came from. He was new to us on this tour and never worked with us again. Bruce grew up across the street from Harold and Ruby, had always been intrigued by ballet, and had just finished his stint in the Army where he'd worked in the Medical Corps. Because of this experience, he was also in charge of our medical box and the dispensing of our malaria pills. Eloise Arnold was Wardrobe Mistress, Wana Kalimos came as Administrative Assistant, and for once Gordon's wife, Dorothy, got to come along. Years later I remember Dorothy telling me how she felt, staying home and going to her office job every day while Gordon went off and did the "glamour stuff"—resentful.

David Adams was our State Department representative from ANTA. He came along with us as Tour Manager. I don't remember him doing much of the actual managing, though; Leon seemed to be doing most of that. I mostly remember him holding orientation sessions before we left San Francisco, then giving us pertinent information about each country as we came to it; local customs, local money, local health problems, what to eat, what to buy, what to watch out for.

The management of this tour, being sponsored by the Government, was a bit odd, in any case. The Government guaranteed only our salaries and transportation costs. It saw that either the USIS (United States Information Service) or the USIA (United States Information Agency) sponsored us in each city where we danced. It, of course, arranged all of our "ambassadorial" duties; going to Embassy receptions, meeting Government officials, meeting artists and teachers, watching local cultural demonstrations, giving ballet demonstrations in return. The demonstrations we gave in return—mostly at English-speaking high schools and universities—were in addition to our regular performances. They were almost "the straw that broke the camel's back", but they probably did more for our goodwill than any of our regular performances.

One thing the Government did not do was make arrangements for our regular performances. Leon had to do that with local impresarios in each city in which we danced. I remember there were certain people in Washington D.C. that Leon was also supposed to work through, but he thought they weren't of much use and preferred working without them. When he stopped using them, however, deals started falling through; when he picked back up with them, deals started materializing, again.

In spite of all the problems, our tour pulled together; we took off from San Francisco's International Airport in high spirits. None of us really knew what to expect—the hardships we might face, the illness and exhaustion—but we didn't worry about it. We'd had so many shots we felt like human pincushions, plus we were young, resilient, and thought we were invincible. We mainly anticipated a great adventure.

An incident that occurred to me while in Colombo, Ceylon (today Sri Lanka) gave me an insight into how lucky we were, though. We were staying at the Mt. Lavinia Hotel, a beautiful, English colonial-style beach resort about twelve miles outside the city, right on the Indian Ocean. A cruise ship had landed, and the passengers were also staying at our hotel. We ran into them in the dining room, on the verandahs, in the gardens, on the beach.

One morning when I was in the writing room, an older lady came up to me and blurted out, "Do you young people realize how fortunate you are?" The tone in her voice was surprisingly vehement. I was somewhat taken aback. Then she continued, "Here I am, finally retired after teaching school all my life. This is my one trip. I've been saving my money and looking forward to it for years and now I'm too tired to enjoy it."

I felt for her. Sometimes we were tired, but not like that. And this wasn't our only trip, and it wasn't taking all our money. In fact, we were being paid to do it.

Our first performance of the tour took place in Taipei, Formosa (today Taiwan) on a gray and blustery January day in a barn-like auditorium. That day began for us at 10:00 AM with a dance program and Chinese pastries in the studio of a local dancing teacher. Next was a luncheon at the Grand Hotel given for us by Major General Teng, our local sponsor— sixteen courses, starting with bird's-nest soup. We then rehearsed at the theater, dashed back for a quick dinner that we assumed was beef, but turned out to be water buffalo, then back to the theater for our first performance. The audience loved us. Major General Teng said they usually didn't clap, but we got quite an ovation at the end. We were the first western dance group they had seen.

From Taipei we flew on to Manila, in the Philippines, where the weather was now beautiful and balmy—their winter. The rest of their year was hot and wet. The first thing we did upon arrival was go to President Magsaysay's palace for an audience. He talked with us for half an hour while photos and movies were taken, then served us refreshments on a beautiful verandah overlooking the Pasig River. I learned the palace was originally built by the Spaniards.

We gave our performances in Quezon City, on the outskirts of Manila, in a huge Quonset hut that had originally been an Army hanger, now converted into a theater for the University of the Philippines. For our last performance, we had a near riot. The house had been over-sold; 7,000 people were trying to cram into a 3,300 seat auditorium. No one could see. People were pushing and shoving and everyone was in an uproar. It took two ballets for them to quiet down. We were afraid to open the curtains for fear people would spill out onto the stage.

In Hong Kong, where the weather was again cold, we danced in a Chinese Opera theater. The stage was most unusual. A large turntable, placed center stage, came up to a point in the middle. It was raked every which way; pirouettes on the diagonal were lots of fun.

Both our theater and our hotel were in the Chinese section of the island, not the European section. One evening—it was drizzling and cold—my friend Christine Bering and I decided to explore the side streets and little shops. Odd-sounding music floated out to us as we walked along the sidewalk. Every now and then we would have to step around women squatting down, cooking over little open braziers. We saw a small child in only a cotton shirt sleeping on the bare pavement. As we walked by in our nicely fashioned high-heeled shoes, a woman spat at our feet. We were told they sometimes maimed their children before sending them out to beg.

Our last day in Hong Kong turned out to be a real catastrophe day. Paula woke up vomiting and had to be taken to the hospital for an emergency appendectomy. Chris was better, but had been quite ill. Gordon was still sick, but had to dance, anyway, plus he got stabbed in the nose by Chris when she missed the back of his neck in **Dryad**, and had to be sewn up. Some of the other kids were sick, too, but somehow we got through that night's show, plus the filming of **Tarot** that morning. I had quite a complicated time in the afternoon getting everything done—doing errands, picking up purchases, getting things ready to ship, saying goodbye to friends—but I did manage to have a luxurious hair-wash and at dinner to have lettuce from California. After the performance I wrote some letters for Paula. I slept an hour-and-a-half before rising at 5:00 AM to catch the launch for the airport.

Paula was going to have to remain in Hong Kong for at least three weeks while we moved on. I felt like a bad mother, leaving her behind, but I didn't have much choice. Just by chance, a mutual friend of both of our families had been living in Hong Kong for years with her husband and had been hospitable to us during our stay. Not knowing what else to do, I phoned her. She graciously offered to keep Paula until Paula was well enough to rejoin us.

Our next stop was Rangoon, Burma, where we returned to sunny, comfortably hot weather. Half the group stayed downtown at the Strand Hotel, but fourteen of us were put up at the Kanbawza Palace, a fantastic place on the outskirts of Rangoon, built fifty years earlier by the owner of the Tiger Balm liniment business. The palace had a tower in which the owner supposedly kept his three wives, each on a separate floor. The first and second floors of the main part of the building had beautiful, spacious sitting rooms divided by delicately carved screens. A Buddhist monastery was just down the road. At sunset the monks, called "pungyis", walked around the hotel grounds. The Russian Circus was also staying here. They were performing in Rangoon, too. They seemed as curious about us as we were about them.

A couple of days later I came down with a bad cold, but went through a long, rugged day, anyway. We got up early and went in costume to noted Rangoon sights for photographs. I had to climb a tree in my *Tarot* costume and pose with the *Shwe Dagon* in the background. We caused a sensation wherever we went. Because of Paula being out, I had to jump into *Barocco* that night, plus do *Nutcracker*. Due to illness, we were now rehearsing all parts five deep. Nancy and I started learning *corps* parts . . . After our performance that evening, we went to the Prime Minister's compound to give him a command performance of *Nutcracker*. I had to do the *Pas de Deux*, again. We just kept on our costumes to go there in the bus. Our gesture was extremely well received, though, and the Prime Minister gave us a midnight banquet.

To this day I hear the story about the leech soup. I don't necessarily remember it as others do, but I remember my cold making me so miserable that at the banquet I could hardly smell, taste, or swallow. We were served some hot, clear soup that I could get down. The warmth of it soothed my throat. Those around me started giving me their soup, too. I thought they were being nice. They later said, amid much laughter, "It smelled so badly we couldn't drink it." The soup was evidently made from leeches.

And this part I don't remember at all, but everyone else insists that I thought the soup was so good that I asked for the recipe. I did collect recipes on this trip, but I have never found one among them for leech soup.

The following day the Russian Circus canceled their show to come see us. Unfortunately, we couldn't do the same for them, though Leon, Wana, and Lew went to see their show while we performed. Until then, we had just been looking at each other from our separate tables in the dining room, but the next morning they seemed decidedly friendly, and Conrad started playing chess with them.

Our next stop was Bangkok, Thailand, where the weather was definitely hotter and stickier. It made us all feel terribly lazy, but at least it was better for our muscles than the cold. For the next two days, besides our regular shows, we both gave, and watched, demonstrations. We were really tired by the time our last performance came around.

Our last performance turned out to be quite an occasion, however. The King of Siam sent Lew a beautiful antique plaque and Nancy, Joce and me the most gorgeous leis I'd ever seen. They were made of hundreds of tiny orchids. The gifts were presented to us formally on stage after the last ballet. The other dancers received lovely flowers, as well. The audience, which had been reserved the first two nights, was now responding enthusiastically. Right after Lew received his gift, Leo, as he always did, first put on a tape of our host country's national anthem and then put on ours. I had never thought of The Star Spangled Banner as being particularly emotional—I had sung it by rote all the way through school— but this night, with all the excitement and us being so far from home; I think all of us had lumps in our throats and tears running down our cheeks.

During our trip, the more tired and uncomfortable we got, the goofier our jokes got. Lew loved puns and made up a whole string of them. The worse they became, the more we groaned. I don't remember them all, but I do remember one in particular. Lew made it on our way to the airport leaving Rangoon for Bangkok. He stood up at the front of the bus and announced, "We all have to put on ties, now. Do you know why?" none of us knew why, "because we're going to Thailand!"

And with that he broke up in gales of laughter while the rest of us groaned as loudly as we could.

We enjoyed making up silly nicknames for each other, too. Leo was "Papa Diner". Leon was "Mother". Some started calling me "Serry Berry" after the way my name was pronounced in places where "l's" were hard to say. Leon said I sounded like a social disease.

I also remember that when we got to Pnom Penh, Cambodia, one of the U.S.I.S. men stationed there taught us to say, "I've had it." in Cambodian. What he taught us to say was something like, "*Con yom chehet hoi.*" At least that's what I wrote down in my journal. We said it a lot.

In Pnom Penh we stayed in the homes of U.S.I.S. people because Leon was afraid to put us up in even the best hotel. The city was really quite lovely, with wide, tree-lined streets, but we were told that ninety-five percent of the Americans got amoebic dysentery. My hostess was recovering from it. She said the cure was even worse than the disease. The life expectancy of Cambodians was around thirty-five years. There was an open crematory near my family's house that burned every day at 1:00 PM—lunch time. I was seated at the dining room table the first time I smelled that smell. I knew instantly what it was.

Our theater in Pnom Penh was a little movie house. The stage was so small that it was like dancing on a postage stamp. We had to re-program and then re-choreograph the ballets we ended up doing. Our closing night was a big success, however. The King loved it. Our appearance was the last of an American Festival the U.S.I.S. had been sponsoring. They were glad to end on an enthusiastic note.

I remember an interesting conversation I had with a member of the Cambodian press. He said his country was like someone waking up after being sealed in an envelope for one hundred years; the length of time they'd been colonized by France, which ended four years before, in 1953. They were now taking a look around, and everyone was courting them, including us.

One afternoon before leaving Cambodia, we crossed the Mekong River and drove through the jungle for two-and-a-half hours to Kampong Cham for a show. Little naked children with swollen bellies and skinny legs waved at us along the way. A little girl at the ferry offered me one of the roasted cockroaches she was eating. The village of Kampong Cham boasted a high school and an English sports club, where we danced. Convicts wearing chains helped Leo, George and Bruce erect our stage on the lawn. During the performance, people from the village kept creeping out of the darkness and up onto the walls surrounding the lawn. They were not our regular audience who sat on folding chairs on the lawn in front of the stage. By the end of the show the walls were jammed. I didn't know where they all came from. The village didn't look that big.

After a supper given for us at the sports club, we drove back through the jungle and arrived in town about 2:00 AM. Our little bus broke down—in town, luckily—and I ended up having to take a *cyclo puce* home by myself. I still remember the streets being absolutely silent except for the swishing sound of the bicycle wheels rolling along the pavement. Skinny dogs, foraging for food, lurked soundlessly in the shadows. I instinctively pulled my legs up under me lest a dog take a chomp out of one. This was another night with little sleep. After about a half-hour's rest, I arose at 3:30; we were going to fly to Angkor Wat and back before having to leave for Singapore at 10:00 AM.

Our Ambassador had been raving about Angkor Wat, magnificent ruins of the Khmer civilization that were discovered about one hundred years before. He said we must get there if at all possible. With great effort and the good will of our charter pilots, we did get there. Our main problem was the rigid rules about take-offs and landings. Our papers said we were taking off from Pnom Penh at 10:00 AM and landing in Singapore at 4:00 PM. Both local governments said these times could not be changed. So our wonderful pilots offered—if we were willing to go without sleep and pay for the gasoline—to take us up to Angkor and back before 10:00 AM. If we took off at 4:00 AM, we could arrive in Angkor at sun up, sightsee for two hours, and then fly back to Pnom Penh in time to depart for Singapore at 10:00 AM.

This side trip was well worth no sleep and the twenty-four dollars apiece it cost us. Words to describe the ruins, which dated from the 9th through 13th Centuries, were hard to find. There were many temples, some of them several stories high, which, naturally, we climbed to the tops of. The stone figures in the friezes along the walls and the intricate decorations surrounding them were carved in such fine detail. We were told the Khmers were originally woodcarvers and transferred their technique to stone. Some of the ruins were out in the open, surrounded by great moats. Others were still smothered by the jungle. One huge stone head had the roots of a tree growing over its nose and down into its mouth. I felt as if the jungle might grow over me if I stood still too long.

After we arrived in Singapore, we heard that our tour was being cut short because of "lack of funds". This didn't seem like the real reason, but we didn't hear any more for several days. We were a gloomy bunch. The manager lady at the hotel thoughtfully gave us a delicious dinner party in order to buoy our spirits. Some of us also drowned our sorrows in "Singapore Slings" at the Raffles Hotel. But then we heard that most of our tour was to be continued. Our spirits rose one-hundred percent, plus I received three letters from home.

The State Department's official reason for the proposed cancellation was that our transportation costs were much higher than anticipated. We had been flying in two chartered DC4's with CAT (Civil Air Transport—originally the Flying Tigers from World War II), one plane for us and one for our gear. Whether there was more to the situation than this, we never did find out. Our State Department representative, David Adams, left us at this point. One thing we did learn, though; Bettine Bayless, Harold Christensen, and San Francisco Mayor George Christopher went to Washington D.C. and threatened to go all the way to President Eisenhower if necessary. Half of our remaining tour was salvaged and some lovely political cartoons showed up in San Francisco newspapers. Editorials proclaimed " . . . The $60,000 needed to continue the tour is small change compared to the profit the Communists can make in holding the shortened tour up to scorn and worldwide ridicule."

On our flight from Singapore to Kuala Lumpur, Malaya our economy kick began. We flew in a cargo carrier; bucket seats, box lunches, and just the shell of the plane for our interior—and a small, bamboo, hand-held fan for air-conditioning.

In Kuala Lumpur some of us stayed at the Majestic Hotel, a lovely, old, colonial hotel that had shutters for windows and a huge tree growing beside it. We were told that monkeys lived in the tree and sometimes came into the rooms and took things. Paula—who had rejoined us by now and was again my roommate—and I carefully put our things out of sight in the bedroom and left our hand-washing to dry in the bathroom. After returning to the hotel that night, we discovered the things we had washed were missing. The next morning we saw our bras, panties, and white gloves hanging in the tall tree outside our room. The monkeys had, indeed, come in and taken them. Room boys had to be rounded up to climb into the tree and rescue them for us.

Later that day, after a morning of sightseeing and a children's matinee in the afternoon, we went to the British Governor General's residence for tea; croquet and all. The Governor General had a delightful sense of humor. He said, "Everyone expects the English to play croquet at tea time, so I oblige." The croquet set was ready for us, and we all played croquet on the huge lawn outside his house, part of a lovely estate set on top of a hill overlooking the countryside. I imagined he—and all the English—would be leaving in August, when Malaya got its independence.

From Malaya we went to Ceylon, then on to Bombay, India. For the nine days we were in Bombay we stayed in the homes of Indian families; to avoid paying Indian income tax. If we looked as though we were earning money in India, we'd have to pay tax on it there as well as in the U.S. Thus we stayed in the homes of our sponsors, the Board of the Times and Talent Club, and danced for their charity. They were so warm and hospitable. They took us right in and treated us like members of their families. We hated to leave them, but it was time to depart for Karachi, Pakistan.

The people we met in Karachi were also warm and hospitable. Some of our local sponsors took a group of us to their hut on the beach one afternoon. We had an Indian style "tea" and sang—of all things—U.S. songs. I remember passing many refugee huts on the way to the beach.

Karachi, itself, was mostly all desert; a lot of camels were pulling carts. Our theater—a bare platform—was erected right in the middle of our hotel's central courtyard. Actually, it wasn't a bad arrangement, coming up to our rooms to rest, make up, and shower right after the show.

From Karachi we went to Tehran, Iran, our last stop of the tour. After weeks of tropical, warm weather, we suddenly found ourselves back in the freezing cold. After a rough flight, by the time we arrived in Teheran, we barely had enough time to unpack—squashed cocktail clothes again—before going to another reception, this one at the U.S. Ambassador's house.

The next day turned even colder, plus there was now rain, thunder and lightning. Many in our group were starting to get sick, again; there were rumors of refrigeration problems at our hotel back in Karachi. And now, with the change in weather, people were really dropping. Virginia Johnson and Louise Lawler had to go to the hospital. Leo should have, but we couldn't spare him. Our transformer never made it from Karachi, and even if it had, we would still have had a problem. The power blew in the movie theater where we were dancing. We had to borrow a generator from the Army. We would not be able to get the show on without Leo. Poor Leo was so sick he couldn't get up off the floor. I thought this was the time for one of my magic pills.

To this day, I'm not sure what was in those pills that my personal physician, Dr. Upton, gave me before leaving home. He gave me four of them. They were in a tiny pill bottle, and were big, square, and pale orange. He told me not to take one unless I was so sick I thought I'd die, but had to go on anyway. I never got that sick, but now poor Leo definitely was. I gave him one of my pills.

Leo not only survived, he was able to get up and get the show on. The next day, after our matinee and evening shows—the last two performances of our tour, he came up to me and said, "Sally, I don't know what was in that 'bullet' you gave me, but I was flying."

Over the years I have sometimes questioned, "Did I do something illegal?" Years later, when I told this story to one of Leo's sons, he loved it so much that he asked me to please tell it to the gathering at Leo's memorial. I did, and everyone started laughing. Then, one by one, people started relating wonderful, funny incidents of Leo. His widow, Iolanda, said it cheered her no end.

The State Department Tours

2: A Marriage of Sorts

BECAUSE OF RUNNING OUT OF MONEY IN SINGAPORE, WE RETURNED home to San Francisco a month earlier than planned. No Spring Season had been booked for us in San Francisco, and not much work was in sight until Opera Season in the fall; just a few single dates out of town, and once again, a week in Salt Lake City with Bill's group in May.

At first, all of us were glad to have the break; we were exhausted, and for me, I would now have time to attend to my wedding plans and see more of John. But for the rest of the Company, once everyone was rested, were these spotty dates enough to keep us together? Though there was talk of another tour for the government—perhaps to Latin America—if it happened, it wouldn't happen for a while, and in the meantime . . .

Shortly after we returned, Conrad Ludlow left for New York and was soon taken into the New York City Ballet by Balanchine. Most everyone else stayed, but we wondered what we'd do for money the next few months. It was at this time—with the Government tour, we had finally earned enough money to qualify—that Leon could start paying into government unemployment insurance so that we could draw unemployment. We used to laugh and say, "Our unemployment checks are the American version of state-supported art."

Richard Carter, who had been alternating Conrad's roles with him on tour, took over most of Conrad's parts. Lew also started giving Roderick Drew, Julien Herrin and Glen Chadwick more to do. While we were dancing in Salt Lake City, two of Bill's young dancers, Michael Smuin and Kent Stowell, also let us know they wanted to join our Company as soon as they were through high school. Conrad and I had noticed them at Christmas during Bill's *Nutcracker.* Now Lew noticed them, too. They were hard not to notice. They were both cocky show-offs, as well as obviously talented. I remember labeling them "the brats from Utah". By fall their names were on our programs.

A nice opportunity came up for us late in the spring. Dave Garroway, host of the New York-based TV show, *Wide, Wide World,* decided to broadcast one of his units from San Francisco. In that the San Francisco Ballet had just returned from a world tour, what would be more fitting than to have us dancing around the Golden Gate Bridge? A jazzy "sailors on leave" number was decided upon. Most of the Company could dance on the roof of the Round House, a round restaurant next to the toll plaza of the bridge. In the middle of the number, all the dancers could point up to the north tower of the bridge where two dancers would be dancing up there. The shots could be spectacular.

Lew chose Glen Chadwick and me to be the ones dancing on top of the north tower. He thought we were the least likely among the group to get hysterical. To reach the top of the tower, which was 500 feet above the roadbed of the bridge and 750 feet above the water, we had to take a little three-man elevator up inside the tower—in the dark, slowly. It took about five minutes and left us off on a platform ten feet below the opening to the outside of the tower. We had to climb up a metal ladder those last ten feet. Once we were outside on the top of the tower, it wasn't particularly scary. The structure was massive, like a huge gymnasium. It was as long as the width of the roadbed of the bridge. The only problem; it was narrow—nine feet wide, to be exact. Sturdy, waist-high railings three feet in from either side took up six of those feet, which left us a space three feet wide and approximately thirty feet deep on which to dance.

The cameraman's situation was much scarier. The beacon light had been removed from the topmost point of the tower and his camera was mounted there. He could stand on the two-foot wide, grillwork platform that surrounded the base of the beacon. This place had a railing, too. I think he actually sat on it while shooting. I remember him telling me he got "hazard pay" for this job.

The show took two days to shoot. It was done "live", which meant that all of our actions had to be coordinated with Garroway in New York. The first day we blocked out every move, every angle. The second day was for "real". Both days we worked almost eight hours. The weather cooperated. I could hardly believe we were so lucky. The Golden Gate is known for its damp fog and freezing cold wind; I wasn't looking forward to being buffeted around in it for two days up on that tower. As it was, we were in still, gorgeous, sunny weather—if anything, looking for shade. The first day my thighs felt weak each time I went near the edge and looked down, but by the second day, that no longer happened. I began to feel quite at home up there. I started climbing around and taking photos. I even climbed up to where the camera was mounted, though I must admit, the grating was a little unnerving to stand on. You could see through it all the way down to the water. I also would not put any of my weight on the railing around it, the railing on which the cameraman sat. I began to understand how the maintenance men could climb out onto the cables—for the show two of them were filmed walking down them—for they, after all, wore safety belts clipped onto wires that ran just above the length of the cables.

Plans moved ahead for John's and my wedding. Somewhere along the line we set the date, though from the sounds of the following clipping from the *Santa Barbara News-Press* (4/30/57), I must have been somewhat coy about it with the Company. " . . . Like all the members of the Ballet, Sally Bailey is single. 'But I'm to be married in June—to a young San Francisco biochemist—only I won't tell the troupe just when,' she said. 'Oh, no she won't,' said a handsome young fellow who dances with her. 'She'll marry another dancer, you'll see.'"

I have no recollection of who said that, or why, but at this time there were several romances going on in the Company. Nancy and Dick Carter started going together soon after the Orient tour—they married the following New Years— and I think Roderick Drew and Sue Loyd were engaged by now, though they broke off their engagement before the South American tour. Glen Chadwick later married a dancer, but I don't think she was yet dancing with the Company.

In any case, John and I announced our wedding date in ample time. We invited everyone. It was a big affair, in a church, the whole bit. Chris was my maid-of-honor, and a scientist friend of John's was his best man. This whole thing was my father's idea. He used to tease both my sister and me, saying that when we were ready to marry, he'd give us the money to elope. It would be cheaper than putting on a wedding. I reminded him of this, but he shook his head and said, "No, not this time. If you're going to marry John, you're going to have a big wedding in the Episcopal Church here in Belvedere, with a reception at our house." He was against our marriage. He was sure it wouldn't work. At the time I just thought he wouldn't like anyone I decided to marry. My mother wasn't against the idea. She liked John. She was just afraid he didn't realize how committed I was to dancing.

She tried to warn him—a number of times—and he'd just say, "Yes, I understand."

I believe the truth of the matter was that both John and I were extremely busy—he studying and I dancing—and we just kept on believing what we wanted to believe. After being engaged all that time, and being apart so much; it wasn't until close to the wedding date that we both began to realize what life together might actually be like. I had started to hunt for an apartment. John didn't like the one I'd picked. I'd already put a deposit on it. A friend of his owned a better place right near the campus; one of those big, old, shingled Berkeley houses that he'd converted into a men's rooming house. His friend's wife was working on her doctorate, and they were going back east for several years. If we would run the rooming house for him—John said he would take care of all that—we could have, cheap, the back porch, the maid's room, the huge old kitchen with its separate pantry, and the dining room for our apartment. It looked awful to me, but I didn't say anything until John wanted to put his big, ugly desk next to the beautiful rosewood furniture I'd had made in Hong Kong. John started to get sharp pains in his stomach. I wasn't feeling too well, myself.

The only real fight we ever had was the night before our wedding. Our argument delayed rehearsal dinner. My mother was thinking, "Oh, my god. It's too late to call everyone and tell them not to come." The machinery was now in high gear and almost impossible to stop. However, by the time John and I joined the others for dinner, we had decided we didn't really want to stop it.

The wedding proceeded as planned. Just as we were leaving for the church, a seagull flew overhead and hit Dad square on the back of his white tuxedo jacket. We had to go back into the house and clean him off. We hadn't allowed time for this and arrived at the church about ten minutes late. John was beginning to panic, thinking I had backed out after all. I remember the look of relief on his face as Dad and I finally walked down the aisle. I also remember having on my stage smile, but being unusually nervous. As we stood in front of the minister, I thought, "This is not the time to throw up."

While I was on our honeymoon, William Dollar—who had worked with Lew and Gisela in the early American Ballet/Ballet Caravan days—came out from New York to set his *Mendelssohn Concerto* for us. It was choreographed to the same piano concerto that Bill Christensen had used for his *Danza Brillante*, the ballet in which I had performed my first solo at Hollywood Bowl.

Lew didn't seem angry about my marriage. He still paid attention to me in class. He, along with everyone else, teased me during my first rehearsal back. He told me to learn the lead in *Mendelssohn* from Nancy, that I could probably perform it for our coming Marin Music Chest performance. I also divided with Nancy what solos there were in Opera Season, and Dick and I alternated *Nutcracker Pas de Deux* with Nancy and Leon Danielian, who joined us again at Christmas time as a guest artist. None of us went to Salt Lake City this year because we had gotten Los Angeles dates that conflicted with Bill's.

But in November, when Lew created *Emperor Norton*—a ballet based on San Francisco's well-loved madman and long-time "ruler"—for the UNESCO Conference on Asia and the West that was being held in San Francisco, Lew used almost everyone in the Company except me.

The following spring Lew did another large new work, *Lady of Shalott*, based on Tennyson's poem. The University of California at Berkeley commissioned it. Author Mark Schorer, who was a professor of English at the University, wrote the program notes. His daughter, Suki, was one of our dancers. Again, Lew used almost everyone in the Company except me.

I was truly disheartened at this point. Even though I was still performing, I had been cast in nothing new except **Mendelssohn**. The only saving grace; by now we knew the State Department tour to Central and South America was on. We'd be leaving in June. I was anxious to go and John knew it. He might not like it, but he agreed that I should go.

In the meantime, I had begun to enjoy living in Berkeley. Never having gone to college, myself, I was impressed with academia in general and post-graduate studies in particular. Several of the men in our rooming house were working on their doctorates, too, and some of them were from other countries. One was from Venezuela; I visited his mother while we were in Caracas. Two others were from Iran; I visited their families in Teheran on our third State Department tour.

At Thanksgiving, John's friend—the owner of the house—bought a great big turkey and asked us to cook it for all the roomers. We had a big open house one weekend that turned out to be lots of fun. All the fellows participated. We had different courses in different rooms. John and I invited some of the Ballet Company girls to come, too.

Somewhere around this time, my menstrual period was over a week late. I was afraid I might be pregnant. These were the days before birth control pills. I had been careful, but one was never quite sure. Everything suddenly turned gray. I wanted children some day, but not now. I remember waiting a few days, then making a doctor's appointment. For some reason, Gordon, who had stopped dancing after the tour and was now full-time Ballet Master, made a crack about impending motherhood. Maybe I had to be excused from rehearsal for my doctor's appointment. At any rate, his remark chilled me. But then I also felt a pang of guilt because I knew how badly he and Dorothy wanted a baby.

In a few days everything straightened itself out; I got my period, I wasn't pregnant, the days seemed bright and sunny again, and I was relieved and thankful. John, I'm sure, was well aware how I was feeling through this. My present husband, Bob, says this was probably the beginning of the end between us.

Many years later, when I badly wanted a child of my own, I remembered how I'd felt at this time. I thought I probably didn't deserve to have a baby. I should be content with the two perfectly fine stepchildren I had as part of my second marriage. However, at age forty-four, I had a baby of my own— a beautiful one. I've always considered him my "special bonus".

Lew spent the remainder of the spring choreographing a lavish new production, **Beauty and the Beast**, for the San Francisco Ballet's Silver Anniversary. It was practically a full-length ballet; five scenes in two acts. Lew decided to use me in this ballet, sharing the lead in the *Roses Waltz Adagio* in Act II with Kent Stowell. The ballet premiered on Opening Night of our 25th Anniversary Gala at the Opera House [with Nancy Johnson as *Beauty* and Richard Carter as *the Beast*], less than a month before we were to leave for Latin America.

CHAPTER SIX

The State Department Tours

3: Latin America—Coming Into My Own

By June 13th we were in Caracas, Venezuela, where Vice-president Richard Nixon had been stoned in a taxicab just two weeks earlier. Our families were nervous about our safety. The people we met in Caracas were mostly embarrassed. No one talked about the incident.

We knew this whole tour was going to be different than our last one. For one thing, South American audiences were more critical; they were used to seeing ballet. European companies came regularly to cities like Rio de Janeiro, Sao Paolo, Montevideo, Buenos Aires and Mexico City. Quite a few cities had ballet companies of their own and lovely well-equipped opera houses. We weren't going to be able to get by on our wholesome charm. But then, we didn't expect to.

We took most of the same repertoire we'd taken to the Orient, plus **Balletino, Filling Station, Mendelssohn Concerto, Emperor Norton** and **Lady of Shalott.** Leon Danielian and Jocelyn Vollmar again came with us as our guest artists. Our regular group of dancers now numbered twenty-two.

Our staff was nearly the same, but now, in that there would be orchestras in most cities, we also brought along our conductor, Earl Murray. Three of our ballets, which were set to piano concertos, needed a solo pianist, so we brought Roy Bogus, our pianist at home, along with us as both solo pianist and assistant conductor. Wana Kalimos stayed home this trip because she was pregnant and having medical problems. Earl's wife, Gloria, came in her place as Administrative Assistant. Gordon Paxman was again Ballet Master, Bruce Kelly moved up to being Stage Manager, and Leo Diner joined us again, though only for half the tour because of his business at home. Bruce and Gordon took over for him when he left.

We opened our tour at the *Teatro Municipal* in Caracas, Venezuela. Curtains were at 9:30 PM; late for us. The house was packed and enthusiastic, though **Con Amore** didn't go over as well as it might. We were told that people here were more used to the old classics—**Con Amore** was a new type of ballet for them.

Two days later, the reviews came out; reactions were half-and-half. Some obviously preferred the old classics, yet some loved the abstract, too. For our second performance we had another full house and Dick and I came over strong in **Nutcracker**.

In the middle of our Caracas engagement, we had two performances away from the city; one in Barquisimeto, about a one-hour flight west from Caracas, and one in Valencia, a wild ride through the mountains of Venezuela on beyond. Barquisimeto was a small, Spanish-colonial city with cattle and jute as its main industries. We were told the people were not particularly interested in art; sometimes only thirty or forty people showed up in the audience. We were pleased, then, when the house was over two-thirds full—and responsive.

Our bus ride from Barquisimeto to Valencia was hair-raising. Some of the curves were more than hairpin and we passed trucks on them. The back half of the bus was hanging out over precipices most of the time. The scenery was gorgeous, though; intense green hills and mountains, orchids growing wild in the trees.

After our performance in Valencia, a reception was given for us at an Old Spanish mansion that was now the *Club de Los Andes*. I spent much of the time speaking Spanish—as a postgraduate "spouse" I'd been able to audit Spanish classes on campus before our trip—with an elderly gentleman who raved about Angel Falls, a 3,000-some-foot waterfall; the world's tallest, he said. Unfortunately, it was hard to get to. We probably wouldn't be able to see it.

The following day we were back in Caracas in the humid rain. We didn't return from Valencia until 4:00 AM and we had two shows—a matinee at 4:30 and an evening at 9:15. I felt as if we were in the theater for forty hours that day. Lew put Roderick Drew, whom we all called Rocky, and me into **Beauty and the Shepherd** for the first time in the evening show. The two of us kept rehearsing in the wings around everything else. We had typical first-time nerves, but it seemed to go pretty well. My costume felt becoming, and the ballet was fun to do. I was getting awfully tired of being wringing wet, though, and of being so thirsty. My muscles cramped up on stage during the evening performance. At Intermission Bruce gave me a salt tablet; to help retain moisture. I had to drink two glasses of water with it, which really made me gurgle, but otherwise I might get sick. That morning, before leaving the hotel, I had called John for our anniversary, which was actually the following day, but the phone lines were easier to get this day then the next. I was so excited to talk to him.

The following day we flew on to Medellin, Colombia. I planned on having a quiet anniversary dinner with Chris in the Grill Room of our Nutibara Hotel. Instead, our dinner turned out to be a big celebration. Some of the kids joined us at our table and Nancy insisted on buying champagne. After a meal of South American muskrat, all the lights went out and the maitre d' brought in a huge platter of carnations, in the center of which sat one tiny cake with one candle on top. The band played "Happy Anniversary" and everyone sang. I burst into tears.

From Medellin we flew on to Bogotá, which was gray and cold most of the time. We stayed at the modern, elegant Tequendama Hotel and were told to remain in the hotel after dark because of the current crime wave. To me the city seemed barren and colorless. However, after going to our theater the next day, I began to change my mind. The theater was in an older part of town that wasn't so barren, and it was just gorgeous; a real little opera house, like a miniature La Scala. We had so much fun dancing here. The 8,000-foot altitude really wasn't so bad. We got a little puffy, and they had oxygen in the wings, but few of us needed it.

The following day I had class, but was not scheduled to dance in the evening, so I did as much sightseeing as possible. Bruce came with me and we went up the *teleferico* to the Church on top of Monserrate, the mountain peak overlooking the city. The Shrine of Christ in Thorns is there. Many *Indios* with their bowlers, wool ponchos and full skirts were wandering about. I saw one *Indio* praying fervently in front of a niche, babbling on in her native tongue. She seemed in a trance. She could have been praying to an Incan god just as well as the Catholic one.

From high, cold Bogotá we went on to hot, tropical Cali, a colorful city full of atmosphere; high black population, lush surrounding country, tree ferns that looked like huge green feathers, a river that ran alongside our hotel. When Chris and I arrived in our room, a fight was going on in the street below our window.

After a swim in the rooftop pool and an interview with the local press, we all went over to the top of another hotel where a minister friend of Paula's and his wife gave a supper party for us. All their friends chipped in on the food. We learned that most of the Colombians here were in farming or cattle. The Americans ran firms like Colgate, Squibb's, and synthetic textiles.

We opened at the *Teatro Municipal,* another little jewel box of an opera house with blue and gold interior. The stage had a steep rake and rough floor, but the audience was placed so nicely that it was fun to dance on, anyway. The audience was wonderful. They loved everything we did; much shouting of bravos with enthusiastic applause.

The following morning we had 9:00 AM class; early for having late performances. It made for a long day. Orchestra rehearsal for **Shallot** seemed to go on forever. That evening Dick and I were scheduled to dance **Nutcracker Pas de Deux** by itself—not as part of the Suite—for the first time. We wanted to be sure to have a good run-through with the orchestra. We finally had our turn at 1:00 PM. That night the audience was smaller than the night before and not as enthusiastic. Technically, our *Pas de Deux* was all right, but it went over like a lead balloon. I could tell we lost the audience half way through the adagio and never got it back.

I remember Leon saying to me afterwards, "Sally, I could see you losing it right there on stage. You didn't look as if you believed you were a ballerina." Then he continued with something I could never imagine Lew saying, "You must always feel you're a ballerina, no matter what."

Our flight over the Andes from Cali to Quito, Ecuador was one of the most spectacular I have ever seen. It really did look like the rooftop of the world. The mountains seemed to push the clouds upward. We had to climb to 17,000 feet to get above them. The steward came by to hand out oxygen masks—our chartered plane was not pressurized—and found almost everyone asleep; or passed out. He said he should have brought the masks at 15,000 feet but forgot. I was still alert, so he asked me if I would like to go up to the cockpit and see the view from there. The pilot could share his oxygen supply with me whenever I needed it. From the cockpit the tops of the mountains—flat, like plateaus, and barren—stretched way out in front of me. The clouds hung in gorges that plunged thousands of feet down into dense jungle. Every now and then I would take a puff of the pilot's oxygen.

I stayed for quite a while, just looking. Finally, I thought I should return to my seat. Without thinking about oxygen, I headed back. The next thing I knew, the floor was in front of my nose. The steward had to help me back up and to my seat. When he handed me my oxygen mask with its simple four-step instructions—turn cap off of oxygen hole, insert tube into hole, put mask over nose, breathe slowly—I could not tell what the words said. They might as well have been in Greek. I started to panic. I was suffocating. The steward had to do everything for me. As soon as I got a few whiffs of oxygen I felt like an idiot.

The steward also gave us our certificates for crossing over the equator. We were now accepted into "the Empyrean Realm of His Exalted Majesty Jupiter Rex, Supreme Potentate of all things above the Surface of the Earth." I could now, and forever after, be known as "Condor Sally".

We arrived in Quito two days before our scheduled performances in order to adjust to the altitude. Quito is at 9,500 feet, and not only the air, but the whole atmosphere is rarefied. The sun always rises and sets at exactly 6:00, and all four seasons occur each day; spring in the morning, summer at noon, fall in the afternoon, and winter at night. That first night, at our reception, I was brave and tackled a martini. It was like having four.

The following day was our 4th of July. During class at the theater that day all of us were in hysterics trying to coordinate. In this altitude muscles didn't react as quickly. Jumping was funny. Everything would be going just fine—you were jumping easily and high—then all of a sudden you got "spaghetti legs", where nothing worked at all. You couldn't tell ahead of time when this was going to happen— a bit scary. I figured we'd just have to "mark full" during performances. In the middle of class Bruce, Gordon, Roy and Leo came marching in wearing **Con Amore** hats, using a stage light for a drum, my pistol for a flute, and whistling "Yankee Doodle Dandy". Happy 4th of July!

One morning we left the hotel by 9:30 AM for a publicity photo session at the monument on the equator, about a one-hour drive from the city. On winding, narrow, bumping, cobblestone roads we passed through several small *Indio* villages. Freshly butchered meat, covered with flies, hung in doorways. The only trees seemed to be eucalyptus. The closer we got to the equator, the dryer the land. The monument was at 8,000 feet and the sun was intense.

Throughout our engagement in Quito, we danced to packed houses at *Teatro Bolivar*, which seemed to be unusual. Evidently this was only the second time in its history that it was full. The altitude didn't seem to bother us much more than in Bogotá, though odd things did happen to us. A lot of the kids had digestive problems. I ate a steak one night and still felt full two days later. Most of us lived on cheese omelets and chocolate bars.

During our last performance, I ran out of oxygen on stage. Dick and I were again doing **Nutcracker**. The *adagio* went fine, but I didn't quite catch my breath during Dick's solo before going back out for mine. I thought I'd be all right, but I got half way through my solo and realized, even though I was breathing all the way in and out, I wasn't getting enough air. I wasn't sure what to do. I could easily have run offstage hysterically laughing, or screaming, or something. I'd heard that people sometimes did that. Instead, I thought I'd better just concentrate on my breathing—counting in two, out two, in two, out two, in time to the music—whether or not I was getting enough air. Luckily, my muscles took over automatically and did what they were supposed to do. I even finished my final *pirouette* to the knee without wobbling. I guess I bowed. Bruce said he noticed my eyes glazing over and my fingertips turning blue, so he brought oxygen to me as I came off stage. I had to be careful not to gulp too much—a big gulp can give you stomach cramps—but immediately I was fine and went back out for the coda.

The following day we flew from high, Andean Quito to sea level, tropical Guayaquil. I felt a little queasy all day, but assumed it would pass. It didn't. Just before going on stage that night in **Con Amore**, I vomited—too late to change casts. I had to dance. I thought I might at least get some sympathy from the others, but not at all. Everyone was delighted I'd finally gotten sick. Lew did, however, stand in the wings holding a bottle of smelling salts for me should I need a whiff.

Our next stop was Lima, Peru, where we stayed for five days. After so many changes in altitude and climate, our bodies welcomed the chance to settle back down. Lima was in its three months of fog, which they get during their winter instead of rain. I noticed the landscape, the minute it wasn't irrigated, was the starkest and driest I'd ever seen. But other than that, the city seemed European. It was the first place we'd been in South America that had streetcars. One morning some local ballerinas came to take class with us in the Opera House. The local newspapers came, too, and so our class, rather than being a warm-up, turned out to be a photo session.

Before leaving Lima, Chris and I learned how to drink "pisco sours". Pisco is the native grape brandy. You take a shot of pisco, half a lemon, and some salt sprinkled on your fist. You sample a little of each by turn, then repeat.

After Lima, and a seven-hour bumpy trip east across the Andes, we arrived in Asuncion, Paraguay in the pouring rain. We got stuck in a traffic jam caused by a funeral for some colonel—all the army was standing in the street—plus roadwork and cows wandering about. Our hotel was originally an auditorium, then a school, and now a hotel. It was in the process of being modernized, but our rooms hadn't been, yet; shared baths, high ceilings with a fan and one dim light bulb hanging down, many mosquitoes. A room boy wielding a "flit" gun came to chase them out, but drove us out instead.

One afternoon, at the end of an excursion to a resort in the countryside arranged by our Embassy, those of us who came home in the bumpy old bus—the good bus didn't have enough room for us all—got to stop by the Presidential Palace. We saw General Stroessner drive off in his official, bulletproof car, and we were allowed inside the Hall of State where all official functions take place. Again, we had *mucha practica en Español* because the two Paraguayan newspapermen who came with us spoke no English. The next day we gave a matinee open free to the public. The mayor sponsored it.

From Asuncion we flew on to Montevideo, Uruguay, which is at the mouth of the *Rio de la Plata,* on the east coast of South America. The weather was again wintry. We arrived at 1:00 AM, and never have I been so glad to touch the ground. Luckily, I had been asleep and was still groggy; otherwise I would have been scared to death. The fog was so thick that the airport had already closed. Our flight was bumpy, the pilot couldn't see a thing, and he missed the runway the first time. As he circled around to go back up and try again, I looked out my window—right into someone's kitchen. We missed that building by feet. Luckily we made it on the next try. Even at that hour, the crash crew and ambulances were waiting for us.

Montevideo is a large, sophisticated, European city. It had a wonderful theater called *S.O.D.R.E. Estudio Auditorio,* which was beautifully equipped with a huge stage, good floor, large seating capacity and a picky audience to fill it. The SODRE had its own ballet company that was performing *Nutcracker* the following month. We met some of the dancers at our Embassy reception, where we also met a girl who had been with our Embassy in Pnom Penh, Cambodia when we were there.

The reviews came out the morning following our opening performance. They liked us as a company, but didn't care for Leon Danielian (whom we now referred to as "Leon D."—to differentiate from Leon Kalimos) and Jocelyn Vollmar (whom we now called "Joce") in *Black Swan,* and took downright offense at *Con Amore.* They didn't appreciate its humor at all; the ballet was an insult to Rossini and to Italians in general—there were lots of Italians in Montevideo. Dick and I did *Nutcracker* that night and it went over extremely well, however; I guess what you would call "bring the house down". After general bows, the two of us took two more calls in front of the curtain.

The following night I danced *Beauty and the Shepherd* with Rocky, and it went over well, too. I felt as if I might be getting an audience here.

But poor *Emperor Norton* died a terrible death in Montevideo. The first evening it was performed, I was through after the first ballet, so went out front with Gloria Murray to watch. She was nervous about the music—Earl and the orchestra had been having trouble with it during rehearsal—but it was at least recognizable. I thought everyone was dancing well. There was absolutely no response from the audience, however. You could feel them getting colder and colder. In this frigid atmosphere the weaknesses in both the music and the ballet stood out. At home, the ballet was loved for its "Old San Francisco" nostalgia, but that didn't count for much here. Poor Lew; he was standing behind us. He couldn't watch it through to the end. He had to leave. He decided to junk the ballet right there and then. It was never performed again.

Luckily, this wasn't our last performance in Montevideo. Though all of us were on edge the following night, the audience response was again warm and friendly. For our last performance, even though the weather had turned stormy and cold, our house was packed. Dick and I did **Nutcracker** again, this time just as the *Pas de Deux,* and this time, unlike Cali, we got across all right. The next morning Dick and I got our first near-rave reviews. Then we were off for Buenos Aires.

We had a lot of difficulty with the local management in Buenos Aires. As Lew nicely put it, "They don't take us seriously, here." We were not dancing at the Colon Opera House. We were dancing in a movie theater and for only two performances—short for an engagement in Buenos Aires, we were told. We couldn't even get into the theater for rehearsals. We jammed into a local ballet studio for class and rehearsal. The orchestra could only rehearse after 11:00 PM, movies ran all afternoon, the stage couldn't be set up, we couldn't rehearse on stage with the orchestra, and the only time we could get on stage at all was from 9:00 to 11:30 AM.

In spite of all this, the Buenos Aires critics gave us good reviews. Suddenly, our local impresario wanted to book us for another engagement right then. Instead, we went on to Brazil, where we danced in eight cities during the month of August.

We started off in the south of Brazil, in Porto Alegre. The weather was freezing. Our hotel was brand new and didn't have any heat. Our theater was brand new, too, and also not quite finished. The stage was small and slippery, plus we had a terrible time with the orchestra, which was actually the Police Band. They had rehearsed long and hard, but it was hopeless; Tchaikowsky was unrecognizable. We had to stop half way through the performance and finish with tapes, even if it might insult them.

From Porto Alegre we flew on to Rio de Janeiro, landing just as the sun was setting. We saw Sugar Loaf and the other jagged mountains jutting out of the bay. The sight was more spectacular than any photo I'd seen. We arrived at our hotel in the center of the city right at rush hour. The place was swarming with people, cars and confusion. We were told that commuters often had to wait in line two hours to catch a bus. Luckily, we were within walking distance of *El Teatro Municipal*, where we were dancing.

The next day, on our way back to the hotel after rehearsal, Chris and I decided to explore some of the city. The sun had already set, and—something that had never happened to me before—I got completely turned around. I couldn't believe it at first because I had an excellent sense of direction; I could usually even tell the time of day by the slant of the sun. I gave Chris quite an argument when she kept insisting, "No, Sally, the hotel is *that* way." We walked blocks before I admitted she was right. I was 180 degrees off. The sun set north of me instead of south. I don't remember this confusing me in other places below the equator, but in the middle of this huge, teaming city, I had nothing else by which to take my bearings. While in Rio, I also noticed that the water circled down the drain the wrong way.

As for our performances, we were the seventh ballet company to come to Rio this year. They seemed to compare us favorably, though. Opening night was a gala affair. The women were beautifully dressed and jeweled; their fashions were at least a year ahead of ours. Ben Sommers of

Capezio's—the maker of our toe shoes—was in town, tying in the opening of his shoe store with our performances. We were included in lots of the entertaining, which was fun, but tiring.

During this time, Harold also flew into town from San Francisco to join us for a month. He didn't have any particular function that I remember—he didn't teach any of our classes—but we all enjoyed having him with us; the same old Harold teasing us in his semi-sarcastic way.

Around this time, Leon suggested that I start wearing more eye makeup off stage, start making myself look more glamorous. He told me that our Brazilian impresario had been quite taken with both my publicity photos and me on stage—he was ready to have me meet the President—but then he met me off stage, and was completely deflated. I didn't look at all the same.

I just laughed. I'd been aware of this transformation I made on stage ever since I started doing solos. I knew people didn't recognize me off stage, and I'd always been sort of glad. I liked the feeling of anonymity. My not being recognized had long been a company joke. Conrad, in particular, always teased me by adding, "You're so beautiful onstage." I remember now saying to myself, "Leon, you can tell me what to do on stage, but not off."

From Rio, after a detour inland for two performances in the planned city of Belo Horizonte, located in the mining district where many gems are mined, we went on to Sao Paolo. We were surrounded by elegance the whole five days we were there. Even our hotel rooms had bathroom walls of marble. The theater was lovely in the old grand manner; wonderful backstage area, tons of room, private dressing rooms, huge stage. Box seats for our shows were fantastically high priced—almost $20 a piece—the same price as for the Bolshoi, and almost sold out I was told.

After another quick trip inland for a show in Riberoa Preto—a charming, Portuguese-colonial town in the middle of the coffee-growing country and not visited by many tourists—we flew on up the East Coast of Brazil to Salvador, Bahia, the original capital of colonial Brazil.

Bahia was a true, tropical paradise. Wonderful long, white beaches stretched for miles. Palm trees swayed in the soft breezes. What a place to stay for a while, which we weren't. The city of Salvador had black-and-white mosaic sidewalks, many buildings of old, French-colonial style we were told, and lace-like grillwork on many of the houses. Our *Teatro*— the auditorium of the normal college—was in the old city, down at the foot of the mountain. The new city was on the top. You could get from one to the other by funicular railway.

On Sunday, some of the consulate people arranged to take us into the slum section of the city—where ninety percent of the town's population lived—to see the *Capoeira*, dances that originated during slave days in Brazil. Slaves hadn't been allowed to carry weapons, so they concealed razor blades in their toes, then kicked and sliced at each other with their feet. The dances were made up of these kicking and slicing motions.

On our way to the mud hut where the *Capoeira* was taking place, we passed a religious parade. A statue of the Virgin Mary, festooned in flowers, was being born on a litter through the muddy streets. Both adults and children—all dressed in their crisp, white, Sunday best—were jogging along behind.

When we reached the hut, we joined the crowd that was already watching two men dance. The two men were also dressed in fresh white shirts and pants. Their hands and feet were on the mud floor—stomachs to the ceiling— and they were making swiping motions at each other with their legs. They never used their arms for anything but support.

The dances were impressive, but what impressed me even more; every man, woman, and child was dressed in immaculately clean, white, perfectly ironed clothes. How did they manage this? They lived in mud houses built along mud streets with raw sewage running in ditches down the middle. They didn't even have running water.

That same evening, after our final performance, a few of us went with our local bus driver in his "best bus" over unpaved back roads in search of the *Condamblé*, or *Macumba* as it was sometimes called. These were voodoo rites, which were frequently performed in Bahia on Sunday nights. Our driver told us that a Catholic priest often began the ceremony by blessing the sacrificial chicken. We stopped at two different places, but neither was working that night.

From Salvador we went on to Recife, the third largest city in Brazil at the time. It was built on two rivers that flowed through the center of town. People called it the Venice of Brazil. But what I remember most about Recife was the huge cockroach that lived in a hole under the sink in the dressing room I shared with Nancy and Joce. I swear he was at least three inches long; much too big to squash. I'm not squeamish about bugs. I grew up in Marin County, a place I once heard described as an entomologist's delight because so many species of insects thrived there. I didn't know what to do about this fellow, though. He and I ended up with a truce. Every time he started to come out of his hole, Nancy or Joce would scream for me, and I'd go over and stamp my feet at him. Then he'd go back into his hole.

Our last city in Brazil was Belem, situated on the Bara River just southeast of the mouth of the Amazon River, only one or two degrees south of the equator. We could see why people called it *"inferno verde"*, green hell. If nothing else, the climate certainly slowed everything down—including us. It was so hard to get started in class. My feet swelled up so much in the heat that I had to exercise for ten minutes before I could get my toe shoes on. Our theater was a lovely, little, European Opera House—a relic of the rubber boom— but it was a bit run down. The extreme humidity made the paint peel.

From Belem we went on to Panama, where we stayed for a week at the luxurious Panama Hilton Hotel. During this time, Nancy left for home. When the tour began, most of us didn't know that she and Dick were expecting their first child, but now she was almost six months pregnant and beginning to look it. She could no longer get by on stage. Lew was afraid, with her shift in weight, that she might injure herself. Dick was worried, too. Harold left with her, and Leon Kalimos also unexpectedly left. Wana had their baby prematurely and the doctors were afraid it wouldn't live. Leon would be back, but it was awfully sad.

Of all the humid places we'd been, Panama was the worst. We were wet all the time. We absolutely dripped the minute we started working. Toe shoes squished immediately. All the light bulbs around our dressing room mirrors had toe shoes balancing on them, trying to dry out. One night I charred the sole of one of my toe shoes; it cracked in half when I put it on. In rehearsal my leotard got so wet that Dick couldn't partner me. His fingers kept getting stuck in the soggy fabric. Chris left wet footprints as she walked across the stage—and she was wearing toe shoes. After my shower, it was useless to try to dry myself off. No matter how many times I toweled, I was still dripping.

While in Panama, I also saw my first transvestite act. We ran into Janet Sassoon—an old friend from Jr. Ballet and Bill Christensen days—at our hotel; she was passing through Panama with the Berliner Ballet and it was her birthday. A group of us took her to Maxim's, a nightclub that boasted a calypso singer who made up songs about people in the audience. One of the acts was performed by a tall, glamorous woman dressed in a skimpy costume and huge Carmen Miranda-like headdress full of fruit. Her songs and dances were quite outrageous—and funny. At the end of her number, she took off her bra top and stood there, a man. Then he threw the oranges that had been in his bra at the audience.

Before leaving Panama, Leon returned. The baby was still all right. We all sighed with relief. Then we headed on up Central America, stopping first at San Jose, Costa Rica, which was at an altitude of 3,870 feet and much cooler and dryer. Pine trees and banana trees grew side by side. Costa Rica is called the Switzerland of Central America and it certainly looked clean and prosperous. One difference, though; everything was covered with a fine gray dust because a volcano in the vicinity was spewing ash.

San Jose had one of the most exquisite little jewel boxes of an opera house I had ever seen. It was perfectly maintained; marble staircases and columns, red plush carpets, crystal chandeliers, gold and white walls, European paintings on the ceiling, seats in the salon upholstered in aqua velvet. It even had a ghost.

Our next stop was Managua, Nicaragua, where the weather was again hot and humid. For our official State Department duty, we went to the Moorish-looking Presidential Palace for an audience with the President and his brother, who was General of the National Army. They were sons of the late President Samoza, who had been assassinated. I remember thinking, "The Samoza Brothers certainly have the government sewed up."

During our three-day stay in Nicaragua, we met two doctors from the U.S. who were trying to vaccinate all

Nicaraguan children against polio; the country was going through a polio epidemic. The doctors took several of us out into the countryside to meet some of the people—quite a different side of Nicaragua than we'd been seeing.

When we arrived in Tegucigalpa, Honduras, the town was in the middle of its Central American Independence Day parade. The only way our bus could reach the hotel was to go way up into the hills, then come back down along narrow, winding, cobblestone streets. Honduras was considered—along with Paraguay—one of the most backward of Latin American countries. At first glance, the people seemed happier here than in other places, though.

In San Salvador, El Salvador we stayed in a brand new hotel that had just opened. It was gorgeous. It was one in the Intercontinental chain. Squatters' thatched huts sat right on the edge of the grounds near the swimming pool. As I looked down at them from my hotel room window, I couldn't help but wonder how they felt seeing us here.

One morning a U.S. colonel whom we'd met at the Embassy reception the night before—a Colonel Hale who was training the Salvadorian Army—took several of us up to the mouth of the volcano, *Boqueron*. We drove up winding mountain roads through lovely, lush countryside for more than an hour. Crude huts along the way were covered with bougainvillea and hibiscus. The colors were unusually brilliant because of the volcanic soil. The mountain was always moist. It was covered in fog every day. People grew flowers around the crater and then took them to market to sell. Their only transportation was by oxen or by foot. They usually walked down the mountain to market one day, and then back up the next.

Our performance in San Salvador turned out to be a strange set-up. Part of the terrace of our hotel was closed over and a makeshift stage was set up. The ceiling was so low that lifts and jumps had to be done very carefully. The most hysterical feature, however, was the glass wall between us and the audience. With the audience in the dark, and the stage lights on us, all we could see were our own reflections in the glass. Our program, shortened to an hour, turned out to be just part of a benefit for some favorite charity of the President's wife. The tickets were expensive and included cocktails, the ballet, supper, and a nightclub show afterwards. Not so complimentary to us, but at least we got dinner.

Guatemala City, Guatemala was next. We were once again in a big city; this one with massive, stone, castle-like public buildings. Our theater was a cinema, nicely equipped, and with a good, flat stage. We also had a fine, live orchestra, again, which was wonderful—we hadn't realized we missed it until we had it again—and a responsive audience. We were thankful because we were all trying to sharpen up for Mexico City, our next and most important stop.

One unsettling thing about Guatemala City; as I left the theater after the show, children swarmed all around me, trying to take my flowers. A lot of children were begging on the streets. If you gave them anything at all, you were overrun; if not, you felt awful.

We finally arrived in Mexico City. Our performance in *Bellas Artes*—Mexico City's Opera House—was especially important. The theater had nicely canceled one of its operas so that we could have at least one performance there; for prestige. Our two performances in the National Auditorium would reflect how well we were liked in *Bellas Artes*.

The performance went well, our audience was enthusiastic, and everyone was happy. The following night we opened in the National Auditorium. When we arrived, we discovered we were sharing space with the International

Poultry Convention. I remember warming up in the hallway next to some exhibits of chickens, eggs, and hatchabators. There were almost 9,000 people in our audience. The stage was so huge—seventy feet square—that I almost lost my bearings during my solo. There were no footlights, the spotlight following me was blinding, the orchestra was so far away I could hardly see Earl conducting and therefore I kept losing center. I didn't know where the sides were because there were no wings. It was strange trying to space my variation on it, and even stranger trying to end my last pirouette facing front.

After Mexico City, we flew on to Guadalajara where we were met at the airport by a Mariachi band. Guadalajara was my idea of a delightful Mexican city; songs, flowers, colorful street markets, the massive stone cathedral with its tiled dome on one side of the main *plaza*, and our columned theater on another. Our final performance was absolutely packed with the most enthusiastic audience we'd ever had. At the end of our show the orchestra broke out with the bullfighting salute.

After Guadalajara we had only two more performances before returning home. One was in San Luis Potosi, a town all by itself in the middle of Mexico, and the other was in Monterrey, not far from the Texas border. San Luis Potosi had no airport, which meant we spent two long days riding the bus across central Mexico. The terrain changed three times; at first it was agricultural, then desert with huge Joshua trees, and then completely barren, almost solid rock. We stopped in a little village for lunch and arrived in the midst of a downpour. Streets were six inches deep in water. By the time we got to San Luis Potosi, I had a dilly of a fever. Instead of going to the reception that night, I went straight to bed.

What I remember most about San Luis Potosi was being semi-delirious with fever. I'd get up to sightsee for a little while, then go back to bed, then get up, again, so that I wouldn't become too weak. I remember my legs killing me while I was putting on my makeup. They hurt so much while I was warming up that I doubted I'd be able to jump. Luckily, my fever broke during the performance. The next day, as we went on to Monterrey, I felt much better.

After our one performance in Monterrey, with a formal reception afterwards, we caught the plane for home at 3:00 AM. I was so excited about returning home to John that I had trouble keeping my mind on that last performance. Letter writing over four months hadn't worked too well, and telephoning was even worse—it was hard getting through, and expensive. I felt as if I'd been gone for years.

The State Department Tours

4: Another Rude Awakening

JOHN MET ME AT THE AIRPORT. I SPOTTED HIM RIGHT AWAY. I WAS so happy to see him, but he looked sort of withdrawn, as if he wasn't too happy to see me. There was so much I wanted to tell him about my trip, but he wasn't interested in hearing about it. He told me about a trip he'd taken to New York the month before, though. I had no idea he'd even gone. He spent a week there. He auditioned some and said it was encouraging. He was glad he went. The desire had been eating in the back of his mind for a while. He used the money I sent home each week from my paycheck.

When we walked into our apartment, the mess overwhelmed me. It looked as if nothing had been cleaned up in the four months I'd been gone. That night, in bed, I felt as if I was lying next to a stranger.

We had a two-week break from classes and rehearsals and it took me most of that time to get things back in order— at least in the house. During that time I found out that John had been having an affair with a girl on campus with whom he had done some singing. I knew her slightly. I didn't ask if he'd taken her to New York with him. I guess he didn't expect to continue the affair while I was home, but I would be leaving again in just three months. Leon had announced that we were going on another State Department tour in January, this one to the Middle East. I couldn't think of not going. Before January we had our regular *Nutcracker* season, plus I would be going to Salt Lake City again—this time with Dick as my partner—for Bill's *Nutcracker*.

I didn't know what to do about my marriage, so I didn't do anything. Neither John nor I seemed to want to end it, but it had certainly changed. I blamed myself, too. If I hadn't gone on tour, he might not have had the affair. Though he never did say he resented my performing, he certainly acted like it. I remember him once making the crack, "You think the world's your oyster, don't you."

On the other hand, I thought I was doing him a favor by staying out of his hair, relieving him of any pressure to pay attention to me. He was in his last year of studies before his orals. He'd told me many times that this was a difficult time for doctoral candidates. They were known to sometimes crack under the pressure.

During this interval between foreign trips, I ran into an old friend of Néné's walking on the street in Berkeley one day. He drove Néné, Conrad and me to Santa Barbara and back for one of our "guest" appearances several years back. He had an old, black hearse; we put our costumes in the back. We drove home up the coast and had a hilarious time. He was now also working on his doctorate and—of all things—living in a rooming house just down the street from us. One afternoon I had coffee with him in his kitchen.

He commented, "Sally, I can't imagine you doing house-wifely things in that house up the street; cleaning, cooking, washing and ironing." I admitted I felt a bit out of place, but there was no reason why I couldn't do such things. It was like playing a role.

I didn't mind playing that role, either. I remember one evening at supper—I'd had a day off during the week and spent most of it puttering around the house—John saying,

"You look relaxed and happy. Not dancing for a day isn't so bad after all, is it?"

Our *Nutcracker* season—and Christmas—came and went. Then Dick and I flew to Salt Lake City to dance in Bill's *Nutcracker*. While we were gone, Lew began choreographing some new ballets for the tour; *Sinfonia*, *Caprice*, and a *pas de trois* called *Divertissements D'Auber*. Our repertoire this trip also included Balanchine's *Serenade*. We hadn't done it in a while, so needed to relearn it. Tony Duquette, who designed our *Beauty and the Beast* production, was designing the costumes and sets for our three new ballets, plus some new costumes for *Serenade*. This is probably the one time in *Serenade*'s history that it wasn't performed in three-quarter-length, pale blue tutus. We were still dressed in pale blue, but in short, Greek tunics, with gold laurel wreaths in our hair.

When Dick and I returned from Utah, we had a lot of catching up to do. Somewhere during all of this, Nancy also gave birth to their baby; a little boy, Eric. Everything was happening at once, and we were to take off January 11th for the Middle East. Nancy would stay home with the baby for the first month, and then join us after that, leaving the baby with her mother.

During rehearsal one afternoon, while Dick and I were learning the adagio from *Caprice*—Dick was dragging me across the floor—he adjusted my position as I lay across his back. I'm not sure how or why it happened, but he suddenly felt a sharp pain in his chest. Later, he learned that he had punctured his lung while leaning over with me on top of him. I, naturally, felt terribly—and you can imagine how I was teased afterwards. One good thing; the injury was not permanent. It would heal in about a month. Dick could stay home with Nancy and the baby, and then the two of them could join us in Istanbul.

There was one major problem, though. Dick was now my main partner. Leon Danielian, who was once again coming with us as a guest artist, couldn't partner me because I was too tall for him. Rocky had already been alternating some of Dick's roles, but he couldn't take on all of them. Kent, Mike, Julien and Glenn were taking on more roles, too, but none of them had yet done *pas de deuxs*. As for covering Nancy, Jocelyn—who was now dancing with us full-time and no longer considered a guest artist—and I were expected to divide her dancing load. Chris, who had grown increasingly restless and unhappy in the Company, left us right after our South American trip and was now in Europe. Fiona Fuerstner, Virginia Johnson and Louise Lawler were already dancing many solo roles, but weren't yet doing *pas de deuxs*, either. There was no getting around it. I couldn't sit out for a month while the hole in Dick's lung healed. I needed another partner. Lew, with the help of Balanchine, managed to come up with one.

Royes Fernandez had been touring with Ballet Theater in Europe when that company's truck carrying all their musical scores, costumes and sets caught fire and burned up. Everything was lost and the company had to disband for an indefinite period of time. All the dancers suddenly found themselves without work.

Balanchine showed great sympathy for their plight and employed as many of them as he could. He particularly liked the way Royes danced and had already hired him when Lew came asking for help. Balanchine lent him to us for the duration of our tour. Royes was at the moment touring with a small group of dancers who had banded together and gotten some bookings, but would be through by the time we left for the Middle East. He could join us at the airport in New York.

Interestingly, Royes and the concert group were appearing at the Oakland Auditorium shortly before our departure. I was anxious to go see what my new partner looked like. Constance Coler, who was married to an Opera Chorus friend of John's, and who was also going again with us on tour—I guess she and her husband, Adrian McNamara, hashed out the long separations better than John and I did—wanted to come to the concert, too. So did Ade. John declined, though, saying he had to study. So Connie, Ade and I went off to the concert and enjoyed it immensely. All three of us were enthusiastic about Royes. He had an open, pleasant manner on stage and was a beautiful dancer. His style was clean and pure—no mannerisms at all—and elegant. He reminded me of a dark version of Erik Bruhn.

The day of our departure came. John was quiet, and I was dubious about what might happen between us during this trip. I half expected him to go back to his girlfriend, except that he might be too busy. This was his last semester of classes; he should be studying harder than ever. At one point I decided not to have money taken out of my paycheck and sent home as I had last time, but then changed my mind. I expected John not to work; just study. At any rate, I felt there was no use worrying the whole time I was gone. This trip I would just go ahead and have a good time, not pine so.

John drove me to the airport and stayed to see me board the plane. Years later, a friend of mine told me that she heard him mutter under his breath, "Never again."

The State Department Tours

5: The Middle East—A Seed of Mistrust

TWENTY-SEVEN HOURS AFTER LEAVING SAN FRANCISCO, WE ARRIVED in Athens, Greece. We were exhausted, but thrilled to be there even so. On the bus into town from the airport we passed the ruins of Zeus's temple, then saw the Academy, the University, and the outline of the Acropolis on a nearby hilltop. It was dark by the time we arrived at our hotel, but before collapsing into bed, several of us walked around a few blocks just to absorb the sense of history.

Our trip had been broken up with a longer-than-expected layover in New York while SABENA Airline readied our charter plane for the flight to Athens. Our long wait in their VIP lounge turned into a roaring cocktail party. Royes joined us here. I was anxious to find out how tall he was; I also thought he might be a bit uncomfortable coming into the company cold like this. He already knew Leon Danielian, but that was all. Therefore, I went over and introduced myself to him, first comparing heights—he wasn't as tall as Dick, but was tall enough—and then being friendly, for soon he and I would be spending a lot of time together.

That first morning in Athens, when we arrived at the theater, we discovered our performances had been pushed up a day. The first performance was to be a command performance—arranged by our embassy—for King Paul, Queen Frederika, and the Princesses of Greece. We also learned that some of our equipment had been waylaid in Belgium. It was being flown out charter that night. If it arrived in time, we would be opening tomorrow night. Royes and I were scheduled to dance *Caprice*. Royes had today and tomorrow before the show to learn the ballet. Then, by the end of the week, we were scheduled to dance *Nutcracker*. After class and around scheduled afternoon and evening orchestra rehearsals, Royes and I started learning ballets.

Royes was a good sport about it. He'd never seen any of our choreography before, he'd never seen me before—until two days ago, and he had no idea how I danced. Luckily, our part in *Caprice* was fairly short and easy. Lew changed the part where Dick punctured his lung.

Nutcracker was a different story. It was longer and harder. Royes probably knew the standard Petipa/Ivanov version, but he didn't know Lew's version. I don't remember whose male solo he ended up doing, or which *virtuoso* steps he chose for the *coda*, but he had to learn the *adagio* from scratch and adjust to partnering me. As we got into it, all the supported turns seemed fine, and the flying jumps to catches worked well, but some of the lifts were quite acrobatic and took time to accomplish. We didn't have that time, so we decided to just stick to big *grand jété* lifts. We decided to make our whole approach "romantic" rather than "spectacular". It turned out to be quite a different *pas de deux* from the one Dick and I performed—and equally successful.

During our dinner break between afternoon and evening rehearsal, I broke a rule I had set for myself concerning alcohol and dancing. I never drank anything alcoholic before dancing, even if there was half a day in between. However, tonight's rehearsal was mostly for the orchestra, Royes and I weren't going to learn anything more today, we were exhausted, and wine tasted good with dinner. I decided this evening wouldn't really matter. Actually, I enjoyed the rehearsal—I floated through it—but I did notice a difference in my muscle response. It was not instantaneous. I realized how much I counted on that instant muscle response for dancing. I decided my rule was a good one. I never broke it, again.

The following day, though it was our Opening and we would probably be in the theater from one o'clock on, several of us got up early and went to the Acropolis. We hired a guide who took us over the entire hill; through the massive entrance, among the Parthenon's ancient marble pillars, past a temple with caryatids holding up part of the roof. Our guide also showed us an excellent view of Mars Hill, the Old Agora, and the cave where Socrates drank his poison and died. We later learned he probably made that last one up.

That evening we opened with **Serenade**. When I found myself standing onstage in front of Greece's Royal Family in my pale-blue Greek tunic and gold laurel wreath in my hair, under soft blue lights, with the opening strains of Tchaikovsky's *Serenade for Strings* beginning to swell; it was almost too much. I still remember the chills running up and down my entire body, the goose bumps, my scalp tingling, the hairs down the outside of my arms standing on end.

After the performance—Royes remembered his part, thank goodness—the U.S. Embassy gave a big, fancy, full-dress reception. Jocelyn and I were asked to help in the receiving line, which gave us a wonderful opportunity to meet all the dignitaries. The Royal Family did not attend, but everyone else was there and anxious to be hospitable. For the past six years, since 1953, Greece had been working hard to pull itself out of the chaos caused first by the German occupation, then by guerrilla warfare against the Communists. They were now constructing new roads, new buildings, new hotels, and were trying to encourage tourism. The crowds hadn't started to come yet, but the Greeks were busily preparing for them.

During most of our stay in Athens I was exhausted, yet keyed up at the same time. I hadn't yet adjusted to the time change, so I stayed out half the night partying, singing, learning Greek dances, and smashing wine glasses in fireplaces. Then I'd fall into a deep sleep in the afternoon, almost as if drugged, before going back to the theater for performances. In between, I rehearsed long hours and squeezed in as much sightseeing as possible.

For one of our afternoon rehearsals we found ourselves having a condensed class and rehearsal with an audience of University students. It was practically a performance. We did *Beauty and the Shepherd*, which Rocky and I hadn't done since Mexico, and Royes and I had to do *Nutcracker Pas de Deux*. That was one way to pull together, fast.

For closing night we performed both those ballets. It was fun doing our Greek myth in Athens. *(Beauty and the Shepherd* was based on the story of Paris and the Golden Apple.) I was glad to be the one doing *Helen*. Rocky was glad to be the one doing *Paris*, too. Royes's and my first *Nutcracker* was a bit rugged, but Royes made it exciting even if, technically, things weren't going so well. At the end of the performance there was a big presentation on stage. Lew received a beautifully mounted, Second Century BC, Greek coin for the company and Joce and I received lovely gardenia corsages.

From Athens we flew on to Salonica, or Thessaloniki, as most of the Greeks still knew it. Salonica is the capitol of Macedonia, the second largest city in Greece, the land of Alexander the Great. His birthplace was right in the city, as well as that of Ataturk, about whom we would hear a lot more once we got to Turkey. The city, built around a crescent-shaped harbor, faced the sea. The hills rose abruptly behind it. Our hotel was right on the water.

The minute we arrived, the U.S.I.S. whisked us off to an official reception, then on to what was probably one of the most genuine goodwill exchanges of our whole trip; a visit to the Thessaloniki Agricultural and Industrial School. This was a farm school where rural youth from all over Greece came to learn modern farming methods, which they then took back to their villages. It was American-sponsored. The boys were at the school for four years. We ate dinner with the senior boys, and then went into their assembly hall for a program of songs and dances. We participated in some of these, and also in some games. Later, we received glowing reports from our consulate. The following day the boys from the farm school came to watch our class and rehearsal at the theater.

For our opening performance, the audience was not demonstrative, but seemed to appreciate our being there, anyway. The Consulate gave us a champagne-and-sandwich reception afterwards. In that the performance didn't even start until 9:30 PM, it was late by the time we got back to the hotel, but Rocky, Royes and I sat in the bar for a chat over tea and cognac, anyway, and analyzed the company situation to date.

Things were going well for the three of us, but others were not so happy. There was a lot of disgruntlement already. Leon D. now had to share "guest artist" billing with Royes instead of Jocelyn. Joce no longer had "guest" status; she still had her "guest" roles, but her name was now down with the rest of ours on the program and she was also dividing Nancy's parts with me. Rocky was taking on more of Dick's parts—which didn't please the other fellows—and doing them well; I saw him do *Mac* in **Filling Station** from out front one night and was surprised at how good he looked. Though I often danced **Con Amore** with Leon D., with Dick out, I had also recently begun doing it with Rocky. I could see that when Nancy and Dick rejoined us in Istanbul, they would be feeling uneasy. Before even thinking of getting their parts back, they would have to get back into shape. Tensions and resentments, which were already in place, would be swirling. Royes would definitely feel in the way.

The weather turned bitter cold the following day. We had both a matinee and evening performance. People kept saying it never snowed here, but it was snowing. I think they believed it, though, because the walls of the auditorium stopped two feet short of the roof, allowing the breezes and snow to blow through. The theater was consequently drafty, damp, and absolutely freezing. The only heat came from two wood-burning stoves. We barely had an hour between shows, so the U.S.I.S. brought in sandwiches that we ate while huddling around the stoves. My feet were like blocks of ice. I couldn't feel them at all, and in *Sinfonia* I had to move fast—nearly impossible.

After a day like this, I was glad when the U.S.I.S. man, who had taken several of us sightseeing the day before, asked us to go with him to one of the popular *tavernas* afterwards for dinner, bazooki music, and dancing. He asked a Greek friend of his to join us. Then the company bus arrived. All of us had a marvelous time, and Leon K. started razzing Connie—who was my roommate this year—and me about going out with "strange men".

Not long after this, on the bus one day, Leon D. and Royes decided to have some fun teasing Connie and me. They said they had something to show the "women" of the company; other than Nancy, we were the only ones married at the time. They had picked up some pornographic ashtrays and were dying to show them to us. The ashtrays were painted in classic Greek style. Each was of a man participating in the ancient spring rite where men strapped on huge phalluses and jumped around. I was amazed at what I saw. I had heard about this, but had never seen anything like it before. The ashtrays were outrageous—and funny. All the fellows were watching us to see our reactions. I decided to play it cool.

The bad weather continued. It moved on to Ankara, Turkey, our next stop. Two days after our arrival, it was still snowing and the airport was still closed. They closed it right after we arrived; actually, they closed it before we arrived, but opened it back up just to let us in. We had been waiting in airports for two days trying to get here, and Leon finally said we couldn't wait any longer. Now we felt as if we might never get back out.

Our hotel was hysterical. Though Connie and I had a suite, it had the barest of necessities. The help was contrary; they didn't understand well and, unlike the Orientals who automatically said "yes", they automatically said "no". If you argued with them long enough you might get what you wanted. Ankara had a newer, more modern hotel, but it didn't have enough room for all of us. Leon K. wanted us all to stay together.

The weather was cold and wet; everything looked muddy and dreary. We weren't the least bit tempted to go outside for a look around. The present city of Ankara was fairly new. It was built in 1923 when Ataturk moved the capital from Istanbul. This whole area had once been the center of Hittite culture, though, and had lots of interesting things to see, but I might never know. Royes and I spent time in the theater making some changes to the pas de deux—for added interest. It still felt a little rough in places, but better in others. I was beginning to straighten out and move more freely, again, rather than just hang on and pull together.

During our stay in Ankara we had several "taxi experiences". Evidently one rarely went anywhere without one. Our first "experience" took place in the middle of the night after our opening performance. The company had been divided among four U.S.I.S. homes for supper parties. The bus, which was supposed to deliver us, never arrived, so we divided up and took taxis. The drivers were all given addresses, but our driver promptly got lost. None of the streets had signs. "The city is expanding so fast," we were told. Our driver spoke only Turkish, seemed completely stupid, stopped in the middle of a boulevard and nearly got us killed. He didn't know where we were, or where we were going, and our host had no telephone. Otty—Ottavio de Rosa, our conductor this trip—at least knew how to get to the home of one of our U.S.I.S. men. He'd been there the day before. So we went there, and the poor man had to leave his party and lead us to ours. I had a good time once we finally got there, but Leon K. and Otty were fit to be tied.

At this point, almost the whole Company started coming down with bad colds and fevers. Therefore, Leon K. cancelled our attendance at any more parties given in our honor. This made things embarrassing for the U.S.I.S. A Turkish man who was writing a ballet book, and whom we had met in San Francisco two years before, was hosting one of the parties. After he was told the company couldn't come, he wrote directly to Leon D. and asked if he, Joce, Royes, Rocky and I would please come. We did go, and a U.S.I.S. couple also attending the party seemed most appreciative.

The following day was a Sunday, and we were free until 6:00 PM class. Leon D., Joce, Royes and I had another invitation; this one to brunch at the home of a lady we had met at the Embassy party the first night, and by whom I'd sat in the PX cafeteria one day at lunch. She wrote criticisms for The Dancing Star Digest. Her name was Ryllis Hesoutra Simpson. In her younger days, she had been a Ruth St. Denis-type dancer and had danced all over the world. She loved having the chance to talk to theater people again. It brought back so many memories for her. I remember her standing in the wings one matinee, watching with such a wistful expression on her face. She had recently been widowed and was now working in communications for the U.S. Government. She cooked us a wonderful sausage, egg and corn muffin breakfast and asked her Turkish landlady, who was also widowed and who published a women's journal in Istanbul, to come join us.

After breakfast, the landlady took us upstairs to her flat for Turkish coffee, then for a short sightseeing trip to Ataturk's imposing mausoleum. She kept stressing that she was an Ataturk child; a modern, liberated, Middle Eastern woman. Ataturk, after World War I, founded the modern Republic of Turkey. He became its first President and made some significant changes that separated it from the rest of Islam—including changing its alphabet.

On the way back to the hotel, we stopped for tea at the landlady's golf club, with still enough time for a rest before theater call. Seeing that I didn't dance until the last ballet this night, and my foot was killing me—I had developed a soft corn that had gotten infected—I decided to miss 6:00 PM class, stay off my foot a little longer, get more rest, then do an extra-long warm-up before going on stage. When I arrived at the theater both Leon K. and Gordon were mad at me. They thought I was goofing off. Though I had told them about my foot, they'd forgotten. When I re-enlightened them, they sort of apologized, but by then I was mad for the rest of the evening. Luckily, **Nut Pas de Deux** went pretty well, so they had no gripes. After the show, our "taxi group"—we were to go in groups in taxis to and from the theater when there was no bus, never by ourselves—went out for a delicious supper, another taxi experience, and much bourbon. I felt thoroughly rebellious and enjoyed myself immensely.

Shortly after this, in the bus on the way back to the hotel one night, Leon K. got up and announced, "There's entirely too much fooling around going on, and I want you guys to stop." He ended by pointing directly at me.

This did it. I thought his remark was entirely uncalled for. I didn't think I'd done anything that could be construed as improper. As far as I was concerned, Leon had declared war, so I shot back, "I haven't fooled around with anyone since I left home."

I hadn't stopped to think what this might sound like,

and of course the whole bus burst into gales of laughter. I
was sitting next to Royes and he completely cracked up. I
was terribly embarrassed and turned beet red. Royes put his
arm around me and let me bury my face in his shoulder.

Things calmed down somewhat after this. I also didn't
miss class, again, and my foot was still killing me.

Our next stop was Izmir. It took us two days to get there,
too, but once there, the weather was beautifully clear, though
still freezing cold. On the way to our hotel from the airport,
we drove up to a castle that had been built by one of
Alexander the Great's generals. From there we had a
spectacular view of the city spreading across the steep hillside
below us and ending at the bay, which opened onto the
Aegean Sea. Izmir was the second largest port in Turkey; a
charming old city with many minarets, old Roman Agora,
the docks, and winding, colorful streets. It was the ancient
city of Smyrna, built on an older city first established in the
third Millennium B.C. People had been living here for 5,000
years.

We had two receptions that first evening; the Turkish-
American Association gave the first one and everyone had
to attend. I met quite a few Turkish people, but most of
them didn't speak English well, so communicating was work.
After two hours of it, I was tired. Then our U.S. Consul
expected about twelve for dinner afterwards. At first I wasn't
going, but Lew wanted me to, so I went. Again, the driver
got lost and didn't know where to go, but we finally arrived.
By that time I didn't feel at all like being charming, so just
relaxed with a gin and tonic. When dinner was served, the
Mayor and his wife escorted Lew and me into the dining
room. They both turned out to be delightful. She was "Miss
Europe" of 1953 and lovely.

The following day we were given a long list of do's and don'ts by our Cultural Affairs Officer, Mr. Humphrey, who treated us as if we'd come straight from the states without ever having been anywhere dirty before. Actually, Izmir was comparatively clean. But he was trying his best, and the Army wives were wonderful in supplying us with toilet paper, drinking water, oranges, and grapefruit juice.

One of our rules was to eat nowhere except at the PX, and soon enough we learned why. The Turkish currency was in crisis and fast becoming valueless. A great effort was being made to stop the flow of all money. We weren't to spend any of it. The few times we had to, no one had bills for making change. I remember one evening trying to pay the taxi driver for our ride. He couldn't give us change. We had to go into the hotel lobby, change our bills at the desk—Leon had seen to it that the desk had enough currency for such emergencies—then come back out and give the driver his exact fare.

Our theater had few regular facilities. The stage surface wasn't too bad because Mr. Humphrey, whom we grew to appreciate more and more, spent the entire night before our opening smoothing it down with a hand plane. Our dressing rooms were makeshift; we sat on the floor, using chairs for our makeup tables. I remember being so crowded that I found myself combing my neighbor's hair along with my own. Evidently there hadn't been much of a toilet, either, because Mr. Humphrey brought one from his house and had it installed backstage.

On opening night, right after the gunshot in *Filling Station,* the power failed. It was fixed shortly, but before the ballet was over, it failed again. Mr. Humphrey had a crew of electricians on hand to hook us to power lines outside in case this should happen, but it took time. Both the audience and we sat in the dark for a while. The power was finally fixed, we finished our program, the Mayor and the Governor brought flowers out on stage, and all ended in grand style, but for a while none of us were too sure.

We stayed over a day to give an extra show, and then the day after that, the Governor and Mayor arranged a trip to Ephesus for us before we took off for Istanbul. They wanted us to see their famous Greek and Roman ruins. Some of the ruins were still quite complete. We posed for photos in the theater, and then walked up a marble road that was flanked by a library on one side and the temple of Hadrian on the other. Behind Hadrian's temple were some baths and some cubicles that were believed to be the red light district of the ancient city.

By the time we got to Istanbul, it was snowing again. The waiting room at Istanbul's airport looked exactly like the one in Ankara, and for one awful moment we all thought, "My God, we've gone back to Ankara by mistake." It was already dark, so we drove straight to the Park Hotel—a spacious, elegant, sprawling sort of place. Nancy and Dick were there to meet us. They both looked well and rested.

A light snow was still falling the next day. I didn't step outside the hotel until 5:00 PM for our U.S.I.S. press reception at the Hilton Hotel. We had class that morning in one of the downstairs bars called "The Snake Pit", where, to our surprise, the management allowed us to put rosin on the floor. After the press reception, Leon D. asked Nancy, Dick and Royes to join him for dinner; a thoughtful thing for him to do. Royes had been visibly uncomfortable all day. This would help smooth things for him.

The following day, after class and a press conference in the hotel, Nancy, Dick and I went sightseeing with some Turkish friends of friends Dick and I had made in Salt Lake City. They were the Ismens, and they drove us along the

Bosphorus to the Rumeli Hisar—a massive stone fortress built shortly before the invasion of Istanbul by Mohammed II. In one of the three huge towers we saw the Byzantine chain that had been stretched across the Golden Horn. After leaving the fortress, we went to the Black Sea end of the Bosphorus to meet a launch provided by Mrs. Ismen's brother, who was a manager of Mobil Oil. He lived on the Asiatic side of the water and wanted us to come for tea. We got a big kick out of crossing the Bosphorus in a boat.

It was late by the time we returned to the hotel, so I found Connie and just ate supper there. After the two of us finished, we sat with Royes while he ate his dinner. He was still feeling uneasy and wanted someone to talk to. After he was through, the three of us went to Connie's and my room, brewed coffee in my traveling percolator, and chatted until quite late. After this, Royes came frequently to our room for coffee and conversation.

A few days later, Lew told all of us to stay in bed until class time. There was lots of illness. The day before, almost the whole company was lined up at the PX dispensary. Maurice Lemus was taken to the hospital; he had meningitis and would be out for three weeks. In *Caprice* Rocky would have to do his part; Dick would have to do Rocky's. Dick was not happy about dancing under Royes for three weeks. Leon Kalimos's fever, after hitting 104 degrees, went back down some, but he was still pretty sick. He was working from his bed. He should have gone to the hospital, but wouldn't. Mike had been dancing the last couple of days with a high fever—from an infected bite on his foot—and so had Julien. Nancy and Dick needed to get back into some kind of shape before they could do too much. We started joking, saying, "If anyone else wants to get sick, he has to go on the waiting list."

I joined the line at the dispensary and finally had my soft corn looked at. It was discouraging. The corn was too deep for the doctor to cut out without proper facilities, of which there were none here. Besides, I'd be off my foot for two weeks. All the doctor could do was to give me some salve that would eventually harden the core and bring it to the surface.

One morning I got up early to see the treasures of the *Topkapi Serai*, Suleiman's huge palace on a promontory overlooking the Golden Horn. It was a terrible morning to go out; freezing cold, windy, snowing. No one would come with me. The palace wasn't open every day, though, and I was afraid of missing it. This day the Harem, Suleiman's Exposition, and the Treasury were open.

As my guide and I walked along massive stone corridors that stretched on and on, the wind and the snow swirled around us like a blizzard. I swathed my head and shoulders in my big woolen stole, over my overcoat, but the poor guide just hunched down in his uniform jacket. He looked miserable. I was the only visitor in the whole place. I'm sure he wished I wasn't there, either.

We first went to the harem, a complex city in itself. One could see how it must really have been like a prison; doors opening upon doors, all guarded by eunuchs. The receiving rooms were straight out of *The Arabian Nights*; low couches covered with silks interwoven with threads of gold and encrusted with pearls and precious stones, lounging cushions, lovely carpets—some of them quite tarnished, but still beautiful. My guide also showed me the mother sultan's apartment, where the coffee drinking ceremony took place. She had a splendid view of the Golden Horn and a fantastically huge, curtained bed.

I kept wondering, "How does anyone make it?"

The Suleiman Exposition held artifacts pertaining to the reign of Suleiman the Magnificent; coins from different countries in the empire, the key to Vienna, maps, Suleiman's weapons and some of his garments. His turban was adorned with fantastic, huge jewels.

The Treasury was filled with so many objects encrusted with pearls, diamonds, rubies, emeralds and turquoise that the concept of value was lost. As the guide pointed out, the value was as much in the time used for workmanship—one lounging couch encrusted with jewels took ten workmen twenty years to make—as in the amount of precious stones used. Even stirrups and a suit of armor were covered with gems.

I got back to the hotel just in time for bus call to the theater for class and rehearsal. More replacing was needed. Virginia Johnson sprained her ankle and Gerrie Bucher went to the hospital with what might be appendicitis.

In the middle of all this, our appearance in Syria was postponed until after the first anniversary of the United Arab Republic [a tenuous political union between Egypt and Syria, with Yemen later joining in]. The U.S. was not popular in Syria. Our government thought it best if we weren't there for the celebrations. This meant we had two weeks to kill.

To fill up some of the time, Leon K. scheduled four performances in Bursa, a skiing and mineral bath resort in the mountains south and across the Marmara Sea from Istanbul. He also made a wonderful deal with the boat that took us there; all personnel, luggage, and our 12,000 lbs. of equipment went for $65.00. For this jaunt we had to leave Gerrie and Maurice behind, as well as our electrician, Dan Winters, who now had meningitis, as well.

After a four-hour boat trip and a drive in taxis through lovely rural countryside, we arrived in Bursa. The resort was located in a long, green valley just at snow line. Our hotel was on the edge of town, right next to the "hammum", the Turkish mineral bathhouse. Joce and I were dying for some chocolate, which was not always easy to find, so we took a horse-drawn buggy into town, but returned fairly soon because it was snowing and cold. I went to bed and read, napped, ate chocolate, spilt some of my precious coffee all over the floor, and Connie and I got on another one of our long talking jags. One night Connie and I remained talking at our dinner table so long that Leon K. finally came over to find out what "two old married girls" were talking about.

The next morning I went downstairs to have my hair washed. They gave me all sorts of treatment, but I think the quantity of my thick hair, which was then halfway down my back, perplexed them. They didn't seem to know what to do with it. In any case, I didn't get a good hair wash. Connie and I then went to see the Green Mosque. We arrived just at prayer time. Not wanting to intrude, we stopped at the doorway, and then peered inside. We could see the deep green tiles for which the mosque was named and hear the prayers. When the prayers were over, the people came back outside, still praying, with their palms turned upwards.

After our opening performance, the Turkish/American Association gave us a reception at the hotel. With the language barrier, there was little mixing. What saved the evening was the dance band. It started out semi-classical and reserved, but gradually warmed up. By the end of the evening, it turned into a regular jam session. Rocky and I did an exhibition Charleston, and those of us remaining danced everything from National Turkish to popular U.S. dances. Some of the Turkish men were excellent at the cha-cha-cha and could jitterbug, too. We danced until 3:00 AM.

The next day finally turned sunny and mild, but instead of sightseeing, we all went to the hospital for throat smear tests. Evidently we couldn't leave Turkey—or perhaps enter Lebanon—until it was certain none of us were carriers of meningitis. There wasn't enough culture for the tests, and after waiting at the hospital for almost an hour, it was decided that we take the tests back at the hotel at 4:00 PM. I thought, "Another day shot", but actually, I was glad to just rest. I was dancing two to three ballets a night, and it was getting to me.

The following day we weren't to return to Istanbul until mid-afternoon. Leon and the impresario arranged a sightseeing trip for the morning, but I decided not to go because I had already seen some of the sights and this might be my one chance to take a Turkish mineral bath on a day I didn't have to dance. I would never take one before dancing, just as I would never swim; my muscles would get too relaxed—another case of "spaghetti legs". The bath was right next door, my body was sore and tired from all the extra dancing, and it would feel wonderful. At this time it never occurred to me that the baths might be for men only. There were no signs saying so, but being the Middle East—even though women were less restricted at that time, particularly in Turkey—maybe it was just assumed. In any case, I took my bathing suit and went. The place was empty except for the attendants and Rocky, who came in not long after I did, and a friendly Turkish dentist who showed us all the different things to do. It was marvelous. I began to feel half-way human once more.

On our trip back to Istanbul it began snowing—again. Leon was mad at me for not coming on the sightseeing trip. He said the impresario was disappointed. Some of the other dancers seemed annoyed with me, too; I supposed for dancing so much. Gerrie Bucher was at the hotel when we returned, her appendix was back to normal without needing an operation, and she turned out to be the one carrying the meningitis. Both Maurice and Dan were still quite sick, but were improving. We left for Beirut the following day.

Our flight to Beirut, Lebanon was another hair-raiser. We were in the center of a snow and lightning storm when the plane was struck by lightning twice; first on one of the propellers, then right on the nose of the cockpit. Our pilot later told us he thought he'd had it for sure. Even with our seat belts on, we were being tossed all over. Gordon was so busy hanging on to the armrests of his seat, trying to keep his head from hitting the cabin ceiling that he forgot to be sick. A priest sitting nearby started praying. Again we heard, "But it never snows here."

Our hotel in Beirut was right in the center of the business district, on one of the main squares. Its rooms took up the eighth and ninth floors of a long office building that also held one of the city's nightclubs on its roof terrace. Our theater, which was a cinema, was down on the corner. We were told we could get to it from inside our building.

On the day of our opening performance, Connie and I went out early to shop and then came back to the hotel to eat and rest. It's lucky we returned when we did. As we started our rest, a riot broke out in the square below. There went our rest. Our room was on the ninth floor on the front so we had a perfect bird's-eye view. I stood on the radiator and started taking pictures. There was lots of shouting and people running back and forth. Shopkeepers scurried to push display carts back inside shops, then lower the grills and lock them up. A streetcar turned onto the square and some fellow started banging at it with a light pole that had already been knocked down. Another streetcar came into view—this one from the Arab section—and someone set it on fire. By now quite a crowd had gathered. There were shots, and then people ran to the other end of the square. Some men in uniform arrived. Suddenly, through my camera lens, I noticed someone in the mob pointing directly at me. I think I froze. The next thing I knew, I was on the floor. Connie had pushed me off the radiator. Leon Kalimos came running down the hall, knocking on everyone's door, telling us to keep our heads out of sight. When he saw that I had been taking pictures he had a fit.

Leon later told me that he had been in the lobby counting money with the hotel manager when the mob suddenly burst in. He and the manager just scooped everything up in their arms and rushed to the elevators, went up to the eighth floor, and then held the two elevators there.

Regardless of the mobs, we had our six o'clock class and nine o'clock opening show. The inside passage from our hotel to the theater proved useful. Amazingly, about 700 people came to see us dance. By show time, the Army had stationed four tanks around the square and announcements had been made over the radio and television saying that people attending our performance would be protected. Bayonet-carrying guards escorted them from their cars into the theater. The Embassy held their reception after the performance, as well. Guards were all over, but everyone was in high spirits. The riots had been going on for the past six months. Some of the Embassy people jokingly remarked they staged one for us so we wouldn't be disappointed. The riots were not anti-American, but anti-Christian; against the Christian faction within the Lebanese Government. We just happened to be in the middle of it. The square outside our hotel and theater was a favorite place for holding demonstrations. Never-the-less, we could be a convenient target.

The following morning I went outside the hotel just long enough to buy some newspapers. I wanted to see if there were any reviews. Traffic was moving normally, but I was unusually aware of the people on the street. The tanks were gone, but there were Army trucks and armed guards stationed all around—two in our hotel lobby. As I turned my back on the square to look at the newspapers, I suddenly felt extremely vulnerable—a feeling I'd never experienced before. I casually turned around, placing my back to the wall, then continued going through the papers.

For the next two days we had matinees and evenings, which meant we were in the theater the whole time. We barely stepped outside. The first day, Joce went to the hospital with an infected ear that had to be drained. This was the first performance she'd ever missed and it upset her. She wouldn't be able to fly in time to go with us to Teheran, either, so Nancy and I would have to cover for her there, as well. This day, Nancy was already doing **Barocco** for Ginny—as we called Virginia Johnson—and was supposed to do **Beauty and the Shepherd**, but she had to go into **Don Q** for Joce, so I ended up doing both **Beauty** and **Nutcracker**. Double shows of that program were a bit heavy for us both. Dick worked into **Nutcracker** for the first time in the afternoon. Luckily it "went". Rehearsal had been terrible—Dick kept saying I was doing everything completely differently—and he was nervous. If I'd gotten nervous, too, it would have been bad. I was changing partners so much during the day that I couldn't let it bother me. I did **Nutcracker** with Royes in the evening and put *fouettés* into the coda just to add to the excitement.

When it came time to leave for Iran, it took us two days to get out of Lebanon. We spent all of the first day sitting at the airport, waiting—and reading pornographic books. A pornographic bookstall was there, and between us, we bought one of everything in stock. We finally had to return to the hotel we'd already checked out of. Most of us ended that day in the nightclub upstairs, eating dinner and making up dirty limericks. I later found out our delay wasn't because of bad weather; some of our plane crew didn't have proper visas. We were now flying charter Ethiopian Airlines. Our plane was a custom-made, deluxe DC6B. It had gold lamé trim, hand-printed curtains of Ethiopian lion hunt scenes, turquoise and metallic gold upholstery, gold air nozzles, and a marvelous steward named John, who gave us steak lunches and all we wanted to drink.

The next day, as we flew over Iraq, we were told we would have to land in Baghdad. Our pilot was taken off the plane for over an hour—to sign all sorts of clearance papers, we were told. We remained inside the plane on the runway, surrounded by armed guards. Leon K. warned, "For heaven's sake, keep cameras out of sight." He meant this for me, and I did.

We finally arrived in Teheran, right away noticing the city to be much more prosperous than it had been two years before. Many new cars and buses were on the streets; lots of building was going on. We stayed in the brand new annex of the Plaza Hotel, whose main building was six blocks away. It wasn't quite finished. The first morning, the hot water from under the sink in Connie's and my bathroom sprayed all over until we could find someone to fix it.

This year, instead of dancing in the old movie theater downtown, we were dancing in the brand new Farhang Hall. The stage was tiny, with quite a rake, a surface that ripped our toe shoes, and there was only one dressing room for all the girls. But one nice thing; Bill Dollar, who had been hired by the Iranian Government to start a national ballet company, had his new studio right next door. He let us use it for class. It was a treat to have *barres* and mirrors again. We performed his **Mendelssohn Concerto** on one of our programs.

Because of Joce's absence, Nancy and I expected to have heavy programs, but I did not expect to jump into a ballet I'd never even understudied before. However, one matinee I found myself jumping into **Dryad** with just one short rehearsal before curtain time. **Dryad** was originally Nancy's ballet. Others had danced it, too, including Joce, but I never had. I had watched it a lot, but that was about it. Sweet Rocky—I was doing it with him—took what time there was after class and before performance to go through the ballet with me step by step. When it came time to go on, I knew the steps so slightly that I didn't even get nervous. Luckily, one of the costumes fit. I remember standing, waiting for my entrance, trying to keep my mind absolutely clear. I knew that if I tried to think of a single step, I'd forget everything. All went surprisingly well. I only made a couple of little mistakes. I went blank once; Rocky said I looked at him with this blank stare, so he just picked me up and put me where I was supposed to go next. If I'd had more time to think about it, it would probably have gone much worse.

After Teheran we flew across the desolate Arabian Peninsula to Addis Ababa, Ethiopia. Addis is at about 8,000 feet, so the days are lovely and warm and the nights cool. The worst of our cold weather was finally behind us. The city seemed African to me, though I was told the eastern influence was strong. There were tall eucalyptus trees, fertile, cultivated soil, whitewashed, round, mud huts with thatched roofs that became squarer the nearer we got to the city. Some of the buildings in the city were quite massive, with corrugated tin replacing the thatch, but the feeling of whitewashed sod prevailed. The airport, our gorgeous new theater, and evidently quite a few other buildings were all named after Emperor Haile Selassie I

Haile Selassie and his queen came to our Opening. Once again our embassy was instrumental in making this happen. There were introductions and the presentation of gold medals. Evidently there had been some discussion beforehand as to who should receive the medals, but in the end everyone in the group received one. Movie cameras captured the event. During intermission, all of us went in costume to the Royal Box where each of us, in turn, was introduced to their Royal Highnesses. Each of us curtsied or bowed—we girls had been instructed to curtsy all the way down to our knees—then shook hands when they offered theirs. We were told not to speak unless spoken to, but when Haile Selassie presented me with my gold medal, I instinctively said, "Oh, thank you." As soon as the words came out of my mouth I realized what I'd done. I was horrified. It must have shown on my face. As I stood there looking at him, wishing the floor would open up and swallow me, not a muscle in his face moved, but his eyes—surprisingly pale and green—started to twinkle. He thought it was funny. I've always loved him for that.

The next day the Emperor issued a decree to all of his subjects that they come see our ballet, and we did have good houses for our remaining performances.

Before leaving Addis Ababa, the U.S.I.S. arranged an exhibition of Ethiopian dances for us. They were performed by tall, wild-looking, loose-limbed men who made faces and lots of jerky movements with their shoulders. We'd never seen such dancing before. One hunting dance in particular—about a lion hunt—was openly erotic and seemed to fascinate Lew. Little did I know at the time that one day I would be trying to reproduce those movements.

We arrived in Khartoum, Sudan on St. Patrick's Day. Both Connie and I, with Irish husbands left at home, were feeling forlorn. What a place to be celebrating St. Patrick's Day. As we stepped off the plane, it felt as if we were walking into an oven. Nancy, Joce and I were greeted with flowers that wilted before we got off the tarmac.

Luckily, our hotel—another wonderful old British colonial-style hotel—was right on the banks of the Blue Nile and a little cooler. A tree-lined street in front of the hotel was the only thing between the river and us. A wide verandah along the front of the hotel overlooked the Nile. Most of the guests spent their evenings there, catching the breeze off the river.

The smocked, turbaned help was not at all friendly to us. Of course, the fact that we were there in the midst of Ramadan, the month-long Moslem New Year observation where everyone fasts from sunup to sundown, could have had something to do with it. We needed to eat at 4:00 PM, when they were all hot, tired and hungry.

The day after our arrival, Nancy, Joce and I went with Lew and Leon to our theater—actually the Cultural Center Club—for a press conference. Our sponsors had gone to great lengths to bring us. They laid a stage for us on top of the cement patio and built a thirty-foot scaffolding for our backdrop. They were dumbfounded when Leon asked for thirty feet; it was the tallest structure in all of Sudan.

For the press conference, we were briefed to keep off politics; not that we knew that much about politics, but recently I had begun reading each week's international issue of *TIME Magazine* from cover to cover. John used to needle me for never knowing what was going on. During the whole conference, we were sure the press was dying to ask us about the recent disruption of school integration in Little Rock, Arkansas. It put U.S. Equal Rights into question and was embarrassing for our government. I remember being given a big glass of mango juice to drink, and Leon watching me closely, making sure my glass was refilled time and again. The pressmen didn't ask us about that, but snuck in a trick question about our reasons for making these tours; what were we hoping to accomplish by them? The men were pleasant and friendly, with humors amazingly like ours, and also sharp. But they were sensitive about the newness of their country; they'd just gotten their independence in 1956, three years before.

The following morning we were taken sightseeing by our local impresario, Suhail, a Palestinian Arab who worked for the Cultural Center. He took us in our bus across the bridge where the Blue and White Niles converge. You could actually see the two distinct colors of the rivers. They were both muddy beige, but one had a distinctly blue tinge and the other a creamy brown. We then drove on to Omdurman, the native capital, to see the gold and ivory market. People were most definite about not wanting us to take their picture. Suhail said they believed the camera lens would take away their spirit—put the evil eye on them.

A few days later, we were flying down the Nile over Aswan Dam and Luxor [the ancient city of Thebes] to Cairo. We were looking forward to Cairo. We would be there for two weeks. We'd have a good theater, a good audience, and wonderful accommodations. Most of us were staying at the Continental Hotel, an elegant, old-fashioned hotel right across the square from the Opera House where we were dancing. Leon D. and Royes were the only ones staying at the brand new Hilton, which was being managed by the same man—an old friend of Leon D's—who had managed the Panama Hilton when we were there. Evidently there had been quite a competition between the two hotels for our business. Connie and I were assigned an elegant suite with spacious bedroom and separate sitting room, each with pale-blue damask furniture and draperies, cream walls, high ceilings, and big glass doors that opened onto a balcony that overlooked the square and the Opera House beyond.

The Opera House was a lovely little theater in the true, old tradition. It was built for the premier of Verdi's opera, **Aida**. The audience, with its horseshoe of beautifully decorated boxes, sat only 700 people, but the stage and backstage areas were full-sized and beautifully equipped. Though the stage had quite a rake, the theater felt wonderful to perform in. A press reception was held for us in the foyer after our class the first day. We met lots of people, including all the directors of the symphony, opera, and ballet. The ballet was new—only four months old—and state supported. A teacher from Russia's Bolshoi Ballet was the new director.

The following morning I was still sound asleep when Gordon phoned to tell me to get dressed and ready in forty-five minutes. We were to meet the Minister of Culture. First, we went to the U.S. Embassy compound to pick up Mr. Lovegrove, our Cultural Affairs Officer, then went on to ex-King Farouk's huge, European palace, where most Egyptian Government officials now were. We went to the second floor of the first section and, amid much photographing, met Egypt's Minister of Culture. We barely made it back to the theater in time for class and orchestra rehearsal.

The day after our opening, I stayed in our room until 2:00 PM class. I felt as if I was wasting a day in Cairo, yet felt luxurious in knowing that we had time to spend here. That afternoon, some of the local dancers joined us for class, and Lew went on much longer than usual. It was late by the time we finished, so Connie and I ordered dinner in our room. Royes, not wanting to go all the way back to his hotel, joined us in our elegant sitting room. The waiter from downstairs set up a regular table for us, and we ate in great style.

The next day was the day of the pyramids. At 9:00 AM the whole company went out to the pyramids for a photo session with the Sphinx and some camels. After the session, several of us stayed on to "do" the pyramids; up, down, inside and out. Two of the girls chickened out, but Maurine Simoneau, Suzanne Hammons, Maurice Lemus—who was now fully recovered from his meningitis—and I climbed right to the top of Cheop's Pyramid, with the help of two guides. It was more of a feat than we had at first thought. The only way up was at the corners, one three-foot high stone block at a time; a steady, twenty-five minute climb. We were tired by the time we got back down, but when the guides offered to take us up inside the pyramid to see the King's tomb, we decided not to care. The passageway leading up to the royal chamber was steep and long, with a low ceiling, and pitch dark. We had to bend over the whole time. The only light came from the two guides' lanterns. However, once inside the chamber, everything was huge. Giant slabs of rose granite lined both the walls and the ceiling. At the topmost point of the ceiling there was an opening through which some star was supposed to be visible. After noticing how huge everything was, and how carefully all had been fitted together, I began to understand the greatness of the engineering feat—and the number of lives it must have taken. All the labor was done by hand.

That night, by show time, my legs had stiffened up and were killing me. I didn't dare say anything because I knew Lew and Leon would kill me. There was a place in *Serenade* where I did a pirouette to the knee, then remained kneeling for twelve counts before standing back up. I nearly didn't make it back up.

As if I hadn't seen enough of pyramids, after the show I went back out to see them in the moonlight. Gerrie Bucher had made friends with an architect who wanted to take her to Sahara City—a few buildings plunked together on the sand behind the pyramids—to see a good Sudanese dancer. He told her to bring along a friend and he would bring one along, too. Lew and Leon were by now disgusted with Gerrie and were threatening to send her home if she misbehaved any more. At first I told her I wouldn't go and that she shouldn't go, either, but I did want to see the pyramids in the moonlight. This was the last night of the full moon, so I decided to heck with it. We went and had a wonderful time. Gerrie's friends couldn't have been nicer or more gentlemanly. The show was officially over by the time we arrived, but half the troupe was still there and in the mood for dancing. They danced for us and then had us join them. I got a lesson in belly dancing.

We had Easter Sunday while still in Cairo; a strange Easter with Ramadan in full swing, and mosques and Arabs all around. The candy stores were filled with Easter eggs, though. The Company was divided among Embassy families for Easter lunch. Connie, Nancy, Dick and I went to the Lovegrove's flat. Their luncheon was informal, so we all just relaxed, talked, and enjoyed ourselves. Lew had put them in the difficult position of refusing most invitations for us. They weren't happy about it, but they also hadn't realized how many hours we spent in the theater each day.

They wanted us to see as much of Cairo as possible, so after lunch they drove us up the mountainside to an old citadel sitting at the city limits, where the desert began. From there we could see all of Cairo, with the Nile and the pyramids beyond. On the way back to town, we also drove past Dead City; block upon block of walled-in mausoleums, eerie even in the middle of the afternoon. It was completely deserted except for a few caretakers. No one else was around. We also drove past squatters in their tattered tents up against the old walls of the city. Some squatters didn't even have tents, just scraps of boards and tin cans tacked together.

While in Cairo, we presented four different programs. For the second program Royes and I did *Nutcracker* as the *Pas de Deux*. We spent a lot of time on it, especially during orchestra rehearsal. Otty's tempos were wonderful, but quite different from those on the tapes. It turned out to be time well spent. The performances went well, and Royes and I got ovations each night. Our last performance went the best it ever had. Everything in the *Pas de Deux* was "on" that night. I felt relaxed and straight, and Royes said he could tell the minute I stepped out on stage. He said he could tell what I was thinking.

I still remember that performance; one of those rare times when everything just clicks. Tchaikovsky's *Grand Pas de Deux* from *The Nutcracker* is indeed grand. When the orchestra plays full out, and you dance full out—feeling every muscle in your body doing exactly as you wish, and you and your partner responding to each other, and the audience responding to the two of you, it is a heady experience. There aren't too many others like it.

With our next change of program we were again in the theater most of that day. Lew made a few changes in the stage effects of **Shalott**. Everyone was excited about them. The ballet seemed much tighter-knit, now, and at points quite ghoulish. "Ballet by Charles Addams Christensen," we all said. Royes went into Dick's part of Lancelot for the first time that night. He was excited about it. He looked wonderful in the costume and the role, even the blond wig. However, it was his catastrophe night. He fell onstage and seriously injured himself. He could hardly put any weight on his right knee. It happened near the end of his solo, which he couldn't finish. He did all the partnering, though, and looked wonderful, but we could see he was in pain. We were all in the wings just dying. My heart dropped to my knees. Royes couldn't walk when he got off stage. A doctor was called; he'd have x-rays in the morning. We were, naturally, all shaken up, but **Beauty and the Shepherd** went much better for Dick and me, anyway, luckily.

I was to have the next two nights free—Nancy and I were sharing the role of *Helen* in **Beauty and the Shepherd** on this program—and I was looking forward to this break. I had class each day and another lecture/demonstration, but as long as nobody else got sick or hurt, I still had evenings free. The first day Joce, Connie and I went to an Armenian tea with Leon D. On the way there, we stopped by the Hilton to see Royes. He was sitting on his bed in a cast from his ankle to the top of his thigh. He had torn the cartilage around his knee and would be in the cast for three weeks. He wasn't sure how serious the injury was, but he was definitely finished for the rest of our tour. He'd probably fly to New York on Sunday. I remember thinking how funny the way things worked out sometimes. As well as working into **Shalott**, Royes was finally going to do **Black Swan** with Joce—he'd already done **Don Q.** with Nancy—and he was dancing so well. He'd been happy about **Nutcracker**, too. It might be better for him to be in New York earlier, though, seeing that he was joining NYC Ballet. It was hard to say.

After the performance that evening, which I watched from out front, the whole Company was invited to the home of Professor Joussef Greiss, an Egyptian composer who had been coming to all of our performances. He had been giving those of us he particularly liked an Egyptian antiquity after the opening of each new program. He and various members of his family lived in a huge old museum of a house right on the banks of the Nile. From his back terrace we walked down steps that led through a garden right down to the water. The whole family evidently haunted auctions because their home was jammed with antiques, paintings, and Egyptian antiquities—of which we were all given one. It was an unusual evening; a marvelous supper, a strange assortment of people, and some of Professor Greiss's compositions that he played for us on the piano.

The following day I slept until noon. I remember being somewhat surprised. I hadn't slept that late the whole tour. That day I only had two o'clock class and, for once, nothing else; just the big Embassy buffet/reception at the Nile Hilton at six o'clock. According to Mrs. Lovegrove, only a portion of the people receiving invitations usually showed up, but today everyone came—perhaps to see the new hotel as much as anything. I remember being in the receiving line part of the time and shaking a lot of hands. There was no liquor at the reception because of Ramadan, but the food was wonderful. Royes came down for the last part of the reception. He said he'd been going mad sitting in his room staring at his cast. It was uncomfortable and certainly made things awkward. It took him an hour to take a bath. He was coming to the performance this evening to take his mind off his leg.

Seeing that I didn't have to be at the theater until "theater call" an hour before curtain—whether we were dancing or not, we always had to appear then, in case of an emergency—I stayed behind with him to keep him company. He was holding onto my arm, limping along as the kids gathered in their taxi groups to leave. I remember Leon K. passing by and saying,

"Awwww." I also remember thinking Leon was being sort of a jerk. Royes and I then went into the bar for a drink.

The Lovegroves were in the bar, too, so we joined them. Royes told us about the trials and tribulations of living in an elegant hotel that wasn't quite ready for guests; the help wasn't well organized, the kitchens would shut down, the electricity kept going off. When it was time to leave for the theater, the Lovegroves gave us a ride. Guards were all around when we arrived. President Nassar was coming to the performance. All the kids were excited. Professor Greiss was backstage and gave me yet another antiquity—a lovely bracelet 3,500 years old. He kept apologizing, saying he had only an incomplete collection; obviously getting less complete all the time.

Leon D. came by and asked me to join him and his Armenian friends for some belly dancing after the show. I was tempted, but with two matinee/evenings coming up, plus a chance to go to the step pyramids at Sakharah with Mrs. Lovegrove and an archeologist friend of hers, I thought it best to just go home to bed early for a change. I remember thinking it a little odd that Leon D. was so insistent this night. He didn't want to take "no" for an answer. He kept pressing me. He usually didn't care one way or the other if I came. I didn't feel I was being rude to his Armenian friends. I'd already spent the afternoon before with them. I thought for once I'd use my head and catch up on my sleep. If I'd used my head a little more, I might have realized what was concerning him. This hadn't even occurred to me at the time, but evidently Leon D. assumed that, in that I declined his invitation, I was planning to spend this free evening of mine—while everyone else was busy—alone with Royes. I, of course, hadn't heard any of the rumors circulating about Royes and me, so I obliviously went on my way.

Two days later Royes left for New York. The night before he left, we all pitched in and gave him a beer party out in the foyer after the show. I was the one who asked Shukri, our local stage manager, for help in arranging the party.

Though liquor is generally not served during Ramadan, this particular day was the anniversary of the day Mohammed finished his book, and liquor could not be served anywhere. Shukri risked being put in jail and paying a $200 fine, but he had beer on ice for us. The party turned out wonderfully, and Royes was touched. Everyone felt sad about his injury, sad that he had to leave. One strange thing, though; neither Leon D. nor Joce came.

The following night we gave our last performance in Cairo. At the end of the show there were many flowers and speeches on stage. Before leaving, Royes had ordered lovely bouquets of roses for Nancy, Joce and me, and they also were presented to us on stage. My roses were red—I remember Rocky commenting on this—Nancy's were yellow, and Joce's were either peach or pink. I thought it was so sweet of Royes to send his three partners flowers. Nancy seemed to appreciate her bouquet, too, but I noticed Joce didn't seem to like hers at all. Her flowers had been in her dressing room, but before leaving the theater, she took them back upstairs and left them backstage—intentionally, it looked like. It made me angry.

The rest of the tour went without incident. We spent the following week in Alexandria. After our opening performance, which was enthusiastically received, we met some of the local dancers. They were talkative and quick to point out that Cairo did not have a discerning audience; they liked everything whether good or bad. But if you were liked in Alexandria, you must really be good. The dancers were sensitive to the fact that few attractions had come through Alexandria recently—only about two ballet companies in the last four years.

Before leaving Alexandria, we witnessed the end of Ramadan. It ended at midnight, and the next morning the streets were jammed with happy, celebrating people. Many were dressed in native dress; men and boys in striped pajamas or nightshirt affairs, little girls with their straight, long dresses and beaded scarves on the backs of their heads, the older women wrapped in black, some even with their black mesh veils on. Many of the shops were closed for the duration. There was a complete holiday feel throughout the city. If you stood alone on a street corner, the din you heard was amazing. Carts along the street were selling every kind of food imaginable—even carts loaded with plain lettuce. The square across from the hotel was thronged with people all day. When I walked through it on my way back from the theater, a man was playing a drum and all the little children near him were dancing to it. After forty days of fasting, I could imagine how glad everyone was to be able to eat again during the day.

From Alexandria we went on to Syria and picked up our postponed engagements in both Damascus and Aleppo. In Damascus we did five shows in three days, plus some sightseeing. Things sort of ran together for me, but I do remember driving along the biblical "Street Called Straight" and seeing the sanctuary window from which St. Paul escaped after being lowered in a basket.

In Aleppo I mostly remember being "out in the sticks", as one U.S.I.S. man put it. We stayed in the only hotel where foreigners could eat without getting sick. An old citadel dominated the city from its natural rise in the center of town. I could imagine it looming there during the Crusades. Connie and I managed to climb up to it one morning before going on to the theater, and also to run through an outer section of the old Souk—the covered market and Caravansary—that spread over fifteen kilometers at the foot of it. The Souk had changed little over the centuries since being on the main silk route to China. I had the distinct feeling I could get lost in it—and never be found. We brushed past Kurds who had come down from the mountains to sell their sheepskins. The skins were piled in a heap on the ground, one on top of the other, and a young woman about my age was standing next them. She was dressed in her best, with a special hairdo, headdress, silver in her ears, and heavy necklaces around her neck. Our eyes met. In her gaze I saw wildness, pride, hostility—and curiosity. I don't think she had ever seen a woman like me before.

In Aleppo, for the first time on our tour, we had half-full, unenthusiastic audiences. I learned that our Consul was feuding with the Consul General in Damascus and was unenthusiastic about bringing us to Aleppo. He was partly to blame for our poor houses.

When we got to Tripoli, our last stop of the tour, we were back to full, enthusiastic houses, though they were mostly Americans from Wheelus Air Force Base. During our stay in Tripoli we met few Libyans. At our U.S. Embassy reception— which really wasn't the Embassy at the moment; the King had moved the capital to Benghazi seven months earlier—we met only two Libyans, both men. We never did meet a Libyan woman. Most of the guests were U.S. military personnel. During our reception, I learned that the hotel where some of us were staying was Rommel's officers' quarters during World War II; the hotel where the rest of the kids were staying was their bordello.

Our theater in Tripoli had one of the steepest rakes of the whole tour. I remember hearing someone say it was twelve percent; one more challenge we didn't need at this point. By now we were all sick of tour and just wanted it to be over. With the end in sight, everyone was giddy with excitement. Lew had to keep reminding us not to let down until the last show was over.

When the final curtain came down, we all let out a big cheer. "Tour is over! We made it!"

The S.F. Ballet, in the Far East under the auspices of the U.S. State Department, having an audience with President Magsaysay of the Philippines, January, 1957.

Conrad Ludlow and Sally Bailey in
Tarot, Colombo, Ceylon, 1957.

The Company arriving in Bombay, India, 1957.

Louise Lawler and Sally Bailey involved in a little cultural
exchange with an Indian troupe, Bombay, 1957.

Glen Chadwick and Sally Bailey dancing on the north tower of the Golden Gate Bridge for Dave Garroway's TV show, *Wide, Wide World*, San Francisco, May 1957.

View from the north tower, May 1957.

Sally Bailey in the *Roses Waltz Adagio* from
Beauty and the Beast, May 1958. Photo by Dale Smith, S.F.

On our 2nd State Department Tour, this one to
Latin America; inside *Teatro Colon* in
Bogota, Colombia, 1958.

Photo session at the Equator Monument, Ecuador, 1958.

Sally Bailey and Nancy Johnson, with Gloria Murray
behind, being greeted at the Guayaquil Airport
by the local ballet, Ecuador, 1958.

From left to right; Bruce Kelly, Leon Danielian, Richard Carter, Jocelyn Vollmar, and Christine Bering relaxing at the pool in San Salvador, El Salvador, 1958.

On our 3rd State Department Tour, this one to the Middle East; we dance after dinner with the boys at the Thessaloniki Agricultural and Industrial School in Salonica, Greece 1959.

Royes Fernandez and Sally Bailey with the troupe in the
Nutcracker finale, Beirut, Lebanon, 1959.

Sally Bailey in *arabesque* on top of Cheop's Pyramid
outside of Cairo, Egypt 1959.

Curtain call for *Masque of the Beauty and the Shepherd.*
Front row from left; Louise Lawler,
Sally Bailey, Richard Carter, Bene Arnold, and
Constance Coler, Cairo, Egypt 1959.

CHAPTER SEVEN

Recognition At Home

1: A Casualty of the Profession

AFTER OUR RETURN FROM THE MIDDLE EAST, LEW GAVE US SEVERAL weeks off before regrouping for what performances were booked for the rest of the spring and summer. Our next steady work wouldn't be until Opera Season in the fall. On the trip home many of the dancers stopped off in New York; some of them didn't return. Others stopped off along the way to visit family and friends. A few of us went straight on through to San Francisco.

I remember the closer we got to home, the more excited we got. But this time, the closer I got, also the more apprehensive I got. I didn't know what to expect from John. I wasn't even sure he'd be at the airport to meet me.

He was there. He did meet me, and we went home. This time, when we got home the house was spotless. I think his mother must have come and scrubbed for two days so I wouldn't come home to a dirty house, again. Even so, I didn't feel joyful about returning this time. We were both uncertain and tense. One thing I knew, though; I was now going to have to deal with those problems I'd set aside four months ago.

How well I dealt with them I'm not sure; probably not well. For one thing, I thought the problems were John's, not mine. At one point he started getting some counseling through the university and asked if I would come with him.

I said no. I was mad and felt he was at fault. I should have gone, anyway, but I didn't. He didn't ask again. Things went from bad to worse.

I remember sitting at a table with John in one of the little cafes along Telegraph Avenue one afternoon shortly after returning, I guess having a cup of coffee. Our rooming house was up at the end of the block. I'm not sure why we stopped here instead of going on home. He seemed moody, full of resentments.

Finally he blurted out, "I've been living like a damned monk these last four months."

I hadn't asked him about his girlfriend.

I don't remember exactly what he said next, but the gist of it was that he thought I hadn't been. I was taken aback by this, and also angry. Just because he had been unfaithful didn't mean that I intended to be. "Getting even" wasn't my style. I took marriage vows seriously—my own and other's— even if he didn't. Was he judging me by how he would act?

I remember saying something like, "Look, I haven't even kissed anyone."

His response was to nearly push the table over. Then there was a long discourse on sins of omission as well as sins of commission. He went on and on.

Another surprise came when John told me he'd been singing each week at the Bocce Ball, an Italian nightclub in San Francisco that featured operatic singing. I thought he was going to use all his time this last semester to study, not work. This was why I changed my mind and had my money sent home, again. I guess he felt he needed the break, though. I know he enjoyed it. He'd continued his voice lessons all along, and this job gave him the opportunity to sing beautiful *basso* arias, make a little extra money, and get some needed ego food.

At the time, I still didn't realize the extent of his ego need. I assumed he had a good image of himself because I had such a good image of him. I remember one day he tried to explain, "Do you have any idea how sub-human a postgraduate can feel? Everyone my age is already out working and making money, and here I am, still a student." I was amazed.

The bad thing about John's singing at the Bocce Ball was that he didn't leave himself enough time to study. In one subject he didn't pull the needed "B" to continue. He was out of the program unless he took two more classes to offset that grade. This, of course, is what his advisor strongly recommended. To me it seemed the logical thing to do; just go ahead and take the two additional classes. However, John couldn't bring himself to do that right now. I felt he'd rather think of ways to put the blame on me.

He would tell me, "I have the knowledge, now. What is a degree, anyway? It's just a piece of paper; something to please your parents."

One morning he yelled at me, "You win!"

I wondered, "Win what?" I didn't even know we were having a contest.

John told me he felt as if he was consistently making the wrong choices. He chose the wrong field; he should have chosen biochemistry instead of biophysics. He chose biophysics because he thought it was going to be the next big field; now it was looking more and more as if biochemistry would be it. I supposed he considered me one of his wrong choices, too.

It must have been about this time that he gave me a copy of Dr. Karl Menninger's book *Man Against Himself* to read. It was about the destructive cycle. I'd never heard of the destructive cycle. Why should anyone want to get on it? I was more interested in attaining goals, not fouling myself up. I always felt that if you wanted something, go ahead and work for it. Do, consistently, whatever it was you needed to do. If you did that, why shouldn't you eventually make it?

One day I said something to this effect in front of one of John's friends. I remember the friend looking at me, shaking his head slightly, and replying, "Sally, you're too tough."

At any rate, I read the book from cover to cover, not understanding much of it at the time.

I thought it might help if we went away for a weekend; perhaps back to Carmel, where we'd spent our honeymoon. Money was a little tight, but John went ahead and made the reservations. He reserved a charming little garden cottage for us. I was delighted with it, except that when we got inside, I saw that it had twin beds. I remember that Sunday morning, getting up quite early, going to a nearby grocery store for fruit, cheese, rolls and the Sunday paper, taking them back to the cottage, spending the rest of the morning snacking and reading while John slept in the other bed.

Nothing I suggested seemed to do any good. I don't remember what we lived on. John must have taken some sort of job while he was deciding what to do next. I saved some money from tour, but it was going. The Ballet had its few single dates, and in between I had unemployment. In June an opportunity came up for me to earn some extra money. A dance teacher in Oregon, who had sponsored the Company there several years before, was putting on a three-week ballet seminar for his students. He invited me to come as guest teacher. I hesitated at first because John's and my anniversary was during this time. It would mean being apart, again, for our anniversary. But the way things were going, it probably wouldn't make much difference, and we could certainly use the money. So I went.

It was during this time, sitting in my Oregon hotel room between classes, that I began writing something other than journal entries. John had been prodding me to "do something" with my mind, so I wrote my first essay. It was about how any job, even one as glamorous as dancing around the world, can become routine—just like any other—when you have to do it day in and day out. I had the use of someone's typewriter. I don't remember whose. At that time

I didn't even know how to type. I showed the essay to John when I got home. He didn't say much about it.

I remember another weekend, one in August; it must have been our last free weekend before Opera Season rehearsals began. It was just before our birthdays, which were four days apart. John wanted to be in Los Angeles for his birthday, so off we drove to L.A. I couldn't stay until his actual birth date because of rehearsals, so I flew back the following Monday morning. This didn't seem to bother him. He promised to return home in time for my birthday. I remember we stayed two nights in a hotel right on the beach in Santa Monica. This time we shared a bed and actually had quite a nice time. John made the comment that I was maturing. I thought things were getting better between us.

As it turned out, John was probably feeling better because he had made up his mind; to take a break from Berkeley and me, go to New York and get some singing out of his system, then, after an unspecified length of time, return to proceed with his studies. At the time I truly believed he would return. I knew how upset he'd been since the spring, and I certainly couldn't object to his going after all the time I'd been away. Our agreement was that I would come visit him in New York over New Years, after *Nutcracker* and before rehearsals for our new, extended spring season were to begin.

So we broke up our apartment, packed up our beautiful wedding gifts, and stored everything at my parents' home. My parents—I hand it to them—kept entirely out of this. I moved in with one of the newer girls in the company, Barbara Culbertson, who could use the financial assistance of a roommate. Her apartment was just two blocks from the studio, a welcome change from commuting back and forth to Berkeley. I didn't bring much with me other than my clothes and John's and my car; a pale chartreuse Chevrolet coupe in which I car-pooled a bunch of us back and forth to the Opera House. I remember also bringing along my dictionary and my set of International Library encyclopedias, and a lightweight portable typewriter I'd recently bought, plus an old typing book of my mother's that had been in a bottom drawer for years. I planned to spend an hour each day between afternoon and evening rehearsals teaching myself to type. I remember Barbara looking at me with a puzzled expression on her face, asking, "Why?"

When all of this happened, the kids in the company looked a bit surprised, but said little. In fact, they were so quiet that I was sure a buzz of speculation was circulating among them. When I gave them my explanation—John was taking a break from school and would probably be back the following semester—they seemed to accept it at face value, then drop the subject.

At any rate, there was a lot else to think about. After last year's absence, the Opera was welcoming us back with some good dance opportunities. They asked Lew for a full-length ballet—he choreographed Stravinsky's **Danses Concertantes** for them, which we performed along with Strauss's short opera **Ariadne auf Naxos**—and asked Bill to choreograph the seldom-performed ballet interlude in Gluck's **Orfeo ed Euridice**. They also gave us the *Spring* section of Carl Orff's **Carmina Burana** to dance. Gita Hager, who with her husband, Paul, was one of the stage directors for the opera, choreographed this piece for us. She had been a dancer in Germany and occasionally choreographed for some of the operas. Gita chose Rocky and me for the young lovers. It turned out to be a surprisingly good part for us. We got some notice from the critics for it.

About this time—during the fall of 1959—we also received prestigious recognition from the Ford Foundation, which was establishing a support project for ballet training. The Foundation chose Balanchine's School of American Ballet in New York and the San Francisco Ballet School as the two organizations to receive grants. Their reasoning; we both had—and other companies did not—well established schools that trained dancers for our companies. Other companies might have schools connected with them, but they didn't necessarily train their own dancers. Most of their dancers came from open auditions. The advantage for both of us was that we could be considered "institutions", with the stability and artistic constancy the term suggested. Therefore, Ford was willing to invest large sums of money in us—in our schools, that is. None of the money was to be used for either company. The investment was to be in future dancers, the future of American ballet.

And today, some forty years later, Ford's investment has proven to be fruitful, indeed. Today there are so many more fine teachers and well-trained dancers than we had in those days.

After Opera Season we jumped right into rehearsals for **Beauty and the Beast** and **Nutcracker.** We were performing both ballets this Holiday Season, which kept us busy right up to the end of the year. Before I knew it, it was time for me to go to New York.

I was excited about going, not only to see John, but also to see Carrie and Jacques D'Amboise, Leon D., Royes, and Chris Bering, who had recently returned to New York from Paris. I'd received a rather disillusioned letter from her. Things at the Marquis de Cuevas Company were not at all as she'd thought. They traveled by train, had to hustle their own luggage, find their own hotels, and buy their own toe shoes—and someone stole hers. She was now hoping to find a place for herself in one of the New York companies.

Rocky seemed excited about my going. All fall he had been attentive to me, almost solicitous. He was in my car pool. We had recently begun reading and discussing books together. He gave me J.D. Salinger's *The Catcher in the Rye* to read while I was in New York. He said we would discuss it when I returned.

I arrived in New York in high spirits. John met me at the limousine terminal in the early evening. It was already dark outside, the weather was cold, and piles of dirty snow lined the slushy sidewalks. We stopped for a bite to eat before going on to his apartment. He still seemed gloomy. One of the first things he said to me after we sat down was, "I'm sorry you came. It's hard on me."

I felt like turning right around and flying back to San Francisco. But I had already made plans with my friends here in New York, and I also wanted to take some classes— and what would I say to the kids back home if I returned early? What would I say to my parents? I decided the best thing to do was just tough it out.

John's apartment was typical; a small, inexpensive, makeshift studio apartment. The kitchen was installed in the entryway right by the front door. The bathroom was actually all right, more modern than many. The single room contained a drab stuffed chair, a coffee table, a brown hide-a-bed couch that when opened up left little room to walk around, and in one corner a large, bright-red, upright piano. Why the bright-red piano, I never did find out.

One morning John's landlord came in to repair something. John wasn't there, and I was still in my robe. I introduced myself as his wife. The landlord answered, "Oh, you don't have to say that. I don't care." I felt affronted, then hurt, then angry. Evidently John hadn't told him he was married. I later found out he had told few people.

Resentments piled one on top of another. Instead of confronting John and having it out, I chose to show my feelings by becoming defiant. I took up smoking because he told me not to. A lot of dancers smoked, some quite heavily, even though everyone agreed it cut one's wind. For one thing, it also cut one's appetite—weight always being a concern—and it was calming. I don't think John had started his technician job at Sloan Kettering Cancer Center, yet, but he had some of the latest information on cancer research. He promptly told me there was suspicion of a link between lung cancer and smoking and I should not smoke.

So I lit up a cigarette and read from the book Rocky gave me. I didn't inhale, though. I was concerned about my wind. Evidently that helped because I never became addicted. A package of cigarettes used to last me days. Several years later, after a bout with the flu, I decided to quit and had no difficulty doing so.

From time to time John would start lecturing me. One idea that appealed to him—he returned to it time and again—was how the wife of some friend of his, her name was Evie, used to walk around with holes in the bottoms of her shoes. She'd just put cardboard inside her shoes to cover the holes. She didn't care at all, just as long as she was with her husband. She didn't want anything more of life. I gathered John wanted me to be more like Evie; and give up what I'd been working so hard for all this time? Join his downward spiral? Why didn't he just come home, take his dumb course over again, and continue?

The days passed, often with us going our separate ways. I took class every day and remember spending New Year's Day with Carrie and Jacques while John went off somewhere else. Most evenings we spent together, though, many of them with Chris. One evening Leon Danielian threw a party for all the ex-SFB dancers. I thought this was so thoughtful of him. I could now see everyone before leaving. I was anxious to go. John was not so anxious, but he did go. We picked up Chris along the way and then continued on to Leon's place on the bus. I don't remember exactly why, but for some reason I wasn't speaking to John—again. I remember the three of us sitting side by side on the bus, me ignoring John, and Chris telling me I was terrible.

As soon as we were inside the door of Leon's apartment, Royes came rushing over and planted the same passionate kiss on my cheek that he always did. This was how he always said "hello" to me. I remember being a little amazed the first time he kissed me this way; it was for a newspaper photo taken the second day in Athens. We had just begun working together and hardly knew each other. It was obviously just one of those things he did. From then on I accepted it as exactly that. But tonight Leon started tugging at Royes, saying, "Royes, this is Sally's husband. This is her *husband*, Royes."

Royes then stopped kissing me and with a cheerful smile turned to John to shake hands. We then bounced on into the room. I made sure John met everyone he didn't already know, but I guess I didn't pay much attention to him the rest of the evening. I was having such a good time that I didn't realize he was seething the whole night.

I so enjoyed seeing Royes, again. I wanted to share his friendship with John, have John get to know him better. Therefore, I invited Royes over for dinner one night before leaving. I remember cooking a stew of some kind. It was simmering on the stove when Royes arrived. We sat down and started talking at length, like we had done so many times on tour. But John, instead of joining in, got up and said he had to go somewhere for a while. He didn't come back for over an hour. The dinner continued simmering on the stove and Royes and I continued talking. Royes told me about all that had happened since his return to New York. He was still having trouble with his knee. Once in class it went out on him completely. He had to have an operation. He may still have been recuperating from that; I know he said he hadn't yet danced one performance for Balanchine, though Balanchine was paying him all this time. He felt that Balanchine was an amazingly kind man.

John finally returned without giving any explanation for his long absence. The three of us then ate dinner. I never found out what Royes thought of John's behavior, but I thought he was rude. It hadn't yet occurred to me that John thought Royes and I became lovers on tour. I have the tendency to be dense and non-thinking about some things.

It wasn't until years later that it finally dawned on me; not only John, but others, too, thought Royes and I became lovers. I was surprised because our relationship hadn't been like that at all. In fact, one of the rumors I *had* heard linked Royes with Rocky. If anything, I thought Royes probably wasn't interested. Perhaps he and I gave that impression because we were so fond of each other, plus we acted like lovers on stage every night. However, I never attached much importance to impressions. I always thought it was what you *did* that mattered. In any case, at that time I still felt very much married, even if not happily, and I wasn't looking for anything else. I don't remember Royes ever not respecting that fact. He seemed an instinctive gentleman. I know my present husband asked, "Didn't he ever make a pass at you?" I don't remember that he ever did—unless he was planning to that night in Cairo in the bar when we ran into the Lovegroves. He said outrageous things sometimes, but that was about all. Actually, I always thought he liked me for wanting to be faithful to my husband.

Soon it was time for me to leave New York and return to San Francisco. I didn't know what to make of John's and my situation, or what to do about it. The only thing I felt I could do was wait. At that time I was still convinced that sooner or later John would return.

By the time I got on the airport limousine, I was feeling miserable all over. To top everything off, I had come down with a bad head cold. John came to the terminal with me. I remember him standing at the curb, alongside a pile of dirty snow, as the bus drove off. I didn't even look back. I just laid my hot forehead against the cool window.

All the way home I kept asking myself, "What happened to the man I married?" It was as if he had died, or something, and was replaced by this man I'd been staying with in New York.

As it turned out, I never saw John again.

Recognition At Home

2: The Campaign Is On

I WAS GLAD TO GET BACK TO SAN FRANCISCO, BACK TO WHERE things were going well for me. With our new spring season coming up, there would be lots of work to do, lots to keep my mind occupied. I wouldn't have time to sit and dwell on what had happened to my marriage. The waiting would be easier.

A lot of excitement was building about the Company's upcoming season. We were going to be dancing Friday and Saturday evenings for eight weekends in the old Alcazar Theater—a smallish 1,100-seat theater I'd hardly even heard about—between February and May. It would be the longest season we'd ever had in San Francisco. The Alcazar was just around the corner from our two downtown theaters, the Geary and the Curran, and had been out of use for some time. It belonged to Randolph Hale, a local businessman and civic leader. He reportedly gave us a good deal on it, allowing us to use it over an extended period right in the middle of the theater season, which couldn't be better for us. The Opera House was never available to us over an extended period, and even if it were, it would be much too expensive.

Everyone was pulling together to make this season of ours a triumphal homecoming. We were opening our *San Francisco Ballet Jubilant* with a special Celebrity Performance featuring Maria Tallchief and Jacques D'Amboise in Balanchine's *Sylvia Pas de Deux*. The occasion was to be topped off with an onstage champagne party afterwards.

The brochure for our season boasted of Lew's "panoramic scope of talents." It stated that audiences would now have the opportunity to see the ballets that had established Lew as a leader in a new, dynamic, all-American ballet concept that required no story and no actors, just lithe, long-limbed dancers who could meet "the rigid demands of human perfection in performance."

We made the cover of Dance Magazine (April 1960) with an excellent photo of Rocky jumping in his *Paris* costume from *A Masque of Beauty and the Shepherd*. Inside was a big spread about our opening celebration, plus an article about us stating, "With a permanent home at last, its status at the Alcazar is similar to that of NYC Ballet at City Center. The company expects to be able to develop a large, devoted audience, financial stability, higher morale and more work for its dancers."

To launch us with the best of "looks" for our new season, Leon Kalimos persuaded the advertising agency, Cunningham & Walsh, to take us on as a "prestige client", free of charge. Though such acts of public service are common enough today, they were not so common then. In any case, because of Leon's efforts, a long and fruitful association with Cunningham & Walsh began, and it made a difference right from the start. Good photos, good layout, and good writing gave us style and stature.

A fine looking souvenir program was produced that included a salute from George Balanchine and Lincoln Kirstein which stated, "It is a very important step for the whole field of theatrical dancing in the United States that the San Francisco Ballet is able to attach itself to its own home theater. While this excellent repertory company is well known all over the world, it has lacked a home base for continuous performances. Without a home, no ballet organization can hope to develop either an audience or a repertory. Without a loyal audience and a creative repertory, a ballet company cannot exist as an institution. The future in America must belong to institutional, rather than speculative theater . . . The New York City Ballet salutes this admirable effort and will lend every material and moral means to sustain it."

Our Ballet Guild Board came through with their part; they raised the money. The party they threw on stage after the Celebrity Performance was a big success. The Winter Olympics were in California this year—at Squaw Valley, near Lake Tahoe—and our Board saw to it that the Olympics officials came to our performance and the party afterwards, lending an international flavor to the occasion. Our Board was a dedicated, hard-working bunch. Some of them had been with us through thick and thin for quite some time.

For us dancers this was indeed a heady time. I know I definitely had the feeling I was in the right place at the right time. There were less of us now than on our last tour, but those of us remaining felt strong and confident. Unfortunately for Nancy, she was pregnant, again, and had to be out a second time.

Lew choreographed two new works to add to our touring repertoire. He set ***Esmeralda Pas de Deux*** for Joce and Dick and created ***Danza Brillante***—the same name as Bill's ballet—for all of us. This ***Danza*** was set to a Mendelssohn Octet. Though abstract, it was unusually romantic in feel for Lew. During our mid-season break, Vida Brown came out from New York and taught us Balanchine's ***Raymonda Pas de Dix*** and restaged his ***Swan Lake***.

This season I also started doing ***Con Amore*** with Mike Smuin as the *Thief* to my *Amazon Captain*. I was normally too tall to dance with Mike, but for this ballet our pairing turned out to be unexpectedly good casting. We were like *Mutt and Jeff* and decided to play it to the hilt. The audiences loved our semi-outrageous interpretation, which created a different sense of comedy than I'd had with any of my other partners.

The critics were most supportive of us. They singled each of us out, by turn, for special qualities we showed in various roles. Mike's spectacular jumps were mentioned in almost every review. At the end of the season, Lew received a wonderful acknowledgment from Jack Loughner of the *News-Call Bulletin*. Loughner had been giving him a bad time all season about his choreography. His final review stated, "Obviously, it is Christensen's influence and his taste that has whipped this group of youngsters into a major, if small-sized, dance company. Their every movement exudes discipline, exuberance, musicality and all the other requisites for first-rate dancing."

The Alcazar turned out to be a wonderful theater for us. We truly did feel at home here. It was kind of old—nothing elegant about it—but comfortable both backstage and out front. The size of the auditorium was small in comparison to the Opera House, but the intimacy of it suited us. When performing, we felt as if we could easily touch everyone in the house. There was only one drawback; if the house were bigger, we could make more money.

I think it was at this time that Lew said repeatedly, "One does need a home. It doesn't have to be fancy, just a good space, but one needs a place in which to work". Lew didn't seem to mind that we were on a shoestring budget, that we performed some of our ballets in leotards, without scenery. In fact, he would often tell us, "If the dancing is good, you don't have to clutter it up with fancy costumes and sets. Lush productions can cover up mediocre dancing and choreography."

I once again remembered Lew saying, "When you're too comfortable you become lazy. You lose your creativity and resourcefulness."

I felt Lew was enjoying himself.

Lew had one disappointment, though. At the end of the season he lost Nancy and Dick, this time two of his principal dancers. With the coming of their second child, they could no longer afford to stay. Dick wasn't earning the kind of money needed to support a growing family, and Nancy was even less likely to dance all the time, now. They were offered a teaching position at the University of San Diego, which they accepted.

Pregnancy has always been a threat to directors— especially in the days before "the pill"—and I think that is why many directors were against their dancers marrying. Babies tended to come, and when babies came, dancers went. For the director's tools, his investments, that was not a good situation to be in. It wasn't that a woman couldn't dance as well, physically, after she'd given birth—once she'd gotten back into shape she could dance just as well—it was simply that when raising a child, dancing couldn't always come first. In order to dance well, dancing must always come first.

In an interview with Debra Sowell (from a transcript dated 9/30/87), Gisella gave an interesting insight into Balanchine's attitude about dancers marrying. Debra had asked Gisella how Balanchine felt when she and Lew married just before American Ballet Caravan went to South America. Gisella didn't seem to think he minded. She answered, "Oh, Balanchine was against a girl getting married while he was using her, but once he was through, he'd let her go. He'd no longer care."

I suppose Lew was wondering about my marriage. I know several of the kids asked if I was going to New York at the end of the season. I couldn't see repeating my last visit, though, especially in the steaming heat of summer. Besides, I thought John would be coming home before long. I'd rather spend what little money I had on moving from Barbara's apartment to one of my own, and getting it ready for John when he returned.

I found a delightful, cheap, studio apartment on the top floor of a three-story building on Sacramento Street—in San Francisco, not Berkeley. I guess I thought John could commute this time. It was about a ten-minute drive from the studio. It faced south and west, the sun poured in all day, and it always seemed bright and airy. I loved that place. It had hardwood floors, which my father helped me refinish, and one day I had a painting party. I made a big pot of Mexican beans, bought some beer, and asked a bunch of the kids over to help me paint the whole place white. When everything was completed, Rocky and his roommate, Jeff (Jeffreys Hobart), helped me move John's and my things from my parent's house. I remember the two of them lugging everything up three flights of stairs.

Over the spring Rocky and I became even better friends. Since my return from New York, we regularly read and discussed books together. One book I remember spending time on was an early work of Gore Vidal's, *The Judgment of Paris*. It was about a young man's search for himself. The protagonist took a year off after graduating from college, traveled to Europe and Egypt, became involved with three women who had the same qualities as *Paris's* three goddesses, and had to choose between what they each offered; political power, wisdom, love. At the end of his year the protagonist chose love.

Rocky often came to Barbara's apartment in the evenings after rehearsal. I remember he was there one night when John phoned from New York. John had injured his leg in a turnstile in the subway and needed medical attention. He kept asking me, "Should I come home, now?"

I kept saying, "I'd like you to come back, if you want to."

He wouldn't say he wanted to. I felt he was trying to get me to make the decision—and I had the distinct feeling that should I do that, he would blame me forever for everything that went wrong; "If only I'd stayed in New York. If only you hadn't told me to come back."

I wasn't going to do that to myself.

I guess we decided that John would get his leg tended to in New York, stay a little longer, and then return in time for the fall semester.

I remember Rocky saying over and over again, "He loves you, Sal. He loves you."

I wasn't at all sure.

I started discussing things with Rocky that I didn't discuss with anyone else. By the end of our Spring Season in May, I was probably using him as a sounding board, trying to figure out what I should do next. I guess he helped me make the decision to move into my own apartment.

Another thing we talked about, and both decided to get involved in, was a new project Mike and Jeff were cooking up. They were calling it "Ballet 1960". Rehearsals would be starting soon. Not all the kids were interested in joining in, but we definitely were.

CHAPTER SEVEN

Recognition At Home

3: Ballet 1960

BALLET 1960 WAS A PROJECT DREAMED UP ENTIRELY BY MICHAEL Smuin and Jeffreys Hobart. They did it all by themselves, without any help from the company. They were counting on using those of us Company dancers who wanted to join in, of course, and the studios for rehearsals, and also could have gotten the original idea from Lew, who helped form Ballet Caravan during that off-season back in 1936, but other than that, it was an independent effort.

Mike was Ballet 1960's Artistic Director and Jeff, who had begun working as Leon's assistant during the spring season, was Managing Director. They were full of ideas and enlisted the enthusiastic help of a surprisingly diverse number of talented people. They not only obtained the use of the little theater at our old Theater Arts Colony location—now the Contemporary Dance Center under the direction of J. Marks—but also managed to get the Contemporary Dancers Foundation to present us.

Ballet 1960 was billed as a "new experimental dance company" offering "innovations in the modern ballet idiom." Mike did most of the choreography, though Lew helped out by contributing his *D'Auber Pas de Trois*, which Mike danced with Fiona (Fuerstner) and Ginny (Virginia Johnson). Mike also brought in another choreographer—a woman, Jeannde Herst—who had a delightful, novel approach to her work that was actually more dance mime than ballet; pointed, funny, social satire. It was completely different from anything we had done before. Her ballet, **By the Side of the Freeway,** was in three parts; O*bstacle Course* was about various kinds of drivers. *I Live by the Side of the Freeway* depicted everyday life when living by one. *Cocktail Party* was a hilarious take on cocktail party stereotypes. Instead of music, Jeannde used a jumble of sounds with bits of conversation mixed in, a truly original score. The "composers" were friends of hers. One of them, John Tomaschke, I later learned also worked with Leo Diner.

Dancer Maurine Simoneau designed and executed all the costumes—we helped her sew—and Bruce Kelley, who had just recently married Sue Loyd, was listed as both Stage Manager and Photographer.

Mike choreographed the other four pieces we presented. Three of them were conventional ballets. *Accent* was an abstract ballet for three couples set to music of Vivaldi. *Troiscouleurs* was a *pas de trois* for Rocky, Frank Ohman and me, set to music of Offenbach. And *Symphony in Jazz,* our closer—definitely showing the influence of Jerome Robbins—was for the whole group and set to music of Liebermann. The fourth piece was a complete novelty at this time, however; Afro/Primitive/Jazz dancing to the accompaniment of a bongo drum, hand clapping, finger snapping and spontaneous vocal calls. Mike called this piece *Session.*

Mike came across a bongo drummer, Kaye Dunham (listed on the program as Ran Kaye), and was anxious to try something that would utilize his talents. We also had a black dancer in our group, Zack Thompson, who had been studying at the School for a while. His specialty was Afro/Primitive/Jazz dancing. This could be a perfect showcase for him, too. And to go along with these two, Mike chose Rocky and me. I don't think either of us had tried any Afro or Primitive dancing before, but we both liked jazz and liked dancing to it.

Actually, I had grown up with jazz, especially New Orleans jazz. It had been around our house all my life. My father loved and understood it and my mother enjoyed it, too. Jazz musicians and other *aficionados* were among my parents' friends. Whenever they came over, I'd sit on the sidelines listening and watching. It's funny, but my sister was just the opposite. She hated jazz and would leave the room as soon as the music started.

Mike set a wonderful solo for Zack, giving him a lot of free rein. When it came time to set something for Rocky and me, Mike would first show a movement to Zack, who would do it his way, and then Rocky and I would copy him. Often one or the other of us would say, "Zack, wait a minute. Do it again. I haven't quite got it." We worked on each step until it flowed.

My solo was a lot of fun. The drum made sort of chattering sounds—in triplets, eight to a bar. Mike gave me hip, rib, elbow and shoulder movements to do. They were slow, sinuous, controlled. Each one took eight triplets to complete. In one section he had me sit down on the floor directly facing the audience, legs spread apart. Opening night I remember sitting there and finding myself eye to eye with our Ballet Guild President, Bettine Bayless. She was sitting in the sixth row looking as if in complete shock. I looked straight at her while I slowly rolled my left shoulder, then my right one, then did a shimmy as I rose back up off the floor, then jauntily went on with my dance.

All of us were having the time of our lives. We were sassy and brash, kicking over the traces, setting everyone on their ears—and we had done it all by ourselves. Both the public and the press responded enthusiastically; tickets sold out and another weekend was added. All the critics gave us good reviews and recognized Mike as a talented young choreographer, full of new ideas, full of promise. We were on top of the world.

Kenneth Rexroth, one of our local poet/writers, had a column in the *Highlights* section of the *San Francisco Examiner* each Sunday. He usually commented on literature, food, the theater, jazz, politics, whatever interested him. For two weekends (7/10/60 & 7/17/60) he devoted his entire column to Ballet 1960.

He raved about us, saying, "If the meal had been enjoyable because everybody seemed to have a good time cooking and serving and mixing drinks, imagine the pleasure of ballet where everybody in the company is having an absolute ball." He continued, "Ballet is terribly hard work. A ballerina works about as hard as a coal miner, or a fry cook and counter man in a skid row restaurant. Most ballet companies are ridden with strife and jealousy. Nothing of this was apparent in 'Ballet 1960'. They all acted like a bunch of model children having a hilarious romp. They knew what they were doing, they loved doing it, and they loved giving it to the audience. The effect on the audience was as might be expected. They went home in a state of profound euphoria."

He went on to mention the perfect rapport and good will that flowed back and forth across the footlights; something that the movies and television could never give. This made "audience personality". When a whole company had it, that was something.

Rexroth had one criticism, however; a rather large one. He devoted most of his second week's column to it. We had called two of our pieces "jazz ballet". He said the pieces were fun to watch, everybody seemed to have a good time doing them, but were they ballet and were they jazz?

Rexroth felt that, to date, there had never been a good jazz ballet. Not enough went on musically in most jazz to give a ballet company enough to do. "Serious" composers who adapted jazz to larger forms invariably did not know what they were doing, and choreographers—and he guessed dancers, too—thought in terms of the popular stereotypes. He said it didn't matter who—Ruth Page, Agnes De Mille, Balanchine—there was a sort of "ballin the jack" figure with snapping fingers in the air that looked like Clara Bow doing the Black Bottom that they all loved to give the chorus every chance they got. He felt it was acutely embarrassing.

Still, he didn't think the problem was insoluble. He had some ideas. First, somebody in ballet should bone up on what was jazz and what wasn't. Forget about Clara Bow and try a calm little mood piece, using a *bona fide*, universally recognized, good jazz orchestra. Then try something that had considerable formal variety, such as the Modern Jazz Quartet's *One Never Knows*. Get a jazz composer to write a suite especially for ballet. He suggested "pure" ballet, but if you needed a plot, it might be a good idea to get a scenario from a poet who understood the depth and breadth of human emotion in the best jazz.

Eight months later, for our Spring 1961 Season, the San Francisco Ballet premiered a new jazz ballet called **Original Sin.** The choreography was by Lew Christensen. John Lewis of the Modern Jazz Quartet composed the musical score. Scenery and costumes were by Los Angeles artist John Furness. And the libretto was by Kenneth Rexroth—with a healthy helping of Jehovah, Rexroth said.

CHAPTER EIGHT

Original Sin

1: *Divorce*

DURING THE EIGHT-MONTH GESTATION PERIOD OF ***ORIGINAL SIN***, we were all busy with Opera Season, then ***Nutcracker***. We didn't even hear about the new ballet until November, just before ***Nutcracker*** rehearsals were to begin, but Lew must have started working on it at the same time he was choreographing for the Opera. This year we were again given good exposure; two full ballets as well as our usual spots in ***Aida, Carmen*** and ***La Traviata***. Lew was expanding Balanchine's ***Raymonda Pas de Dix*** into a longer ballet called ***Glazounoff Variations de Ballet***, which was to be presented with the opera ***La Sonambula***. Our other ballet was ***Con Amore***, which would be presented on the same program with the opera ***Gianni Schicchi*** for the Student Matinees.

By the time Opera Season started—which was also when UC Berkeley's fall semester began—John still had not returned. By now I was thinking, "Oh, to hell with the whole thing. He'll either come back or he won't." I had no idea what to do about my marriage, so I didn't do anything.

I was not unhappy. We were all still high from our summer success, and I was continuing to enjoy my friendship with Rocky. I remember he started giving me comic strip nicknames. He often called me "Beetle", for Beetle Bailey. He also gave me a middle name. He thought "Olive"—for Popeye's Olive Oil—was just right; then my initials could be

S.O.B. For my birthday in August, he gave me a copy of Joy Adamson's book, *Born Free*, about Elsa the lioness. He wrote an inscription on the inside cover, "To my wonderful Sally Olive Bailey. Love Rocky."

One night in early September, after a particularly boring Opera rehearsal that finished early, Rocky and I decided to go out together for supper. The following day was going to be heavy—we had a demonstration of **Pas De Dix** for S.F. State University's theater department in the morning and the *Polonaise* from **Beauty and the Beast** for the Opera Ball/Fol de Rol in the evening—but we had plenty of time for a nice leisurely dinner tonight.

We decided on the Old Spaghetti Factory, a lively restaurant in North Beach that offered flamenco dancing on certain nights of the week, though not this particular evening. We enjoyed a tasty pasta dinner and all that went along with it, then topped off our dinner with a drink at the bar afterwards.

While we were sitting at the bar talking, Rocky suddenly stopped and turned around to look directly at me, then ask bluntly, "What are you going to do about your marriage?"

I sort of shrugged and didn't say anything at first. It was pretty obvious I hadn't been doing much lately. I didn't know what there was to do. The only thing I could think of, now, was to end it. Actually, it had ended a while ago and I honestly didn't feel there was anything I could do to get it going again—unless I quit dancing and moved to New York? Berkeley? Where? Would this be good for either one of us? I doubted it. At least I knew it wouldn't be good for me. I couldn't do it.

I finally said, "I think I'm going to divorce him."

We discussed this for a while. I would be the first in my family to divorce. Rocky asked me questions, as if trying to see whether or not I really meant it, whether or not I'd change my mind.

Finally he asked simply, "Can I come home with you?"

I didn't answer him at first. I just looked at him.

It took a little while for me to adjust my thinking to what he was asking. Though I knew he had had some homosexual encounters, he had never seemed the least bit so around me. In fact, he once made some comment about homosexuals staying out of the way when a woman was involved. I remember watching him as he leaned forward on the bar, sort of taking a deep breath, looking straight ahead—looking so vulnerable. He'd laid himself wide open.

Finally, hesitantly, he looked at me out of the corner of his eye. He looked miserable.

I smiled, and nodded, "Yes."

That night we spoke of many things we had never talked about before. Rocky said he first realized he was attracted to me when we were in Bursa, Turkey. He had evidently walked by the hotel beauty salon while I was having my hair washed. He saw all this thick hair waving around my shoulders and down my back. He said he stood and watched for a few minutes—probably while the poor beauty operators were wondering what on earth to do with it all. He said he would love to have run his toes through it.

One of the first things he asked of me this night was to take the pins out of my hair. We were facing each other on the bed—I was leaning against his bent legs—and after I had loosened my hair, he kept running his hands through it over and over again. At one point I noticed I still had on my wedding rings, so I took them off and handed them to him. He turned and set them down on the bedside table, then turned back to me and drew me close. His kiss was one of the sweetest I'd ever experienced. I never put those rings on again.

The last thing he said, as we turned off the light—he looked at me hard—was, "Sally, don't laugh at me."

A little while later, he sat up in bed and cried out, "Thanks a lot, Mother!" He was in anguish. He confided that his sister had been conceived out of wedlock, and ever since he was a little boy, his mother had admonished, "Don't ever touch a woman until you marry her." He cursed her several times, and then moaned, "She's smothered me, Beetle, she's smothered me."

I must admit, his outburst unnerved me some, but soon enough he calmed down, and in that it was quite late by then, we soon fell asleep in each other's arms. We were still entwined when we awoke the next morning. He left about 6:00 AM to go home, shave and get ready for our demonstration/rehearsal at 10:00 AM. As he was getting dressed, he leaned over and kissed me once more. At this point, though we knew there were problems, I think we both felt we were starting something beautiful.

I arrived at the studio shortly before 10:00 AM and Rocky was already there. When he saw me, he just beamed. I guess I beamed, too. I tried not to be too obvious about it, but I was so glad to have someone responding to me again. We danced together in **Pas de Dix**, and I guess it showed.

It hadn't occurred to me that Rocky would not be discreet, but by the time our demonstration was over, several of the fellows—including Jeff—started making pointed remarks to me about Rocky. It's true that Jeff was his roommate and probably knew what time he came home, but was this the first time he ever returned home at dawn? Even if we went to dinner together, wasn't it possible he could have gone on somewhere else after leaving me off?

Then one of the younger girls, who was sort of a brat, asked, "Sally, why don't you have your wedding rings on?"

That night, for the Opera Fol de Rol, Rocky and I danced together in the *Roses Waltz* part of the *Polonaise* from **Beauty and the Beast**. Each time I'd catch his eye he'd beam back at me. We had always enjoyed dancing together, but now it was even better.

After the show, Rocky went straight home. He didn't

stay for the party afterwards. I stayed for a while; I was keyed up. I was going to have to tell my parents I wanted a divorce, and then notify John of my intentions, then start divorce proceedings—however one did that. I just hoped Rocky would keep his mouth shut. I didn't want a scandal to accompany this. He was not the reason for my divorce and he knew that perfectly well. He was just making it easier.

On my next free night I went home to have dinner with my parents and told them what I proposed to do. My father's first reaction was "Well, it's about time."

My father had been doing business with one of John's brothers-in-law, the husband of John's older sister, who had evidently been asking for some time, "When is she going to dump him?"

I was a little hurt that they found him so easy to write off. I know my father never felt John was the husband for me, but I had taken him seriously and had loved him—I thought. At the time we married I didn't expect to ever divorce. But now, I didn't blame him entirely for the disintegration of our marriage. I hadn't been the greatest wife for him. He hadn't had too good a time, either.

My mother was mainly sorry; sorry that I was unhappy, sorry that John was unhappy, sorry that our marriage hadn't worked out, sorry we were going to have to go through this. But she remarked in her practical way, "You never had a real marriage, anyway." She seemed to agree that divorce was the answer.

A good friend of ours, Nathan Rowley, who lived just down the street with his wife, Carlisle, was a lawyer. He recommended that I see a friend and colleague of his who specialized in divorces. Kay Gehrels would be able to help me. And she did. She was wonderful.

The divorce was simple. I could have used desertion for grounds, or incompatibility, but she thought the catchall "irreconcilable differences" was preferable. The only community property we had between us was the car and the wedding gifts. I didn't want alimony, so she thought I should at least keep those things. John was to pay the legal fees.

I wrote to John and heard back from him. He answered that he'd found he could not love me and agreed that divorce was probably the best thing for both of us. Kay Gehrels was able to get a court date the beginning of December for my interlocutory decree hearing—I'd be glad when that was over—then it would be a year before my divorce was final.

One afternoon during all of this, Mike and I were sitting together on the steps outside the upstairs studio during a rehearsal break. Nobody else was around. Mike got this funny look on his face, then came right out and asked, "Sally, I'm determined to find out. Did Rocky make it?"

I looked at him in astonishment; astonishment that he would ask such a question. Without saying a word, I got up and walked away.

I knew there was a lot of competition between these two, but how far did it go? What all went on in the fellows' dressing room, anyway? I think I was glad I didn't know. I thought of the night we'd had a dress rehearsal for ***Traviata.*** This was before Rocky and I had gotten involved. Rocky and I had been dancing together when his tight toreador pants split up the front. While we were dancing, everyone ignored it, but the minute we got off stage, all the fellows—including Lew—started laughing and giving him a bad time. Then he started laughing, too.

I wasn't offended then, but I was beginning to be offended now. Why was Rocky talking so much? Was he just using me after all? This thought took the edge off my euphoria, to say the least. I instinctively withdrew some. I didn't like feeling used, I didn't like being on display, and I didn't like being the center of a scandal. I should have told him, right then, how I felt, but I didn't. I'd always found it hard to talk about the things that really bothered me. Certainly with John I had.

I was now also beginning to wonder what was really going on with our relationship. Though Rocky had talked a great deal, he and I hadn't been together alone since that one night. When opportunities arose, he hesitated, and I didn't want to push him. Was he beginning to regret having gotten into this? Was I? Should we try to go back to being just friends? Had he already done too much boasting? One thing for sure, we certainly weren't communicating well any more, and we were no longer close friends.

In all the time I'd worked with Rocky, and in all the time we'd been good friends, the one thing I'd never considered was our age difference. He would be twenty-one on his next birthday and I'd just had my twenty-eighth. It had never made any difference at all, but it probably was making a difference now. He, at least, wasn't really ready for this.

By the time we went to Los Angeles with the Opera I didn't know what to think. Before leaving San Francisco, Rocky had announced to me during rehearsal one day that he was getting the wedding suite at the good old Figueroa Hotel. Why was he telling me this—here—now? Was it for the benefit of those within earshot? Was he expecting me to spend a good deal of time with him there? And give everyone a blow by blow account? With some of John's friends still in the chorus, and all of us staying at the same hotel?

I didn't want to do that to John or me. Rocky was driving me crazy. I needed someone to talk to, and now I couldn't even talk to him.

I couldn't talk to anyone else in the Company because they'd just gossip about whatever I said. I wasn't seeing much of Connie at this point—she had already stopped dancing—though I must have talked to her and Ade about divorcing John. Chris had recently come back to San Francisco in hopes of rejoining our company, and she agreed to go to court with me in December as my divorce witness, so I assumed she was sympathetic with me about that, but I wasn't so sure how she'd feel about Rocky. It's funny, but I don't remember caring how anyone else felt about him. Anyway, I wanted to get my interlocutory decree over and done with before starting to talk about anyone else.

Bud Bibbins was in Los Angeles with the Opera, still playing with the orchestra. He and Pat had been such good friends for so long, especially when I first started dating John. Pat was like a big sister, taking me under her wing, always looking out for me. When I was living at home and commuting from Marin, she often had me spend the night if we were particularly late. I felt at home in their guest bedroom. Years later Bud laughingly remarked, "You were like 'The Man Who Came to Dinner'." For several years I drove back and forth to Los Angeles with them during Opera Season and usually rode in their car while there. I must have been a pest sometimes, as younger sisters can be.

I hadn't seen much of Pat and Bud in the last couple of years. Pat had stopped dancing, and with my getting married, then traveling outside the country so much, I just hadn't seen them. I still considered them close friends, though. This year Pat was having health problems, so Bud came to Los Angeles by himself.

On one of the ballet's free evenings, I went to see the opera—it was at least something to do—and rode back and forth to the Shrine Auditorium with Bud, as I had so often done in the past. I was glad to have an old friend to talk to, plus I felt I owed him an explanation of what happened to John's and my marriage.

When we got back to the hotel, the bar that opened off the lobby was crowded with Opera people, Rocky included. It did not seem the best place for Bud and me to talk. When Bud suggested his room, I did not think of it as being improper. How many times had I talked with people late into the night in hotel rooms? Everyone seated with Rocky— when they saw me look at Bud's room key before going up in the elevator—thought it was improper, however.

The next day Rocky was in a rage. He hardly spoke to

me during class or rehearsal. We had a performance together that evening. One of his pals, whom I'd also considered a friend, passed me on the stairs backstage at the theater and said, "My, I didn't know you were so wanton."

I was furious. I felt like kicking him—hard—all the way down the stairs. I felt like retorting, "Just what do you mean by that?" But I didn't say anything. I kept thinking, "He who protesteth too much." Besides, why should I have to defend myself when I hadn't done anything wrong?

What actually happened was that when Bud and I started talking, I found out that his and Pat's marriage was also in trouble. Pat refused to come down to Los Angeles with him this year. I could see her sitting home alone, hurt that he wasn't more insistent that she come, but too proud to show it.

I told Bud, "Please, leave me out of this. I'm in enough of a mess as it is. You call Pat. Tell her you love her, you miss her, and you want her to come down and join you."

He didn't think she'd come.

I answered, "Even if she says 'no' five or six times, just keep asking her until she comes." I guess he did because Pat came down the following day.

I left the two of them pretty much to themselves for the rest of our stay in Los Angeles. I found other things to take up my time. One interesting assignment; I went with Lew and Jocelyn to various ballet schools in the area to observe classes. We were looking for potential scholarship recipients for our new Ford Foundation Grant. They were to be between the ages of fourteen and nineteen, both boys and girls. More than how well they danced in class, we were to judge their body type, their sense of rhythm, how they responded to their teacher, their trainability. There were many good teachers and good dancers in the Los Angeles area. We were encouraged.

It was at this time that we picked up two gorgeous fourteen-year-old girls whom Balanchine had noticed on a visit to L.A. He thought we should offer scholarships to Cynthia Gregory and Nancy Robinson. I guess we did exactly that, because, by the following summer, their names were on our Ballet 1961 program.

Near the end of our Los Angeles run, an opera that included the ballet was scheduled for San Diego. Everyone in the production was bussed down for the single performance. Rocky and I were the soloists that night. We were still hardly speaking outside of rehearsals; I was as mad at him for assuming the worst, as he was at me. I kept thinking, "You idiot. Can't you see what happened?"

I suppose it wasn't nice of me—I think I did it mostly for spite—but I sat with Bud on the bus on the way down and had supper with him before the performance. This upset Rocky even more, but I didn't care, and I was glad to hear that things were going better between Bud and Pat.

On the way back—enough of us were through before the opera's end so that one bus could leave early—I sat in one double seat by myself and Rocky sat two seats away, also by himself. We both glowered at each other, but neither of us would go join the other. Later that night, alone in my hotel room, I was already sorry I left him looking so troubled, already regretting that I didn't go sit next to him and explain what had actually happened. I kept wishing he would phone. I didn't feel I could call him. Unlike today, girls didn't call boys. We waited for them to call us. I would have died before I'd call a man.

Soon enough Opera Season was over. I was relieved. Everything had become so emotional. I felt as if my life had suddenly gone haywire. I was hoping, now that we were back in San Francisco and moving into our Christmas Season, that things would calm down. I was to dance the *Grand Pas de Deux* in **Nutcracker** with Rocky this year. We couldn't afford to still be feuding.

Around this time, Lew began telling us about the new ballet he'd been working on all fall. It was to be called **Original Sin,** the story of Adam and Eve. He told us about the music, the costumes, and some of the casting. Rocky was to be *Adam* and I was to be *Eve.* The company was buzzing; again; still.

My divorce court appearance was coming up. It was supposed to be relatively simple. I wanted to make sure it stayed that way. I thought I really must have a serious talk with Rocky, so we arranged to go to lunch together; not where all the kids usually ate. When we walked into this other restaurant, there were Lew and Leon sitting in a booth. As we passed them, Lew said, "When I cast you two as Adam and Eve I didn't necessarily mean you had to live the parts."

I thought, "Oh, great."

Rocky just sort of smiled and looked pleased with himself.

I could see where, if he was named co-respondent in my divorce, he could get back at people who had hurt him, who had given him a bad time about his manhood. He would like nothing better.

As we ate lunch I told him, "Rocky, you'd really better 'cool it'. It's not that I regret the change in our relationship, but you know as well as I do that you didn't make one single advance towards me until you were sure I was going to divorce John."

I filled Rocky in on all that was going on with my interlocutory proceedings and told him that I would let him know—quietly—when my hearing was over. Neither of us mentioned what had or hadn't happened with Bud.

As for the divorce, John had not shown any opposition to it, though he had been slow in signing and returning the papers. The last paper didn't arrive until 6:00 AM the morning of the hearing, which made both my lawyer and me extremely anxious, but once it arrived, everything went quite simply. The courtroom was empty except for the judge, Kathryn Gehrels, Chris, and me. I remember answering the questions the judge asked me. Chris also answered some questions, and Kay said a few things. Then that was that. In a year my divorce would be final.

It seemed deceptively easy. I was surprised how long it took me to pull all the threads of that marriage out of my life.

Original Sin

2: The Ballet

WE BEGAN WORKING ON *ORIGINAL SIN* IN EARNEST RIGHT AFTER the first of the year. All of us were curious about this ballet and could hardly wait to see each variation as it was set. Each day Lew would take just one, two, or three dancers into rehearsal and shut the door. Unlike most other rehearsals, which were open to any of us who wanted to come in, these were closed. At the end of the day, though, Lew would usually have a run-through and let everyone see what he had done.

When Lew set the *pas de deux* for Rocky and me, the rehearsal stayed closed until we were finished, however. It took several days. The *adagio* was, after all, about discovering each other. It was intended to be sensational, and Lew wanted to go as far as possible without getting us kicked off stage. The three of us needed to feel our way carefully through this one. We didn't want any outside reaction until we were finished. I remember these great expectant looks from the kids as we came out of rehearsal each day.

Looking back on the setting of this *adagio*, I think the experience was different from any other I'd had working on a *pas de deux* with Lew. For one thing, the steps he chose were not particularly identifiable as ballet steps. They were more just movements. And, interestingly, today I can't seem to remember many of them, even when I listen to the music. I can usually remember any ballet when I hear the music.

One other difference; I had to have hair. A great part of my costume, and the *adagio,* had to do with hair—a beautiful, expensive, hip-length red wig. It was made of real human hair; I had to fly to Hollywood to have it specially fitted. It cost $400. To put that price in perspective, the most expensive seats in the house were $3.50 and tickets for our Opening Gala were $20. The hair was choreographed right into the movements. I remember thinking to myself, "Hmm, Lew likes hair, too." Before we could start rehearsing, I had to sew three long falls of hair onto a band that I could tie on my head, then rehearse with it on each day.

For our interpretation, we—as did Rexroth—went straight to the bible. Many people assume sex was the original sin, but it wasn't. The sin was disobeying God, eating the fruit from the tree of knowledge after being warned they must not, for they would die if they did so. The serpent tempted Eve by saying, "Ye shall not surely die: For God doth know that in the day ye eat thereof, then your eyes shall be opened, and ye shall be as gods, knowing good and evil." Being as gods, knowing good and evil; this was Adam and Eve's undoing, why they were thrown out of Eden.

Our *adagio* came before the temptation scene and the eating of the apple. It was about sex, but sex in innocence, sex as something natural and beautiful. When Lew started choreographing it, as we came to each new musical phrase, he would either tell or demonstrate what he had in mind. If what we did turned out not to be what he wanted, he'd suggest something else.

"Here, let's try this."

"No, that doesn't look right, either."

Maybe I hadn't bent enough a certain way. "Try this instead." And he would come over and move my body into another position.

"Now hold that, right there."

"Good!"

We felt our way through each section—experimenting, changing, modifying—until it clicked. During all of this, we constantly checked the mirror to see what we looked like. By the time we got to the climax of the *adagio,* Lew had Rocky holding me around the waist with both of my legs almost straight up in the air. We took one look in the mirror. All three of us recognized it at once; we looked just like the pornographic ashtrays Royes and Leon D. had bought in Greece—obscene, and terribly funny.

We cracked up on the spot. Rocky was laughing so hard that he lost his grip on me and I slipped through his arms, heading straight towards the floor, bottom first. He scooted underneath me in time to break the fall; there the two of us were, a jumble of arms and legs in a heap on the floor, laughing uncontrollably. Lew was laughing as hard as we were. It took a good five minutes to recover sufficiently to continue.

The position we ended up with was actually quite similar, but Lew adjusted it just enough to bring it back over the line of decency. When we were finally done with the whole *pas de deux,* Lew allowed the other kids into rehearsal for a look. It did cause a sensation—there, and on stage—but I don't think it ever offended anyone. Lew's integrity always managed to be impeccable.

Debra Sowell, in one of her interviews with Harold (9/27/87), asked for his views on Lew's handling of sex in his ballets—***Original Sin*** in particular. Harold immediately became defensive. "Lew never did anything lewd. He never did anything in bad taste." He said that after the premiere of ***Original Sin***, he ran into Mrs. Upton in the lobby during intermission. She was ecstatic about the ballet. She loved Lew's interpretation of the Bible story. She said, "You know, Harold, that ballet would be suitable for Sunday school children." He then mentioned that, though Rocky and I performed the *pas de deux* in flesh-colored tights, it was beautiful. He kept repeating, "You know, every Sunday school child should see that ballet. Every Sunday school child should see that ballet."

Original Sin premiered at our Gala Spring Opening in March. Even though we were presenting other new works this season—we were also doing Balanchine's *Symphony in "C"* and another new ballet of Lew's, *St. George and the Dragon*—it sort of monopolized everyone's attention. It was being counted on to sell the season. As *SF Examiner* critic Alexander Fried wrote (3/12/61), "The San Francisco Ballet is about to take the longest, costliest, riskiest forward leap of its career. Never before has it put on so many performances in a home season as it has billed for the Alcazar Theater . . . The leap may land the troupe more firmly than ever in its ambition to be a permanent dance repertory theater. Or it may plop it into red ink. The company is willing to take the chance."

Articles kept appearing in the newspapers about *Original Sin*. Photos of the new ballet made the covers of two Sunday supplements. All of the artwork for this year's programs and posters featured *Eve* and her apple. Those dancers not cast in the ballet felt really "out of it".

All of this pre-publicity generated a lot of interest, but one thing it did not generate—thank goodness—was scandal. It's not that Jeff didn't try; most likely with Rocky's full backing. One thing Rocky loved to say was, "Bad publicity is better than none". I remember Jeff coming into the studio during rehearsal one day, sort of pleading with Lew, and Lew motioning, "No, absolutely not!" Jeff needed Lew's permission before he could slip any item to a columnist. I sighed with relief and said to myself, "Thank you, Lew."

Even with no scandal, the audience was well primed for this ballet. When they arrived at the theater, cartloads of free apples greeted them in the lobby. The premiere was a huge success. As reported by critic Dean Wallace, the audience "rose to its feet in a frenzied ovation for its own home-grown and occasionally neglected ballet company."

A big, gala fundraising party took place on stage afterwards in the "Garden of Eden". Mrs. Upton was Gala Chairman. Trader Vic's, a famous local restaurant, concocted a special drink for the occasion, calling it "Eve's Potion". Everyone was there and everyone was excited.

The next day our event hit all the newspapers. The *News-Call Bulletin* called it "San Francisco Ballet's boldest venture to date . . . a huge, crashing success in concept and taste." Alfred Frankenstein's review in the *SF Chronicle* stated that *Original Sin* was the title of the new piece unveiled at the Alcazar, but primal innocence was its theme; it had a kind of sweetness and inwardly illumined quality. He wrote, "Adam himself is altogether aflame, thanks to Christensen's choreography and Roderick Drew's magnificent performance thereof, and Sally Bailey's Eve is the perfect lyric counterpart to him. These two are an Adam and Eve such as one might see in a particularly inspired drawing by William Blake."

Even *TIME Magazine* (March 24, 1961) wrote an article about the ballet, accompanied by a photo of Rocky and me. It told about both of our births, how Rocky was poked into life from a pile of mud by the swords of the angels Raphael and Lucifer. It described his acquaintance with the animals in the Garden of Eden; how he played with them, then how, weary at last, "Adam rests on the gnarled, raised roots of a tree. It is then that Eve (Sally Bailey) emerges from underneath him. For Choreographer Christensen, the biggest problem was the birth of Eve. 'I sat at my desk for days, thinking—how do I do that? Drew pictures, and all that.'"

As it turned out, I had to crouch in the hollow of that tree from the beginning of the ballet until time for me to slip from Adam's rib. That time span was exactly thirteen minutes and thirty-six seconds. I remember it well. I had a somewhat unconventional balance to make shortly after my birth and I worried that if my muscles should go dead—which they well might, sitting in that cramped position for so long—I wouldn't be able to sustain it. I remember sitting inside the tree's hollow, perched on a couple of cross beams, flexing my thigh, fanny and back muscles in time to the music to keep them toned until time to emerge. Then, on musical cue, I'd slowly lower myself feet first through the space in between the crossbeams—from out front literally the crotch of the tree. Adam and his ribs were draped across the roots just above me. It was quite graphic. I was a breach-birth from Adam's ribs.

Other columnists besides the critics began writing about the ballet. Society columnist Millie Robbins devoted one whole column to it. She started out with, "Still lurking in the minds of many American males (and females, too, for that matter) is the feeling that there's something effete about ballet." She suggested that anyone harboring such preconceived notions run, not walk, to the Alcazar box office and buy a ticket for a performance of *Original Sin*. She continued, "This exciting new ballet by Lew Christensen (himself a handsome, husky six-foot-plus hunk of masculinity) had its world premiere last weekend, and left that brilliant, socialite-studded audience limp." She went on to say she was especially entertained in the lobby during intermission to hear women of assorted ages rhapsodizing about Roderick Drew. Of Rocky she wrote, "Now here's a muscular, athletic lad who oozes virility and was a magnificent foil for the ultra-feminine Eve as portrayed by Sally Bailey."

Our five scheduled performances quickly sold out. Nine more were added and they sold out, too. We were drawing in a new and different audience. We were even reaching the financial district. Bright-eyed young businessmen were coming in droves. Our photos started appearing all over the place. Before the season was through, a record of John Lewis's original musical score was released—with the season's poster of Eve and her apple on the cover.

And now, more than matrons were swooning over Rocky. The homosexuals were, as well. Women and men, alike, were admiring him. I think it went to his head. That's not surprising, considering how young he was.

All of this must have brought back memories for Lew. I remember once hearing a story—I think it was Gisella's sister, Clelia, who told it to me—about Lew during his *Apollo* days. When he walked into a room, the women lined up along one side, the homosexuals along the other, and Gisella walked with him down the middle.

I remember Clelia over the years occasionally making snide comments about Lew. At a shower given for Gisella just before Chris was born, I remember Clelia remarking, "This is the wonder baby." I don't think she and Lew got along too well; they had a sort of truce because they both needed Gisella. Though Clelia had a daughter of her own, she often lived with the two them. She was eighteen years older than Gisella and something of a mother figure. Also, with Lew gone so much, Clelia kept Gisella company and helped her with Chris. We felt Lew avoided going home when she was there. He'd make excuses, and then say "They *talk* so much!" I know he sometimes laughingly made a play on Gisella's last name, Caccialanza, calling her, "Gisella Cackle-onza." He'd call the two of them "The Cackle-onza Sisters".

I like to talk a lot, too, and sometimes Lew would just stop and stare at me, then start making "yakking" motions with his fingers. Then I'd realize that I, too, was talking too much.

Several times I heard that, of all the male dancers Lew trained, he was particularly fond of Rocky. I think Lew saw in Rocky some of himself as a young man. They were both gorgeous in their youth, and they both represented the epitome of manhood in a ballet—Lew as the Greek god Apollo in **Apollon Musagette**, and Rocky as the biblical Adam in **Original Sin.** I have seen photos of Lew as Apollo, and they do, indeed, remind me of that Greek sculpture in the Vatican. And to me, Rocky looked like Michelangelo's Adam. In the ballet his light brown hair was covered with a black wig, and he looked as if he'd just stepped down off the ceiling of the Sistine Chapel.

I could relate to what this was like for them for I, too, represented an epitome in a ballet—the epitome of womanhood. I was, after all, the biblical temptress, Eve. I remember someone telling me they overheard a woman as she was leaving the theater say, "I didn't know Eve had red hair." I also heard that those bright-eyed young businessmen from the financial district were asking, "What's she like off stage?"

Once again I reminded myself of the wisdom of keeping illusions just that. I knew that I was much plainer off stage than on. These young businessmen could well meet me off stage and be disappointed—the old "Oh! I didn't recognize you. You look so different!" Rather than trying to live up to my "on stage" image, I thought it best to just ignore it.

Years later I actually did meet one of those bright-eyed, young businessmen. Tom McLean was a fourth grade teacher at my son's elementary school. I ended up volunteer-teaching drug education to his fourth grade students one semester. He had been in insurance in those days. He told me he used to go to practically every performance of Rocky's and mine.

He said, "You were so romantic. I just loved it."

This is something Rocky and I were able to do night after night; capture the essence of love—sex, romance, heartbreak, whatever—and project it to the audience. We felt sort of like alchemists.

Tom followed us for some time. He knew of Rocky's eventual suicide. He was one of the first people to ever discuss it with me.

Chapter Eight

Original Sin

3: A Desperate Situation

EVERYONE WAS GOOD AND TIRED BY THE TIME OUR SPRING SEASON was over. Some of the kids were disgruntled by all the attention Rocky and I had been receiving. They felt they'd worked just as hard as we had, and they were just as good. Though **Original Sin**'s great success was lucky for us all, that fact didn't make them feel much better. I had the feeling they were just waiting for Rocky and me to have more troubles of our own. They had been brewing.

All season the two of us had been working together—all day every day—and well. There was no question about that, but that was about it. Afterwards we'd go our separate ways. I knew that Rocky's admirers were lionizing him, and he didn't seem at all anxious to include me. I don't think I did much socializing at all this season, other than go out after a performance with family or a few friends. I think I mostly just went home and collapsed.

By now I was utterly discouraged. I didn't know what was going on. I didn't know where I was headed, or where Rocky was headed. When all the commotion died down, I don't think Rocky knew either. I hesitated to talk to him about it because I didn't want to push. He might have changed his mind. I felt as if, once again, I was caught in limbo. I was in limbo, anyway, until my divorce was final in December. All I could do—again—was wait and see what would happen.

Right after the season, Lew gave us all a needed, short vacation. I went home to Belvedere to keep house for my father while my mother went to Denmark for the birth of my sister's second child. In the evenings I remember playing chess with my father, or the ancient Japanese war game of *go*. I got really good at *go*; quite ruthless, almost unbeatable. That took care of me. I don't know what Rocky did during this time. I didn't ask him and he didn't tell me.

After vacation, those of us who were interested put on another workshop season in July, this year called Ballets '61; and this year firmly under the thumb of the Ballet Company. We were now being sponsored by the Ballet Guild and we were dancing at the S.F. Ballet School. The three upstairs studios, which were separated by moveable walls, could be opened up into a makeshift theater. The top studio was three feet higher than the other two, and when black drapes, black flats and some lights were put in place, it made an adequate stage. Portable risers were put in the middle studio, with folding chairs set up on them for the audience. The front studio was left empty for the audience during intermissions. This arrangement took the financial burden off of us, and the workshops continued here each summer through 1973, but no season was ever again as daring or as exhilarating as that first one.

Lew choreographed two new works for us this year, **Prokofiev Waltzes** and **Shadows.** Joce joined in, as did Kent, who had returned from his Army duty in time for our Spring Season. [During the '50's and '60's, between the Korean and Vietnam Wars, six months of Armed Service training was mandatory for all able-bodied men.] Kent also tried his hand at choreography and moved into a director position with Mike, who was up for his Army stint this summer. Mike now assigned himself General Director, Kent Artistic Director, and Jeff, still, Managing Director.

Before Mike left, he choreographed a new abstract piece to Stravinsky's **Ebony Concerto**. Kent choreographed a balletic version of Arthur Miller's **The Crucible,** and the two of them together re-choreographed **Session,** this year using different dancers and calling it **Session II.** Kaye Dunham was still the drummer, but neither Rocky nor I were in it—or Zack Thompson, for that matter.

Kent did choreograph a *pas de deux* to Shostokovich music for Rocky and me, however. He had been one of the dancers resentful of Rocky's success in the spring, and he made Rocky's part as technically difficult as possible. Whether it was from rehearsing this or from something else, I don't remember, but Rocky injured himself before the season opened, and Kent ended up having to dance that stinker of a part, himself. He didn't have the nerve to change it. I remember Lew laughing, thinking it terribly funny, and saying, "There's some kind of justice in this."

Rocky took time off to let his injury heal. He didn't come around the school. I was still in Belvedere with my father and I didn't know where he was. All sorts of rumors were, of course, flying.

In July, half way through our workshop season, we gave our annual Sunday Matinee performance at Stern Grove. Rocky came to the performance and came backstage afterwards. He looked pale and alarmingly thin. He had an ace bandage on his left wrist. I immediately sensed something serious had happened.

He smiled at me and said, "Hi, Beetle. My sister is here with me. Will you come meet her?"

I changed my clothes as quickly as I could, then went out front with him to meet her.

The story unfolded. Two weeks before, Rocky had tried to kill himself by slashing his wrist. He tried a second time after he was already in the men's psycho ward at San Francisco General Hospital. Somehow he had managed to smuggle in some razor blades and aspirin.

His sister, who was married and living with her family in San Diego, came up at once when this happened. The doctors felt she was the only member of his immediate family with whom he'd be safe at this point. Rocky felt such anger towards both his mother and father that they were told to stay away. His sister had now been up for two weeks and she needed to go back to her own family.

Would I help them? Would I be responsible for Rocky while he was in the hospital? I guess the doctors felt he would be safe with me. How could I say no?

The three of us went together to their parents' house before Rocky's sister took him back to the hospital. It was there that I had the first of many long conversations with his mother and father. I had never noticed before, but Rocky had the same eyes as his father, except his father's were blue and his were green.

His parents were alarmed, frightened, bewildered, hurt, and helpless to do anything themselves. I don't remember any anger in them; just a great questioning. I grew very fond of them. I'd call them on the telephone after each of my visits with Rocky, and we'd talk and talk.

I wasn't the only one they asked to help; they asked Jocelyn and Jeff, too. We would take turns visiting Rocky at the hospital and taking him things to eat—he wouldn't eat the hospital food. I remember baking lots of bran muffins. Sometimes Jeff would drive me there and back, usually when we were going to take Rocky out somewhere. I was the only person who could sign Rocky in and out of the hospital, though.

I remember one time Jeff and I took Rocky swimming. Rocky wanted to go to the city-owned indoor pool near Stern Grove. This day was gray and cold. The fog was blowing in— I turn blue in swimming pools even on nice days—and this was probably the last thing either Jeff or I wanted to do, but the three of us went swimming.

While all of this was going on, classes, rehearsals and

performances continued as usual. I think I was mostly numb the whole time, running on automatic. Actually, I was glad to have a schedule to keep. Otherwise, I might have just sat on the edge of the bed and stared into space. I don't know if anyone told Lew or Leon what had happened. Someone certainly should have. This is the kind of thing anyone in charge of a group of people needs to know. Maybe Joce or Jeff told them. Maybe Rocky's parents did; I guess they were the ones who should have. All I know is that I didn't. I didn't say anything to anyone—except, of course, to Joce and Jeff. Rocky didn't want the kids to know, and I couldn't blame him. Could you see me saying, "Oh, he's in the psycho ward for a little while; I'm not sure when he'll be out."

I did tell my parents, however. My mother was by now back from Denmark. They were both extremely concerned about the position I was putting myself into, but I will hand it to them, they didn't say a word. I think they both thought that if they kept quiet, I might come to my senses faster.

The only comment my father made during this whole time was a rather oblique one, made while I was keeping house for him, before all of this had happened. I was reading *The Alexandria Quartet* by Lawrence Durrell. I probably started reading it with Rocky before the end of the season. Dad commented, "Why do you always look under rocks for things hidden there? Some things you're better off not knowing about."

I remember countering, "Actually, I think the more you know, the better off you are." This conversation between us recurred numerous times over the years, and neither of us ever changed our positions.

My mother was somewhat familiar with the situation Rocky was now in. She had volunteered as a Red Cross "Gray Lady" in the Army's Letterman Hospital psycho ward for several years. The psycho ward was usually not open to volunteers, but she was good at communicating with the patients. She could sometimes get them to talk before the doctors could. She asked me to bring Rocky over to our house for Sunday lunch several times. He seemed to enjoy coming. He always had me stop on the way so that he could buy her a bouquet of flowers.

One Sunday, as I arrived at the hospital to pick Rocky up, one of the nurses told me, "He's been up and ready for hours. He's been waiting for you." He was improving.

I remember the first time I took Rocky out of the hospital; he wanted to see—of all things—Federico Fellini's movie, **La Dolce Vita**. It had recently come out and was making quite a stir. The movie deals with the decadent Italian high life, not really *dolce* (sweet) at all. The main character squanders his talent and wastes his life because he can't quite make himself leave *la dolce vita*. His close friend kills his two children, then himself, out of hopelessness.

On the way to the movie, Rocky wanted to stop at the grocery store to buy cookies and fruit. He wanted me to stay in the car. I didn't know if I was supposed to let him go in by himself or not. He looked at me, daring me not to trust him. When he came back out, it was all I could do to keep from blurting, "Show me what you have in that bag."

Later that day, on the way back to the hospital, he told me that he hadn't expected to survive the second suicide attempt. It was just a fluke that he did. He was so afraid of the pain that he took too many aspirins. His heartbeat was so slow that he hadn't yet bled to death when the hospital staff found him.

I tried not to react. I simply asked, "How did you feel when you woke up?"

I remember him answering, "At first I couldn't believe it. I was supposed to be dead. But I was still alive." Then he sort of shook his head and sighed, "It's so hard, Beetle. It's so hard."

I then responded with something like, "Well, at least you have help. Do you like your doctor?"

He answered, "Yes, I do. But some of our sessions are pretty rough. Sometimes I get sick."

I think I also asked him how all of this was being paid for. Not as many people had health insurance in those days, and I knew his parents didn't have much money; his father was a high school custodian. He told me, "The State. When you don't have anything, the State pays for it."

I was at least glad of that.

I tried to figure out what drove Rocky to do this and came up with an explanation that at least made sense to me. Rocky had for so long wanted this marvelous, virile image that he now had. Though he had identified himself with the homosexuals, had probably used them to get ahead—maybe even used them to stay out of the Army—and was most likely attracted to them, he hated himself for it. He wanted to be manly. He knew that one got along much better in this world if one was manly. But now that he had this wonderful, masculine image, what was he going to do with it? I think he felt it was making a mockery of him. He knew to what extent it was pretense. He had managed to fake it so far, but he couldn't do that indefinitely. Time was passing. My divorce would be final in six months. If he didn't marry me then, what kind of statement would he be making about himself?

This saying of Oscar Wilde's—a favorite of my present husband's—applies so well here. "In this world there are only two tragedies. One is not getting what one wants, and the other is getting it."

Rocky was now in real trouble and he was wise enough to know it. He needed help. I think his first suicide attempt—with the injury beforehand—was a cry for help. If I remember correctly, he committed himself into the hospital.

This was in 1961, when doctors believed that homosexuality was a mental disorder, that it was curable—just like impotence. It wasn't until 1974 that the American

Psychiatric Association (*TIME Magazine,* July 26, 1993) began to suspect there might be a genetic factor involved.

I'm not so sure about Rocky's second suicide attempt, though; I think he got so discouraged when, after getting help, he saw what he was going to have to go through, and thought it would be just too hard.

By the end of this first outing of ours, Rocky seemed more relaxed and almost cheerful. When I signed him back into the hospital he asked if I would like to come on in and see his "new place". I was allowed inside. He showed me his room. It contained two metal beds and two dressers. I don't remember there being any chairs. He introduced me to his roommate. He pointed down the hall to where the bathrooms and showers were located. He took me into the occupational therapy room—"O.T.", he called it—where they did crafts.

"We've been making moccasins this week. Last week we made ash trays."

"Can I see them?" I asked.

"No, they're in there," and he pointed to some locked cupboards underneath a counter that lined one wall under a row of windows.

He said, "There's going to be a dance in here one night during the week. Would you like to come?"

I answered, "Sure." Whether or not there was a rehearsal, I would come.

He then said, "I'll call you when I know for sure."

The dance did, indeed, take place one night during the week, and I came.

One doesn't often go to a dance in a psycho ward, but looking back on it, I don't remember anyone—there were other guests besides me—looking as if they thought it was strange to be behind two sets of locked doors with two staff members in white coats hanging around.

The room wasn't large. There might have been twelve of us altogether. I seem to remember a three-piece combo, especially a big *bass viol,* though that seems unlikely. The music probably came from a record player. At any rate, I remember—clearly—standing in front of Rocky, waiting for him to take my outstretched hand and start dancing. We just stood there facing each other. It seemed forever. He began to perspire. He didn't move. Then he broke out in a real sweat, and droplets started trickling down his face. He began to shake, and his shirt became drenched. Suddenly he started shaking so violently that I thought he would collapse in a wet heap at my feet. I can still see myself standing there, smiling, as if nothing was amiss; one of my best acting jobs, ever. Out of the corner of my eye I could see the staff's eyes riveted on us. Rocky managed to remain standing. His shaking gradually subsided and he finally, hesitantly, took my hand in his. And slowly, carefully, we began to dance.

Before the evening was over, we were cutting loose, as we had so often done in the past—and sort of took over the dance floor.

I guess this was the turning point for Rocky, when he decided to give life another try. From this point on, his therapy progressed surprisingly quickly. That's not to say it always went easily. Sometimes he would call and postpone our visits for a day or two. But by September 18th, the opening night of Opera Season, he was on stage in a solo role in the opera **Blood Moon.**

CHAPTER EIGHT

Original Sin

4: A Recovery

I DON'T REMEMBER WHAT ROCKY TOLD THE KIDS WHEN HE
returned to the School. Maybe he just said that his injury
had now healed. I'm left with the impression that everything
went smoothly and quietly for a change. Rocky looked good.
He'd gained back the weight he'd lost and he got back into
shape quickly. Opera Season seemed to progress normally.
Lew gave him nice things to do.

For this year's Fol De Rol/Opera Ball, Lew set a piece
using eight fellows plus Rocky and me that was probably the
sexiest, steamiest thing he ever choreographed. In the
program it was listed as **Voodoo Dance**. The music was credited
as being *Traditional*. It sounded much like the ethnic music
we'd heard throughout the Middle East. The number was
sort of a "white goddess" thing. I was totally white; leotard,
tights, shoes, headdress, necklace, skirt, hands, neck and
face were all white. The fellows were all black; body-paint,
loincloths, neckpieces and wild straw hair were all black.

I recognized some of the movements Lew set for us; they
were just like those we'd seen in that wild, erotic, lion dance
in Ethiopia. In one place Lew had the fellows jerking around
me in a circle—I don't exactly remember what I was doing
in the middle. In another place he had Rocky rolling back
and forth on the floor while I pranced over his legs. But
Lew kept the lid on the steaminess by making everything

just slightly kooky. The whole audience was chuckling by the time the fellows followed me off stage.

Because the artists always donated their services for the Fol De Rol, there was, of course, no budget for costumes. As usual, we put together our costumes as best we could. This time Lew and I ended up assembling the costumes for the Voodoo Dance. We bought my leotard, tights and all the body paint, but we had to make headdresses, neckpieces, loincloths, and my skirt of beads. It was fun. Lew sent me to the library to look up African headdresses. I remember making sketches of about five. We chose one, then he helped me make it. His special touch was the white straw hair flowing out the back. My headdress and the beads for my necklace and skirt were made of a fabric that hardened after being dipped in a special solution; one of Hollywood's inventions introduced to us by Tony Duquette when he designed ***Beauty and the Beast***. I remember rolling hundreds of strips of solution-soaked fabric into little tubes for the beads. When they were dry, Lew and I strung them together and sprayed them white. Lew was clever with his hands, almost as clever as he was with dance steps.

The two of us spent hours together in the back room working on these creations. One evening, while we were working away, he started telling me about some of his disappointments. I'm not sure what triggered this, but I remember him saying, "I don't know that what I'm doing is what I want to do, but at least I'm doing something." Then he added, "I don't really know what else I could do, anyway."

Then Lew told me how he felt on leaving New York for good. It was not his official stance of, "I wanted to be more creative, to have the opportunity to build something of my own." What he confided to me that evening was, "Sal, they wouldn't let me in; I wanted to be a director along with them, but they wouldn't let me in."

I think this must have been around 1948 or 1949, when Balanchine and Lincoln reorganized their company for its first season at New York City Center, when they changed the name from "Ballet Society" to "New York City Ballet", when Lew and Gisella returned to San Francisco.

Lew had been helping Balanchine run his company since the beginning, except for the four years he was in the war. Lincoln always acknowledged this and seemed grateful. Lew, himself, knew how useful he'd been and felt he'd earned a position equal in status to the two of them. He felt he should be a director, too, not just ballet master.

But they wouldn't give the position to him, and this time—perhaps it was the only time—Lincoln didn't back him up. I think Lew was deeply hurt and now felt he had no choice but to leave. I also think he spent the rest of his life wishing he were back working with Balanchine. True, Balanchine and he continued to work together until Balanchine's death—as long as there was a continent between them.

In Bernard Taper's biography of Balanchine, Taper refers several times to Balanchine's ability to forget the past, to accept his present situation, and try not to second-guess his future. Balanchine believed that "to calculate too finely is to presume on God's role, and he who does so can expect to meet with frustration, disappointment, and humiliation . . . All that a person ought to do is make the best of whatever turns up."

Too bad Lew didn't absorb these beliefs of Balanchine's along with so many of his others. He might have gotten more satisfaction out of what he was doing in San Francisco. It's funny, but I have always thought Lew's best ballets were those he did on his own, where Balanchine's influence didn't show so much.

Another thing Taper wrote that particularly interested me; "Of all those attracted to the company in the early years, the most important to its future was Jerome Robbins." During the New York City Ballet's first season, Robbins was evidently so affected by a performance he attended that he wrote

Balanchine a fan letter stating how much it would mean to him to become part of such a company. He offered to serve in any capacity—as dancer, choreographer, handyman, whatever. Balanchine engaged him in the fall of 1948 and in 1949 made him Associate Artistic Director, the position Lew had asked for.

By then, Lew's admiration for Balanchine was not starry-eyed. He knew the problems too well. Also, by then, he'd had some successes of his own, while Balanchine's work was still disliked. Gisella made an interesting comment to Debra Sowell (transcript dated 12/5/87) about Balanchine's feelings toward Lew during those early years, "Once Balanchine commented to me, 'the audience likes what Lew is doing *big*, but not what I'm doing.'"

In any case, Balanchine perceived Lew's ballets as not complementary to his own. He now preferred the starry-eyed Jerry Robbins, who did, indeed, turn out to be a great asset not only to his ballet company, but to theater in general.

Near the end of Opera Season Rocky took me to Alexis's of Tangiers—one of San Francisco's fanciest restaurants—for a deluxe, black-tie dinner before the gala opening of the Bolshoi Ballet, which was being sponsored by our Ballet Guild. We flew up from Los Angeles for the occasion. Rocky looked especially handsome in his rented tuxedo. I wore my fur, my best jewelry, and a strapless, short evening dress I'd made out of fabric I'd bought in Damascus.

I didn't know what the kids were making of this dinner of ours. I wondered if Rocky's parents were hoping it would lead to a wedding; mine were most likely hoping it wouldn't. Before the evening was through, I understood that it was a "thank you", a payback for all I'd done for Rocky over the summer—and a release from further obligation.

Whether I liked it or not, I could see that he needed to be on his own for a while, without me around. I'd had way too much power over him, for which he could hate me about now. He was going to have to get his self-respect back before he'd come back to me—if he was going to come back. I felt that the choices he made now were critical.

As soon as we returned to Los Angeles, Rocky made a beeline for the Duquettes and their crowd, among whom were many homosexuals. He was deliberate about it. He made sure I knew. He even asked me to press his pants for him one afternoon, like his mother had done so often. I had a traveling iron, and he showed me how to do the pressing on the floor of my hotel room.

I was mad, and when we had both finished with his pants I asked him, "Are you trying to make me into your mother, now?"

He paused and sort of looked at me. He never asked me to press his pants again.

I was upset over the choices he was making. True, he was being courted like mad by the homosexuals—with the corresponding slings and arrows directed at me—but he didn't have to go along with them if he didn't want to. I was sick. What had this whole past summer been about, anyway? He was undoing everything he'd worked so hard on. He would end up right back where he started, again hating himself for it, and one day succeeding in killing himself— and next time I wouldn't be able to do a thing about it.

I wondered, "What purpose have I been serving in all this?" I was confused and hurt, and speaking of feeling unwanted; this was different, much worse than having a husband be unfaithful with another woman. In that case you could still compete. Your whole gender wasn't being rejected, wasn't being looked upon as repulsive.

Rocky would never make a clean break with me, though. He always wanted to keep hold of some little thread. I think what he really wanted of me was a good nursemaid; not a wife. If I went along with him on this, he would probably keep me up on a shelf and trot me out only when he needed to look as if he had a wife. It would be a completely counterfeit situation, and I've never liked anything fake.

I guess I was, once again, the one to make the break final. I did it, perhaps subconsciously, at the same time I got my final divorce decree from John. I remember going to see my divorce attorney the day it was final. She told me, "You don't have to pick it up right now. People usually don't come for these until they're ready to remarry." But I just wanted to be free of the whole mess, get rid of all the things in my life that weren't working, tie up all the loose ends in a firm knot and move on.

It's funny, but I thought that once I got the decree in my hand, I'd feel decisive and relieved, ready for a celebration. I'd even spent too much money on a pair of Austrian crystal drop earrings to mark the occasion. But once the time arrived, I didn't feel like celebrating at all. Instead, that evening I went back to the Ballet School and took an extra class.

I took lots of extra classes. That gave me something to do. Besides, I danced better for it. Quite often, after class, I would go on to one of the theaters—all of which I could now walk into free—and see whatever was playing. Keeping current with what was happening in the theater was not only good for my spirits, it was good for my dancing. There were definite professional advantages to being alone.

Around this time I also started keeping a daily journal, not just a travel journal as I had kept for each of my trips, but something to help keep in perspective what was going on around me. I was now even more reticent to talk about things that were bothering me. I also, once again, felt I had no one to talk to. Joce had been supportive while Rocky was in the hospital, but now that he was out, she seemed to be siding with the homosexuals; so was Jeff. And I certainly could no longer talk with Rocky's parents.

While putting together this book, I regretted no longer having those journals. I kept all the others, but not those. Eleven years later, as I was packing up my belongings before remarrying, I read them again. They were terrible. We all sounded as if we were mad. They also described a type of viciousness from the homosexual community that I'd never before encountered. They made for ugly reading. I did not want them coming into my new life with me so I burned them in my apartment's fireplace, section at a time. I watched until the last page went up in flames.

I still have my scrapbooks from this period, though, with all their clippings, programs and photos. I just take one look and the memories come rushing back. Three things, in particular, I remember.

The first occurred during a Christmas matinee while I was dancing **Nutcracker** with Rocky; for one brief moment during the *adagio* I felt as if I was blacking out right on stage. It alarmed me. I had never blacked out in my whole life, but now my lips were tingling, and I felt light-headed. Suddenly the footlights dipped, then swiveled 360 degrees. Luckily, the sensation lasted for only a moment, but it was long enough for Rocky to notice. He was, after all, supporting me. He could tell if I suddenly lost my balance. I sensed he was secretly pleased. I realized I must get a better grip on myself.

The second thing I remember; Mike and Paula, who had been dating since South America, got married right after Christmas.

The third thing; by the year's end I was repeating to myself this uncharitable quote, "Walk with a cripple for a year and you'll end up with a limp."

CHAPTER NINE

The U.S. Cross-Country Tours

1: One Cold, White Blur

THERE WAS A LOT ABOUT THE WINTER AND SPRING OF 1962 THAT I don't remember, even though we were on our first cross-country U.S. tour for a good portion of it. I purposefully removed myself mentally, if not physically, from what was going on around me. I thought I'd survive better if I ignored everything—especially Rocky, who was continuing to flaunt his homosexual escapades.

I do remember the winter weather, however. It was unusually severe. We were right in the thick of it for six weeks. We saw snow every single day. Our first stop was St. Paul, Minnesota; we arrived just after a blizzard. I remember high piles of snow along the sidewalk outside the theater. Our train from San Francisco took three days to get to St. Paul. It was rerouted through Kansas City because of the weather. I remember our train being stuck in the snow one evening, and some of us getting off the train to watch men shoveling it off the tracks.

We picked up our chartered Greyhound buses in St. Paul—one for the orchestra and one for us—and used them for the bulk of our tour. I mostly remember driving by miles and miles of white snow fields with corn stalks sticking out, pushing on to the next town before the next storm set in. I remember walking in Saginaw, Michigan in a wind so cold that I thought the moisture in my eyes would freeze.

Adjusting to our rigorous new schedule was not easy. One-night stands are like no other kind of touring. We had to be up each morning at 6:15 in order to get "bags and baggage" on the bus by 8:00 AM. The bus left on the dot. We were screamed at if we were late. We'd stop along the way for lunch—our main meal—around noon, arrive in the next town at 2:00 or 3:00 PM, settle into our rooms, then be in the theater by 5:00 PM for class and a run-through of that evening's program. We'd stop an hour before curtain— curtains were usually 8:00 or 8:30 PM—to make up and prepare for the performance. We'd finish around 11:00 PM, get a bite to eat, bathe and wash out tights and underwear, get to bed around 1:00 AM, and then do the same thing all over again the following day. We thought for sure we'd die, but then everyone learned to sleep on the bus.

To make matters worse for me, I started off the tour with a bad chest cold. I was still feverish and taking antibiotics when we left San Francisco. I had a husky, sexy voice and bad cough for the first several weeks. I just about recovered from that when I developed stomach problems—unusual for me. For about three days I couldn't keep food from going through me. I could still dance, but I remember Lew watching me with increasing concern. I guess I started dropping weight.

I remember one night after some performance; our local sponsor invited Lew, Leon and us principal dancers to supper. It was a delicious supper. I could eat it, all right. It's just that it went on through me. Before dinner was over, I had to excuse myself from the table and go to the ladies' room. I remember Lew's eyes following me with that same watchful look of the hospital staff's in Rocky's psycho ward.

A day or two later, Rocky and I were scheduled to dance *Nutcracker Pas de Deux* for the first time this tour. Until now we had been dancing together in ballets like **Sin** and **Caprice**, but nothing as strenuous as the **Grand Pas de Deux**. Of late I had not enjoyed dancing with Rocky. For one thing, he was shifting his interpretation of *Adam* to that of an innocent being seduced by an all-knowing *Eve*. This wasn't how either of us had played it before. Soon enough Lew decided to change casts, and had the two of us teach our roles to others. I didn't mind in the least. But now I think Lew was wondering if I had the strength to get through **Nutcracker**. He had Rocky and me rehearse it with him on stage before the performance. Rocky was so solicitous as he practically carried me through the *adagio* that he infuriated me. I decided to just relax and take it one step at a time, and all went just fine, thank you. After the performance I started eating again, with no more stomach problems.

It's funny; by now Rocky and I were barely speaking to each other, but we could still "pull it off" together on stage. I remember a performance in Bloomington, Indiana at the University. We were closing with **Nutcracker Suite** [at this time **The Nutcracker Ballet** was still not widely performed and we often used the suite of dances from **ACT II** as a closer] and Rocky and I were again scheduled to dance the *Pas de Deux*. This particular night, as we took our bows at the end, we received a standing ovation—a completely different experience than any other kind of ovation.

During bows, usually the performer and the audience play a little game together, egg each other on. But this isn't a game at all. It's completely spontaneous—it just happens. For a moment, after you've finished, there is no sound at all. The silence is long enough that you begin to think, "My God, they don't like us." Then—you don't see it happen because you can't see the audience; it's more something you feel and hear—the audience stands up in unison. There is a definite sound to a house full of people all rising from their seats at the same time. The applause breaks out after this. It rolls in great waves. Everybody loves everybody. This is another heady experience.

Because of my new detachment from the group, I could have been lonely this trip, but I made a new friend, a flutist in our pick-up orchestra. Our orchestra was assembled especially for this tour. The players came from various places, gathering in St. Paul just in time for one rehearsal before our first performance. Dottie Lee was from outside Chicago. She was about my age, had many of the same interests I did, and was also a little lonely. She had recently married and had to leave her husband at home. Each day at our lunch stop, after getting off our respective buses, we'd meet and eat lunch together. There were many Howard Johnson Restaurants along our route, and we often stopped at one of them. At that time their place mats showed a map of the United States with stars marking their locations in each state. I saved one of the place mats with our itinerary marked on it. I found it in my scrapbook. Dottie and I used to spend a lot of time studying those maps, trying to figure out where we'd been and where we were going. We kept crisscrossing the Midwest—I remember passing through Indianapolis three times—and this confused my sense of geography. To this day I'm still mixed up about the Midwest. In the snow, every place looked alike.

In Chicago, the last stop on our tour, we danced at McCormick Place, a large convention center complex with a huge 6,000-seat auditorium. I don't remember anything being particularly wrong with our performances there—or the size of our audiences for that matter—but we had a new experience; bad reviews. I don't think we'd ever had bad reviews before. In fact, we'd sort of gotten used to raves.

Well, Chicago critic Claudia Cassidy was lying in wait for us. But then, from what we'd heard, she lay in wait for everyone. Among performers she'd earned the nickname "Acid-y Cassidy".

Quoting from her review in the *Chicago Sunday Tribune*, March 25, 1962, "The most important thing about **Original Sin** is that it lies in the young company's vernacular of movement, which is lithe, easy and pleasant to watch, when not pushed beyond its sharply defined technical limitations." Of Balanchine's **Swan Lake** she wrote, "[It] was so short of virtuosity and the grand style as to be pathetic. I could not bear to see the same thing happen to **Symphony in 'C'**, so I took **Original Sin** as the valid coin of the San Francisco Ballet's realm, and departed."

I guess we took her remarks in stride. But still, we didn't like being blasted. Lew bolstered our spirits as best he could by saying we should just ignore her and get out there and dance. His attitude towards all reviews—both good and bad—remained the same; don't pay any attention to them. They are only one man's opinion. However, I do remember him confiding to me once, "If I paid attention to bad reviews, I'd never choreograph again."

My personal response to "Acid-y Cassidy" was, "Too bad you didn't stay for **Symphony in 'C'**. You might have liked it." We had all worked hard on this ballet. I was especially pleased when Lew gave the 2nd Movement to me. I thought maybe he wouldn't. It has that one long balance in 2nd Position *en pointe* where your partner lets go of one hand, then walks around behind you before taking your other hand. I remember Lew yelling at me in rehearsal, "Sal, you look like you're balancing on top of a flag pole!"

It was definitely a technical challenge for me, and in my usual fashion, I responded to it by making myself accomplish it. In performance I was always glad when it was over. Once it was past, I loved dancing the rest, for now I had the chance to reproduce what I had so loved about Danish ballerina Mona Vangsaa's interpretation.

For me this was a special role for another reason, too. It was often placed on the same program as **Original Sin**. The pure dancing of it contrasted well with my rather sensational *Eve*.

I remember once in a *"C"* rehearsal—I was leaning against the *barre* waiting for my entrance—when Jeff came up to me and said, in reference to all the attention I'd been getting for **Sin**, "Sally, you don't even have to dance. All you have to do is stand there."

I looked at him evenly and added, "But I can also dance."

After we got back from tour, we had a late Spring Season in San Francisco. Unfortunately, since last year, our wonderful old Alcazar Theater had been torn down and replaced—to our great dismay—by a motel and parking garage. We had to move up the street to the Geary Theater, which wasn't nearly as suitable for us. It was comparable in size, but the stage was narrower and deeper, and the audience was so close to the stage that I had to practically look straight up to see the top row. This made me feel as if I'd fall over backwards; not good for balance. None of us liked dancing at the Geary and we were there for three spring seasons. I think this must have been when Lew started his campaign for a new theater in earnest.

The centerpiece for this season was Lew's new **Jest of Cards**, his venture into the *avant-garde*. We were all a pack of cards. The ballet featured Michael Smuin as the *Joker* and the rest of us as the different suits of the deck—three soloists to each suit. Our costumes consisted of all-over tights, with headdresses that denoted our suits and covered most of our faces.

Visually, this ballet was quite unusual. Some of our dancers were fourteen feet tall. Our royalty walked around on stilts, were faceless like the rest of us, and wore huge, cumbersome costumes of oriental splendor. They were actually more like walking scenery. Tony Duquette designed the production, and—we were told—got some of his ideas from the Japanese Kabuki Theater.

The most novel thing about the ballet, however, was the sound. One could hardly call it music. It was composed by atonal composer Ernst Krenek, and called *Marginal Sounds*. The piece was composed for conventional instruments, but none to be played conventionally. The pianist played the keys with his forearm and strummed the strings under the piano's lid with his fingers. The violins tried to sound like electronic music. I remember hearing that, besides regular percussion instruments, four brake drums were used. Someone had scoured auto junkyards in search of brake drums that could produce a perfectly pitched C, D, or A.

Jest of Cards caused a lot of excitement and also got us good press coverage. *LIFE Magazine* gave the ballet a nice two-page spread. At the end of our San Francisco Season we took it, along with the rest of our repertoire, to the Seattle World's Fair for one week. A new Opera House was built for the Fair; we were the first performers to use it. We "broke it in", worked out some of the bugs, but I remember it as being a nice theater.

I don't remember much else about our stay, except trying to see the Fair's attractions around our dancing schedule. I remember the Space Needle and hearing John Glenn tell what it was like being the first American astronaut to circle the earth. He was one of the speakers at a conference on space exploration that used the Opera House one afternoon. I could come and go through the backstage entrance, so this afternoon I sat on the floor in the wings and listened to him speak.

By this time I'd mastered ignoring all the kids' goings on around me. My obliviousness gave me a nice protective shield. Should anyone still want to sling something my way, they might as well throw it at a brick wall. I felt I was again in pretty good shape, enjoying things as they came along. I came across a Seattle newspaper interview of me that stated, "She talks a mile-a-minute, and laughs a lot, often at herself."

The only drawback; when seven of the kids left at the end of our Seattle run, I was taken completely by surprise. I hadn't been aware of more discord than usual, certainly not enough to cause a general walkout. Both Mike and Kent left. That surprised me because both of them—Mike in particular—had gotten good breaks this spring. They shouldn't have had any gripes. They were both also listed in our programs as assistants to Lew. Paula, of course, left with Mike, then a few others left, too—and so did Rocky, though he was supposed to return before fall.

It's odd how I missed all the drama. I'd made plans to stay over in Seattle after we closed with an old friend of mine who now lived there with her husband and children. They invited me to stay with them for a few days. Leon gave me my ticket so I could come home separately. I don't think I even said good-by to anyone.

When I got back to San Francisco, there was much speculation about the grand departure in the newspapers.

"Stars Quit SF Ballet—Dissension or Pay?"

"'No Walk-Out,' Ballet Says."

Lew and Leon downplayed the situation. They said it was the usual post-season dilemma the company faced every year. There was no work here for the dancers this time of year, so they went elsewhere to find some. "They all like to take off and try their wings in New York," they said.

Critic Alexander Fried wrote, "Knowledgeable rumors suggest the dancers' restlessness is caused by chronically low pay, and perhaps other distresses."

Today, as I look back on this blow-up, I'm still unclear on all that happened, but one thing I do know is that—then as well as now—dancers know they have only so much time in which to "make it". When they think they're ready, they go where they think they'll get ahead fastest. Loyalty doesn't have much to do with it.

The U.S. Cross-Country Tours

2: A Rats Nest

THOSE OF US WHO REMAINED IN SAN FRANCISCO DID BALLET '62 during that summer. Almost no one from Ballet '60 was left. It seemed completely different. Two Ivy-Leaguers from back east, who ran a local booking agency called Dana Attractions, suddenly appeared on our program as Managing Directors. Leon said they were helping him with bookings. Some of our younger dancers took over the other Director positions. Robert Gladstein and Terry Orr became the Artistic Directors and Michael Rubino became General Director.

For this summer's repertoire Lew choreographed a new work called **Bach Concert**. Bobby Gladstein tried his hand at choreography, too, and did a work called **Opus One.** Carlos Carvajal, who had recently returned to the Company after dancing in Europe for a few years, also set a piece—a *pas de deux* for Bobby and me—to Rossini's overture, **Voyage a Rheims**.

During this same time, Harold, Lew and Leon put on a week-long seminar sponsored by the Ford Foundation, offered free to teachers from all over the West. It was part of the Foundation's project to upgrade the quality of U.S. ballet instruction. Harold gave both formal lectures and informal discussions on ballet technique; Lew explained different facets of choreography and allowed participants to watch him rehearse; Everett Mason, our makeup man, explained the theory behind theatrical makeup; our stage manager, Bruce Kelley, demonstrated the use of lights and "gels" in creating special effects with fabric and color; Mrs. Arnold shared her insights on costume making—drawings, fabrics, color, and texture. She also gave a workshop on tutu construction, stating it often took sixteen hours per tutu.

In the midst of all this, Rocky returned. Before doing so, however, he sent a letter to one of his special "pals" who had remained with the Company. For a whole week that letter stayed conspicuously on a ledge in our lounge area that was used for setting out Company mail. From the way the kids would look at it, then at me, I gathered I was supposed to open it and read it. I was damned if I was going to open that letter. To this day I refrain from opening other people's mail. If Rocky had something to say to me, why didn't he write to me? No one was dealing with me directly anymore, and I wasn't going anywhere with anyone unless they did.

One afternoon I walked back into the studio after rehearsal and there was Rocky. He bounded down the stairs toward me with love in his eyes. I guess he expected me to pick up right where we'd left off last fall, without any discussion, even, of his behavior since then. I greeted him pleasantly enough, asked him how his summer had gone, things like that. Then I went off home by myself.

I suddenly felt so light, so free. It was as if I'd been struggling for a long time to climb up out of a deep, dark hole, and now I'd finally made it over the rim. I wasn't going to fall back in.

Ballet '62 was still going on and this year it was to continue throughout the fall with single dates, booked by Dana Attractions around our Opera Season schedule, for various Community Concert Series. I don't remember that Rocky started rehearsing with us again, but I know he took class every day and seemed somewhat depressed.

And soon enough, he injured himself—again. I immediately thought, "Oh, oh, the pattern." He knew I'd recognize it. I felt he was trying to manipulate me, and this made me just mad enough that I went to him and said, "Come on Rocky, let's not try that one again."

During this time, one of the Dana Attractions partners—the kids called him "Hurok Jr." because he worked for Sol Hurok at one time—started showing some interest in me. At least I thought he did; we'd been exchanging pleasantries backstage. At this point I would be glad to find someone new, but so far I hadn't even had a cup of coffee with him. However, Rocky must have picked up on this and evidently flew into a jealous rage. I could tell by his friends' reactions to Junior. Shortly after this, Rocky and his injury went off again.

After our closing performance of Summer Ballet '62, Junior and his business partner gave a cast party for us at their bachelor pad—a rented mansion off Union Street in Cow Hollow, an affluent area of San Francisco. Rocky's friends were being sort of nasty, but everyone went. Leon took great pains to make sure I went. I think he had one of the younger girls ask me for a ride. She was careful to assure me that she had a ride home, though. I was uncomfortable from the time I arrived. It seemed like a set-up to me. Junior still had done no more than say hello to me and now he was not much friendlier. He was mostly just watching me from across the room. I got the distinct feeling I was expected to stay on afterwards. I felt like a piece of meat on a platter, with Leon as the chef. I decided to leave early. As I went out the door, Bobby, with a smirk on his face, asked, "Sally, are you leaving so soon?"

Now Junior was mad at me, too—and Leon.

All sorts of undercurrents kept flowing around Opera Season and our various Fall Ballet '62 dates. Rocky's friends were particularly obnoxious, plus I felt Junior was now playing cat and mouse games, and Lew and Leon seemed mad at me, too.

I was probably becoming paranoid. I felt I had no real friends any more. Various people tried to get me to confide in them, but I felt they were after information that could be used to manipulate me, rather than help me. I felt safest by myself. I kept my own counsel. I wrote in my journal every day, hoping it would help me keep my balance. Anyway, I once again did my best to ignore everybody.

As our Christmas season of *Beauty and the Beast* and *Nutcracker* approached, it became obvious that Rocky wasn't going to be dancing. I didn't know if his injury was still not healed, or what. Though our younger male dancers showed promise, they weren't yet ready to carry these two ballets. We needed some first dancers—now.

Lew brought Dick Carter back from San Diego for *Beauty and the Beast* and found Thatcher Clarke, who had recently been touring with a small concert group of Rudolph Nureyev's, in Los Angeles, and hired him to be first dancer for *Nutcracker*. Thatcher was a good dancer with particularly fine jumps. He was to be my partner. I was too tall for him—we were both about the same height, not counting toe shoes—but we were scheduled to open *Nutcracker*, anyway. Thatcher was a good sport. Luckily he was broad and strong, and I was thin and bent a lot.

During a break in one of our first rehearsals, we began chatting and getting to know each other a little—flirting terribly according to some accounts, though neither of us took it that way. Now there was even more uproar, particularly from Junior, Lew and Leon. Luckily, Thatcher thought it was funny.

I was cast out of *Beauty and the Beast* this year, however, and Bobby Gladstein, who was tall, danced *Nutcracker* with Joce, who was several inches shorter than I. Dick could have danced with me in *Nutcracker* as well as with Joce in *Beauty*, but he didn't. I had the feeling Lew was intentionally trying to make me look bad, which I didn't think was good artistic judgment on his part. People were, after all, still paying good money to come see these performances.

I ended the year fed up with everyone. This was the third time something like this had happened; everyone assuming the worst of me. Each time it happened, I was both hurt and infuriated, plus there were always bad results afterwards. Why didn't someone bother to find out what really happened? Why didn't someone ask me? I began to see that gossip was controlling my life. I didn't like that at all. I began to rebel against the whole idea and consequently felt much the stronger for it.

The U.S. Cross-Country Tours

3: Staying Out of the Hole

THIS YEAR EVERYTHING ABOUT OUR SPRING TOUR SEEMED EASIER. For one thing, we began in Phoenix rather than in St. Paul. The milder weather made a big difference. It was much easier climbing aboard the bus at 8:00 AM each morning when it wasn't cold and snowing.

Also, we now knew what to expect; including where to sit on the bus, what dressing room to use, which line to stand in for class. Hierarchy had a lot to do with it. Lew and Leon sat together in the front seat to the right of the driver—the "office". Our two conductors, Gerhard Samuel and Lawrence Foster, sat in the seat right behind the driver. They both traveled with us on our bus rather than with the orchestra on their bus. Joce and I sat behind them. The other principals sat in the other front seats. The newest members of the *corps de ballet* bounced along in the back of the bus, next to the lavatory.

A lot of the kids slept most of each daily four-hour bus trip. I wasn't sure all the sleeping was from exhaustion. It could well have been because they didn't know what else to do. I remember some of them saying they felt as if they were in a daze until they got to the theater each late afternoon.

I know I didn't like sleeping all that time. About one hour's snooze mid-morning was better for me. I usually spent the rest of the time on the bus reading. Leon worked on business things each morning, then he, too, took just a short nap, then read the rest of the time. He shared his *U.S. News and World Reports* with me. Gary and Larry read and discussed things with me, too.

I remember one particular morning everyone was asleep except Gary, Larry and me. We had a big discussion going on about something we were reading. Finally Lew bellowed, "Will you guys shut up!"

I answered, "But Lew, it's 10:00 o'clock in the morning. How can you complain when someone is talking at 10:00 in the morning?"

"Just shut up, will you?"

The whole bus cheered.

The three of us sort of looked at each other, then went back to our reading. When we had something to say, we would whisper.

Then Leon woke up because he wanted to know what we were whispering about.

Cynthia Gregory's mother, Marcelle, came along with us as wardrobe mistress this year. She replaced Mrs. Arnold who, sadly, retired because of poor health. Amy Sarris, wife of our head carpenter, Danny Sarris, came along to help Marcelle. Thatcher also decided to join us. He said he really loved the Company and wanted to help fix what he thought was wrong with it. He had all of these "causes", one of which was to get the Company to provide more security for its dancers. His strongest backers were among the *corps* fellows who hardly did any dancing. I was beginning to get impatient with Thatcher and his ideas.

I had noticed a growing tendency among the dancers to want to "mother" each other and be "mothered" in return. This exasperated me. They wanted to solve each other's problems instead of their own. I thought they were like a pack of cards, all having to lean on each other in order to stand up at all. Why didn't they just feel obligated to take care of themselves? I wondered; should a person join an organization in order to be taken care of, or in order to be given an opportunity to produce something?

Thatcher said he cared so much about his ideals that he would rather do without than compromise. If he couldn't find what he wanted here, he would go elsewhere. Then I asked myself; if you can't find exactly what you want one place, should you keep searching elsewhere? Or should you stick it out in one place, work towards your end, compromise when you have to, but always aim in the same direction?

From the Southwest, our tour took us on through Texas into the Deep South. We were in Houston for opening day of the big Fat Stock Show and Parade. The Stock Show took place in the arena right next door to our theater. Ginny posed backstage with one of the young, up-and-coming cowboys. My cousin and her family lived in Houston at the time. She told me the schools had given all the kids a holiday in order to see the parade, though not the one for Washington's Birthday.

In Corpus Christi, Texas, our show was postponed for forty-five minutes so that the citizenry could see *Route 66* on TV. This particular show was filmed there.

As we crossed into Mississippi, we soon became aware of the tensions the integration issue was causing. We were dancing at "Ole Miss" University in Oxford, staying overnight at the Alumni House on campus and eating at the Student Union. This was during the time James Meredith, the black man, was enrolled there and having a grim time. We were aware of armed policemen standing around. That afternoon Thatcher sought out Meredith, went to his house, and brought him to the theater to see our performance.

We noticed a distinct unfriendliness towards us; so different from the expansive friendliness of the Texans. The people of Mississippi had taken a stand against the world on the black situation and were sticking together against all "outsiders". The students stared at us as if we were from another planet—a completely different species. A boy in the snack shop at the Student Union had the grace to become embarrassed when he realized I'd overheard him say, "Ah guiess they're suh'posed to be human, but they cian't even tawlk."

At first I thought he was kidding, but he was dead serious; so different from the cute girls that helped us dress backstage last year at Middle Tennessee State University in Murfreesboro who laughed and said, "Y'all hiave the funniest accents we evah did heah."

Also, our waitress at the hotel in Jackson, Mississippi glared at us when we left our grits on our plates and warned, "You girls had better eat them grits." We knew she wasn't joking.

The next day on the bus, as we were leaving "Ole Miss U", I finally got hold of Bobby's issue of *SHOW Magazine* with the Graham Greene story, *May We Borrow Your Husband?*, in it. I had been dying to read this story, but every time I went to borrow it, it would disappear. This particular morning I got on the bus before Bobby. His magazine was in plain view, so I borrowed it and sat there reading by the time he boarded. He looked disconcerted as he came upon me sitting there, story in hand.

The story is marvelous—and deadly. It is about a marriage between a young girl and a homosexual. They are newlyweds on their honeymoon in Antibes. Greene's protagonist watches two homosexuals seduce the young man away from his bride right before her eyes. She is so young and inexperienced that she doesn't realize what is happening. Greene's protagonist ponders—I read this part aloud to no one in particular, in reverse order from what was written— "If she were ignorant of the situation it would be a comedy, even a farce; if she recognized it, it would be a tragedy."

Amy Sarris came right out and said, "Sally, you're wise in not getting yourself in for a life of real unhappiness."

Nobody said much during the rest of that day's trip.

Over the years I have had opportunities to observe marriages between women and homosexual men. Some don't last long; others last a long time. But regardless of their length, those that I have observed seem sad for the woman, or else a situation of complete pretense. I don't think the pretense is so great for the man, either, but in this world he survives much better if he has a "wife".

One couple with whom I was acquainted led a glamorous life. He was a Hollywood designer who did beautiful work. His productions were magical—so were his homes. I saw one as it was being remodeled. One of his artisans was painting French tiles on the kitchen walls that day. The whole house looked like a movie set. The furnishings in his wife's bedroom were those used in the movie *Cleopatra*. His wife was beautiful. She was pale blonde and always wore her hair slicked back like a ballerina. I never saw her when she wasn't perfectly dressed, perfectly groomed, wearing lovely jewelry, and always with a sweet, gentle smile on her face. We always exchanged pleasant greetings each time we met, but that was about it. I never got below her beautiful surface to see what she was like as a person. I sometimes wondered what she did with her time during each day—or during each night, for that matter. I wondered if she slept in Cleopatra's bed all by herself.

Another couple was in the Ballet Company. At this time there had been a rash of marriages within the Company. Dancers often marry other dancers because they have little opportunity to meet anyone else. Some of the marriages work, some of them don't. Some involve homosexuality, some don't. I think this particular one did, and it didn't seem happy to me. One time we were on tour; I was coming back to the hotel after seeing a movie by myself. I ran into the husband, also by himself. There was nothing wrong with me seeing him by himself—he could have been out looking for a paper, or getting a cup of coffee—but he had this slightly embarrassed expression on his face when I ran into him, as if I'd caught him at something; like cruising? I didn't ask him where his wife was. I felt she was probably sitting alone in their room, forlorn, reluctant to be seen at this time of night without her husband.

I met one other couple after I'd stopped dancing. I was working for the Ballet Guild at the time. They were nice to me, and we became good friends. I was in and out of their apartment frequently. They entertained beautifully; I was often included in their parties. Everything they owned was exquisite—I think the money was hers. One day I asked for a glass of water and received it in Baccarat crystal. Another time it was her birthday. He'd had a key ring made for her which duplicated one Prince Albert had given to Queen Victoria. He'd read a description of it in some book. He told me the two of them had a little game they played in private; she was Victoria and he was Albert. Once or twice he referred to her as "Victoria" in my presence.

But then I remember one Christmas Eve, about 4:00 in the afternoon; she phoned and asked me in this sad little voice, "Have you heard from my husband? He's been gone for three days. He was supposed to be home by now." She sounded so hurt and lonely. My heart went out to her. I wouldn't have been in her shoes for all the Baccarat crystal in the world.

A few days later, on the bus, Marcelle Gregory showed Leon a newspaper clipping she received from home stating that Dana Attractions was closing its San Francisco office.

Joce popped up with "Perhaps they've gone bankrupt."

After reading the clipping, Leon said, "Junior is an egotistical ass. He'll probably go back east."

Several days before, Leon had mentioned the Ballets '63 tour might be canceled because of stage requirement difficulties. There was no mention of the work I suspected Junior was still doing for Leon. I refused to react.

A couple of weeks after that we arrived in Durham, North Carolina to find Rocky waiting for us in the hotel lobby of the Jack Tar Hotel, where we were staying. I immediately wondered if this had all been planned in advance. Just that morning at breakfast I sat with Joce. We had a long discussion about what and how Rocky was doing. She mentioned that Rocky was the one dancer Lew really missed out of the whole bunch that left last year.

When Rocky and I met in the lobby I shook hands with him cordially and asked how his injury was doing. He said his leg was all right, now. He looked well, though was a bit on the plump side. I then went on my way, leaving him visiting with the other kids. He evidently had been talking with Danny earlier; Danny told me he was considering coming back. This would be good for the Company. I was sure Rocky and I could still work together well. I trusted he knew that neither of us should expect more from the other. I knew I didn't have the least desire to change my mind.

In New Orleans we did a promotion-type appearance at the horse races. A race was named in honor of the San Francisco Ballet and some of us handed out the trophy. As we walked through the crowd, down onto the track—I had on a red knit coatdress—Leon commented to me, "Did you see how those guys were looking at you? They're not used to seeing bodies like yours. Yours are like fine race horses."

That same race I won a little money. I picked a horse as I would a ballet dancer—long legs and straight back.

Leon said, "Maybe your luck is changing."

The U.S. Cross-Country Tours

4: Holding My Own

SOON AFTER WE RETURNED TO SAN FRANCISCO WE HAD A SHORT spring season at the Geary Theater. Dana Attractions, with no explanation as far as I could tell, reappeared on the scene. Junior and his pal were backstage almost every night. Neither was more than just civil to me. Junior posted the Ballets '63 flyer. The management was listed as Columbia Artists, not Dana Attractions. I still didn't know if they actually had closed their office. They were still bringing in attractions for the next two months.

Everyone was out of sorts, both the kids and the management. A lot of resentments were floating around. Bobby, in particular, was directing his resentments toward me, I guess because I'd given up on Rocky. Some of the critics were unusually harsh on us, too. They didn't like *Fantasma*, one of our new ballets this year, and kept referring to the fellows who'd left last year. I wondered why they didn't just drop the subject and write about who was dancing now.

Other people, including some of our Board members, kept asking, "Why aren't you doing more of the classics?" Lew's position was that the classics were no longer new and vital. They could perhaps be done freshly again someday, but not now. A clean break needed to be made. He said we weren't discarding them, but developing on from where they left off. We had to keep doing new and vital things in order to grow, even if it sometimes meant making mistakes.

I found myself defending Lew whenever people complained to me. I wondered how to educate people to recognize artistic quality. They paid high prices to see the standards, or things with glamour or curiosity value, anything foreign—especially if it came from the Soviet Union. If they weren't of high artistic quality, few seemed to know the difference. Encouragingly, something was being done about it. People like Balanchine, Kirstein, Lew, Leon, and impresarios like Hurok—and Junior—and critics like Frankenstein were all working to make people aware of those differences.

As a break from Company goings-on, I saw as much as I could of a small circle of "outside" friends. These friendships were not always easy to maintain; we might plan dinner together, then I'd have to cancel because of a night rehearsal, or we'd go off on tour for three months. Never-the-less, these friendships did take hold and became increasingly important to me—another aid in keeping my balance, so to speak.

One such friendship was with a couple, Mary and Bob Jasperson, whom I met two years before during *Original Sin.* We met at an Easter party given by some mutual friends of Mary's and my parents. Mary and Bob had just moved to the Bay Area and our friends were helping them meet people their own age. We clicked. Soon they were coming to my performances and meeting me afterwards. We'd either go out for a bite to eat or they'd come on to my apartment. Sometimes they brought other friends with them.

One evening I went with Mary and Bob to the Masonic Auditorium to hear the black writer, James Baldwin, speak. He had recently published his book, *The Fire Next Time.* This was at the height of the Birmingham, Alabama integration issue; the Freedom Riders had been attacked by mobs as they got off their bus in Birmingham, Alabama. [They had been riding through the South in buses to test the Supreme Court's 1960 ruling that segregation was illegal in bus stations open to interstate travel.] About 3,000 people came to the hear Baldwin speak. The place was packed. There were about as many whites as blacks in the audience. Most were well dressed and educated looking; little of the "beat" element in evidence. Baldwin had none of the rabble-rouser in him—though some of his CORE sponsors did. He had logic of steel.

I liked a lot of what Baldwin said. In particular, "Color in itself is not important. What is important is what is behind the color."

He asked the question "When will the black man be judged as a person?" He also asked, "How many blacks hide behind their color?"

But the idea of Baldwin's that struck me most; "People who cannot suffer can never grow up, can never discover who they are. That man who is forced each day to snatch his identity out of the fire of human cruelty knows something about himself and human life that no school on earth—and, indeed, no church—can teach. He achieves his own authority, and that is unshakable."

At some point during this spring of 1963, Mary started a book study group with several of her woman friends. She asked me to join them. I was pleased to be included. Mary and some of the others were trying to write. I loved the stimulation, such a welcome change for me. I was so tired of the Company.

By the end of the Season I had such bad casting that, rather than being scared, I became rebellious. I felt that everything the Direction was doing was intentional; in order to control me, to keep me off balance. I felt they were being totally unfair. I tried complaining, but it didn't do any good. Then I heard that Rocky passed through town—again—this time riling up some of the kids about Ballet '63. Some had already committed to doing it, because they probably thought I wouldn't, but I was definitely planning to do it, no matter what Junior did or did not do.

I was so tired of all this nonsense that I decided to figure out what levers I could pull in order to force the Direction to come around. I found a few. One was the fact that the whole Stanford Dance Department came to hear my talk to the Peninsula Ballet Guild. Interest in bringing professional people into college performing arts was definitely growing. Also, the classes I was teaching for Harold were going well.

I was dreadfully polite and correct to everyone and, as I figured, things straightened out beautifully. It just angered me that I had to threaten to get results. But then I realized an even better result; by threatening, I was discovering new opportunities.

Ballets '63, with all but a few kids participating, opened early in the summer with a surprising amount of interest; good houses and good press. There seemed little more the "intriguers" could do to upset things. I now thought it wise to try to make peace with everyone. There was no point in hanging on to hurts, suspicions, and grudges.

The summer continued well for me. Not only was my dancing going well, I ended up with a regular teaching schedule. There were so many advanced students for the summer session—the "Foreign Legions", as we called them—that Harold had to split his class. He gave half to me.

For this year's Teachers' Week we tried to establish all the new principles that Harold, Lew and Balanchine had formalized during their sessions in New York. It was stimulating and worked out perfectly for me, though performing and teaching at the same time was a bit much.

Along with everything else, I continued to socialize as much as I could. I was determined not to let the fear of gossip deter me. Another couple I frequently saw at this time ushered regularly at the Opera House; I knew a lot of the ushers because I walked in and out of the theater so much. This couple made a special effort to come see me when we danced elsewhere, too. We usually went out together afterwards. They even showed up at a couple of rehearsals.

One evening, after a performance, the wife rode back to my apartment with me in my car while her husband and some friends followed behind. She started talking about loneliness—mine in particular—and how I was leading such a lonely life. Something in the way she said it made me wary.

I remember glancing over at her, then looking back at the street ahead of me and carefully answering, "Actually, I don't mind it. At any rate, it's preferable to anything else I can think of at the moment."

They weren't quite so attentive after this.

This same summer Rudolph Nureyev came to visit our school. I heard that he was interested in some of the new ideas we were working on. I also heard about a comment he made to our ethnic dance teacher, Anatol Joukowsky, a fellow Slav. After watching a Ballets '63 rehearsal where everyone was bossing each other around, he remarked, "It is a truly democratic company," then added, "That can be dangerous."

The U.S. Cross-Country Tours

5: Columbia Artists Management

BY MID-SEPTEMBER TWELVE OF US WERE READY FOR OUR BALLET '63 Concert Tour. We were going to fifty-four cities in nine weeks. We were going as far east as Illinois and even into Mexico in our "Blue Butt Bus", affectionately dubbed this because it was pale blue and had a big, rounded, windowless rear end that looked like an elephant's behind. For repertoire we used the most successful of our workshop ballets. All of our performances were sponsored by Community Concerts Associations, under Columbia Artists Management out of New York—booked by Junior.

As one of our press releases stated, "This marks a new page in the success story of a company that began as summer stock to introduce new ballets." We were publicized as "Ballet '63, Soloists of the San Francisco Ballet". Banners on each side of our bus announced that. In the program Lew was listed as General Director and Leon as Managing Director. Neither of them came with us, though; neither did Bobby, who was listed as one of the Artistic Directors. On the actual tour, Terry Orr acted as Artistic Director, Michael Rubino as General Director, and Ron Poindexter as Ballet Master. Junior was listed as Personal Representation, but he didn't travel with us, either. Both he and Leon turned up along the way, however. The rest of the Company stayed home to do Opera Season.

All arrangements were made for us in advance. All we had to do was arrive on time, put on a good show, and clean up after ourselves before leaving. We were a much simpler operation than the spring tours for the full Company. For those tours, besides the two buses for dancers and orchestra, we needed a moving van for costumes and sets and a camper for our stage crew, who had to drive on to the next town as soon as they struck the sets. They slept while we came on in our buses, then went to the theater a couple of hours ahead of us to set up the next show.

On this tour we were self-contained in our one bus. The seats from the back half of the bus were removed so that costumes, shoes, black drops, props, lighting equipment, and sound equipment all fit in nicely. There was plenty of room for twelve dancers, one stage manager, one assistant stage manager, and one bus driver in the front half of the bus. Each of us had a whole seat to ourselves. In that we were all considered soloists, none of us cared where we sat.

Our attitude towards chores was equally democratic. All the fellows, including the bus driver, unpacked and repacked the bus each night, and whichever of us dancers was through first started gathering up shoe bags and costumes. No one person was always through first, so no one felt put upon. Everyone pitched in and it worked well. We could do this because we were usually in school auditoriums, not union houses. The few times we were in union theaters, where union people had to be hired for all jobs [We were union dancers under AGMA (American Guild of Musical Artists). In order to make these tours, we received special wavers from the union.], we weren't even allowed to zip up each other's costumes.

About our only problem was the bus, itself. It kept breaking down. I think its fuel line kept getting clogged. I remember sitting on a dusty logging road outside of Ukiah, in the heart of Northern California's logging country, waiting for help. We were on our way to a remote lumber town where we were giving a concert at the local high school. We were late. The audience was already there by the time we arrived. They just sat and waited while we got ready.

Another time our door blew off. A great gust of wind caught it while we were in the parking lot at Carlsbad Caverns. Our bus driver had brought us here for a sightseeing excursion. He fixed the door with a wire coat hanger from the back of the bus; it remained that way for the rest of the tour.

Our driver was wonderful. He was a long-time tour bus driver. He was accustomed to moving people around and cheering them on. He would often stand in the wings and watch our performances, rather than go off for a break while we were working. One of our ballets, **The Set**—a jazzy sort of ballet by Ron Poindexter, set to music of Dave Brubeck— had a place in it where the girls do a take-off on ballet's academic *port de bras,* the standardized arm movements that pass through ballet's five basic arm positions. One night, there was our driver standing in the wings, grinning, and doing the arm movements along with us. We all cracked up.

Our driver tried to arrange our trips so that we could see as many sights as possible. On our trip from Idaho Falls to Rock Springs, Wyoming he offered to take the long way around so that we could see the Grand Tetons. All we had to do was chip in to buy the extra gasoline. Our stage manager didn't want to do this and got mad when we out-voted him. Instead of enjoying the sight of those gorgeous mountains, he slept the whole time we drove by.

I also remember a scenic trip along the spine of the Rockies from Cheyenne to Denver. Berthoud Pass wound along for quite a while at 11,000 feet. We gazed out over the spectacular panorama and down thousands of feet of mountainside as our bus gasped and jerked along.

And I remember one scary trip; we were going down the "Grapevine" from Los Angeles to Bakersfield near the end of our tour. Our brakes nearly burned out. I could see the tenseness on our driver's face in the rear-view mirror.

Luckily we didn't have to use one of those runaway truck lanes.

A pall had already settled over us by then. President Kennedy had been assassinated three days earlier. We were in the Los Angeles area for several days and were staying at the Roosevelt Hotel, right on Hollywood Boulevard. I remember sitting in my street clothes near the pool; we'd started to gather for bus call when we heard the news. People just stopped whatever they were doing, then grouped around radios and TV sets in stunned silence. Our performance that night was canceled.

I remember feeling stranded. We didn't know what to do. We started wandering down Hollywood Boulevard as all the shops began closing. Some of the restaurants must have stayed open, though, because I don't remember going hungry.

Two afternoons later, while sitting in the hotel lobby, again waiting for bus call and wondering whether or not we'd dance that night, we watched the cortège. Jackie was standing there in her black coat and veil looking so brave and calm, holding the hands of her children, Caroline and John John. Little John John was holding the American flag. This time we got on the bus and went to the theater, and this time we did dance. We started the performance with a bare, lit stage and a span of silence.

On this tour I began reading some works of David Ogilvy, owner of one of Madison Avenue's larger advertising agencies. I first came across him in an issue of *VOGUE Magazine*. He wrote an article entitled *How to Get to the Top of the Creative Tree*. I enjoyed it so much that I bought his book, *Confessions of an Ad Man*. I loved his Scottish, straightforward way of thinking—so different from all the Byzantine intrigue I had been enduring. My Scottish blood really responded to him.

Ogilvy wrote about how he ran his ad agency, what was

important to him as a leader, what he liked in people and what he disliked, what he expected from people, and what they could expect from him. He liked people who worked hard and "with gusto", who had first-class brains and intellectual honesty. He couldn't stand "toadies who suck up to their bosses". He wouldn't allow nepotism in his company; it bred politics. He expected people to be excellent craftsmen, well organized, deliver their work on time, and be respectful—not jealous—of others. He tried always to be respectful, to be fair, to make unpopular decisions without cowardice, to listen more than talk, and to work as hard as, or harder than, anyone under him.

His ideas made absolute sense to me. I thought, "If I should ever be in charge, I'll use his style."

And soon enough I found myself in charge. I began the tour with no special position of authority, but before it ended, I felt I'd better just take one if things were to continue running. The fellows didn't seem to mind at all—as long as they kept their titles. That was fine with me. Something I was learning on this tour; people love titles of authority, and often the less the real authority, the longer the title.

Ogilvy's writings were like a road map for me to follow. His ideas worked. The tour ended a success and plans were begun for another tour the following fall.

The Ballet '63 tour being a success was almost more than the homosexual contingent could bear. With **Nutcracker,** our feud finally came to a head, even to the point of coming out in the newspapers. One of the critics, who was of that group, was not above being personal in his reviews. It wasn't so much what he wrote about me—I was dancing the *Pas de Deux* with Bobby, for the first time, and we could well have been a little rugged—it was more the way he wrote it that seemed pettish; not only to me but to others, as well. I later found out that Joce had given a party—excluding me—the day before the review came out. Some of the critics were there. I surmised the whole bunch was trying to undermine my confidence.

As the season progressed, Bobby's and my performances got better, not worse. I expected as much, but I noticed others seemed bothered by this fact. My guess was that they had reached the bottom of their list of psychological war games, all of which proved ineffectual. I overheard one fellow say, " . . . all except Sally. She's indestructible."

I knew I had gotten good at combating psychological warfare—mostly by refusing to acknowledge it—but that didn't mean I enjoyed it. I shed pounds, and my teeth started cracking and falling out.

I ended the year feeling that my feud with the management was also coming to a head, with friendliness on their part and anger on mine; they should give me what they knew I deserved. As my Dad pointed out, they were willing to give it to me if I'd come take it, but not if I was waiting for them to hand it to me. That seemed a strange philosophy to me, but if that's what they wanted, that's what they'd get.

That New Year's Eve I went off with Bob and Mary Jasperson to two parties. I didn't see a single ballet person and loved it. I remember Bob being excited because he was starting a new job in a new field of law—conservation law—right after the first of the year.

Many years later Bob told me of that night, "At midnight I tried to give you a New Year's kiss on the mouth, but you turned your head slightly and I got your cheek, instead."

This reaction of mine was instinctive when it came to husbands of my friends. They were "off limits".

I also remember that nine years later, after Bob and Mary were divorced, Bob and I were together one evening when I realized he was no longer the husband of a friend of mine; he was a date. I felt funny at first, but we were married six months later.

The U.S. Cross-Country Tours

6: Riding High

1964 started out with a bang. Margot Fonteyn and Rudolph Nureyev danced with us as guest stars for a short Opera House Season in January, then toured with us as far as St. Louis and Chicago. How such a *coup* came about, I didn't even question at the time. Things just happened. But as I was browsing through my scrapbooks I found this item, a "SCOUPS DU JOUR" written by *SF Chronicle* columnist Herb Caen in the fall of 1963. "Fonteyn and Nureyev, not having to be back in London for several months, melted before Guild President Jim Ludwig's relentless charm, and agreed to dance as guest artists with the Ballet."

Another item I found, this one written in January 1964 by *Chronicle* critic Alfred Frankenstein, was headlined, "Grant for SF Ballet, $644,000 from Ford Foundation." This grant was part of Ford Foundation's $7,756,000 they were distributing among a select group of ballet companies and schools, including NYC Ballet and SF Ballet—much to the consternation of those not included. The $644,000 was to be paid over a period of ten years, contingent upon $250,000 being raised during the same period of time. Frankenstein stated, "James J. Ludwig, President of the San Francisco Ballet Guild, says he hopes to secure the whole $250,000 in 1964, thereby obtaining the entire Ford Foundation grant in a lump, and profiting by the interest it would bring."

Ludwig's goal was reached, due in large part to our sold-out performances with guest stars Fonteyn and Nureyev.

In connection with these performances, I was asked by the *SF Examiner* to write a 250-word article for their Sunday Magazine section, *Pictorial Living,* on the importance of mirrors in a dancer's life. I'm not sure how this project came about, either, but I wrote the article, and a photographer from the *Examiner* came and took my picture in front of one of the studio mirrors. The article and the photo, plus a publicity blurb about me, came out in the newspaper (*S.F. Examiner's Pictorial Living,* 1/19/64) the day I went into Joce's role in *Fantasma* for the first time.

Not one person in the Company mentioned my article except Joce. I finally said something about it to Leon, and all he said was, "I'm glad you don't always do your own writing."

Our five performances in San Francisco were packed, even though Frankenstein picked up the line about Nureyev being overrated and possibly not living up to his advance billing. Frankenstein did state, however, that there was no dancer in the world more adept at flourishes on the sidelines that said "Now you are going to see the most sensational thing that ever happened."

There were those who said Nureyev attached himself to Fonteyn in her waning years to advance his own career and she to him in order to prolong hers. But whatever the reasons, I felt no one could deny they made magic together on stage. They were wonderful artists.

Fonteyn's husband Roberto (Tito) Arias—a Panamanian diplomat from a political family whose father and one uncle were Presidents of Panama—joined her in San Francisco for the festivities. By this time the two of them were part of the international "jet set"; she the beautiful ballerina, he the handsome Latin American diplomat. They certainly made a glamorous addition to any gathering. In talking to her, I got the feeling she was preparing to retire fairly soon, perhaps looking forward to a life of globetrotting, parties, and interesting people.

I remember one day asking Fonteyn about teaching; she was honorary head of the Royal Academy of Dance. She said she didn't really like it much. She didn't like analyzing things. She preferred to just "do". She didn't seem particularly interested in the newer ballets we were doing, either. She had carved out a successful niche for herself—that of the beautiful, charming, enchanted princess—and at this point, she probably didn't want to rock the boat.

Where on the other hand, Nureyev—though he obviously had great fun being the handsome prince with all his flourishes—was interested in every idea he came across. He was also interested in teaching. He taught our company class on stage one day; a simple, basic class. There was nothing complicated or "dance-y" about it. However, by the time we were through, we were completely warmed up. Lew had been watching from out front; I remember him coming up on stage afterwards, kind of laughing and saying, "Well, he certainly picked out the Company weakness in a hurry." He didn't waste any time in giving us exercises to correct it, either. The weakness had to do with our upper backs. I had always thought the Russians had marvelous, arched upper backs. I started working on mine right then and there.

Six months later, Fonteyn's husband was shot while campaigning for the position of Deputy of the Assembly of Panama. He was permanently paralyzed and confined to a wheelchair for the rest of his life. Fonteyn's future turned out to be quite different from what I had imagined for her.

After Chicago, we continued on with our tour. Our guest stars were now gone, and so was the glamour. Everyone was discouraged because the Chicago critics once again ripped us to shreds. They said we looked even worse performing with such artists as Fonteyn and Nureyev. They seemed particularly angry that we'd been chosen for the Ford Foundation money when their favored groups had not. David Anderson and I were the only ones in the Company to get a good review—for our performance in *Fantasma*.

Morale was low. The kids started developing all sorts of complaints; minor illnesses, injuries, the bus trips were too long or too short, the dancers were being taken advantage of, no one was giving them any consideration.

My casting got noticeably worse. When I made some crack to Leon about it, all he said was, "We have to make the whole Company look good, now, and sell it. Once we get the European tour set, things can be different." I decided there was nothing more I could do, so I escaped into my reading on the bus.

I started reading Thornton Wilder's *Ides of March*, his re-creation of the last two weeks of Julius Caesar's life, mostly done through letters and documents of key players. To me it was brilliant.

I loved what he had Caesar say: About augurs and soothsayers—horoscopes being big among our dancers, "They remove from men's shoulders the obligation to act. They flatter passivity and console inadequacy."

On responsibility, "Responsibility is liberty; the more decisions you are forced to make alone, the more you are aware of your freedom to choose."

On the feelings men hold towards those who have authority over them, "What deference and loyalty masking what contempt and hatred! The deference and loyalty proceed from a man's gratitude that his superior relieves him of responsibility. The contempt and hatred stem from his resentment against the man who limits his freedom."

And on keeping people in the dark, "I am not oriental and have not kept the people in ignorance of what they should know, nor have I lied to them." This went back to my argument with Leon about Balanchine's use of scare-tactics to control his personnel. Both Leon and Balanchine—Greek and Georgian respectively—had eastern mentalities, but they were dealing primarily with Anglo/Saxons, who instinctively rebel against such ways—except Lew, who was Danish, but seemed to go along with them on this.

In the middle of February, as we headed into South Carolina, Leon one day started reading all sorts of things to me on the bus; about finance and investments, Repertory Theater, a letter to Bournonville (Director of the Royal Danish Ballet in the mid 1800's) that was reprinted in Dance Magazine. The letter was from one of Bournonville's French contemporaries, complaining of intrigue in his company—caused by one ballerina in particular—and the philosophical approach needed to withstand it. He thanked Bournonville for sending him one, honest, hard-working, pleasing, male dancer. When Leon came over to read it to me, Joce wanted to hear, too.

All afternoon Joce had been engrossed in a book she kept covered with a paper bag. She usually played cards with Lew, but Lew wasn't here today; he'd gone back to Sacramento for a meeting of the newly formed California State Arts Council. Of late Lew had been spending a lot of time with Joce; I thought to wean her away from the troublemakers. But Leon now commented to me, "Lew has a real monkey on his back and it's going to take some doing to get it off."

Leon also started talking to me about marriage in general. He said there was no reason for it if you didn't want children. He had always felt he would never marry, but when he met Wana, and still felt like seeing her after six months, he thought he'd better make some changes in his way of life.

As we came into the New York area, Junior appeared again in both Brooklyn and in Princeton, where his ex-

partner—they actually had closed their S.F. office last fall—
was now managing the theater at the University. I felt a lot
of below-the-surface play was still going on. At times I thought
I was imagining the whole thing, but then I'd find out some
fact that indicated I wasn't. I decided the safest tack for me
was one of slight rudeness.

Junior was still helping Leon with Columbia Artists,
though from the New York end. I noticed he was listed in
our St. Louis and Chicago programs as personal New York
representative for the Fonteyn/Nureyev performances. I
knew he was arranging the Ballets '64 tour. He said he would
be in San Francisco in June. I asked myself, after a year-and-
a-half of this nonsense, why did I even still care?

Our performance in Brooklyn was like old home week.
With the exception of Rocky, everyone who had left our
Company in the past few years came to see us. My eastern
cousins also turned out in full force for the show. I went out
with them afterwards. I had a wonderful time—except for
the casting. I only danced in *Jest of Cards*.

Another disappointment for the Company; the reviews
for our Brooklyn Academy performance were not good,
either. Walter Terry said in his *New York Herald Tribune* review
(2/24/64), "Something pretty good and something very bad
have happened to the San Francisco Ballet since its first
Atlantic-States performance eight years ago on Ted Shawn's
Jacob's Pillow Dance Festival. The something good is that
since that time what was once a local, or at least regional,
ballet company has attained international stature through
its foreign tours under the auspices of the U.S. State
Department. The something bad is that the youthful vitality
(and I'm talking about the exuberant air of an entire
company, not just individuals) displayed at Jacob's Pillow has
disappeared." He also mentioned that we were in line to
receive more than half a million dollars from the Ford
Foundation, a grant available to only a few ballet companies
and schools.

Our tour went on for almost another month. Lew seemed to withstand the blasts from the New York press well enough, at least as far as I could tell—we had enthusiastic audiences and good reviews in other places—but the morale of the kids did not improve. Their behavior grew more and more childish.

I finally spouted off one day after a bus window was broken in a snowball fight between two of our fellows. No one would own up to it when our bus driver asked who did it. Leon encouraged us all to say a group of kids, whom we didn't know, were having a snowball fight. One of them hit the bus. Somehow this did it for me; I let them have it.

Afterwards, I admitted to myself that part of the reason I got so mad was because I was sick and tired of people making trouble for me, thinking they could punish me for things I didn't do. But I also felt this use of deceit indicated a way of thinking that was pervasive and not good. Why shouldn't people be straightforward and honest? Why shouldn't they "take their own rap" rather than push it onto someone else? Why shouldn't they be responsible for their own actions?

After this incident everyone was fairly wary of me. I mostly kept my nose buried in my book about Caesar's last days, with his wonderful insights on power, intrigue, and betrayal.

Our tour ended with Leon being arrested and detained in Dallas. While boarding the plane for Little Rock, our last stop, the stewardess asked Leon what he had in his funny-looking Styrofoam typewriter case. He kiddingly answered, "A bomb." This was a dumb thing for him to say, but after coping with the mentality of our Company for the past few weeks, I could understand why he made such a smart-aleck remark.

We had a late Spring Season at the Geary Theater after our return. The new effort this season was Lew's re-working of Balanchine's choreography for the Kurt Weil/Bertold Brecht opera *Seven Deadly Sins*. Balanchine did this for New York City Ballet some years before and lent us his production. Cynthia Gregory danced the role of Anna. As the *Oakland Tribune* (4/25/64) stated, "Miss Gregory, the Season's hit in *The Seven Deadly Sins*, generates electricity in anything she attempts."

Casting-wise, the season started out so badly for me that it really began to be noticed. Frankenstein, in his *Chronicle* criticism of *Seven Deadly Sins*, came right out and said, "It seems unjust to complain that Sally Bailey is not being used enough, but she isn't; one small role in 'Sinfonia' does not do justice to the company's finest artist."

The *Dance News* review of our Brooklyn performance also stated, "Sally Bailey, a dancer we remember with pleasure from her stint with New York City Ballet when that company first staged Con Amore, was left with a single appearance in Jest of Cards. As a Club, she had a mask over her face and was confined to a few acrobatics over the backs of the male dancers."

The San Francisco audiences were always asking at the box office when I was dancing, and the Guild even had a meeting in which—as Leon informed me—I was the main topic. When Leon teasingly asked me how much I'd paid Frankenstein, I retorted, "I'd have to be a millionaire to pay off him, *Dance News*, Chicago, the Guild, and everyone who has been asking the same question". I really began to find it funny.

After this, things improved for me enough that by the end of the season my father was saying, "This is the year of the Bailey." To top it off, Harold gave me all of his classes to teach while he and Lew went auditioning for Ford Foundation scholarship students.

Ballet '64 started in mid June with a great amount of petty intrigue. This year Joce and Bobby were the Company

Coordinators. Junior and his partner were back in town, though neither of their names appeared with the staff's on the program. Bobby was in one of his rages, again, and showed marked bad feelings toward Junior. He and the 'group' were making it obvious they would be terribly upset if Junior and I ever did work anything out. I guess they felt I would be deserting them.

I stayed out of the turmoil. I danced what roles I was assigned and taught the classes Harold gave me to teach.

For this summer's workshop, quite a few of the dancers tried their hand at choreography. That in itself was good. That's what the workshops were about; get an idea, choreograph a ballet, take chances—whether successful or not didn't matter—just get it on stage. However, I saw this year turning into a big "me too" season, short on new ideas and long on copycat. I nastily dubbed it "remembrance of things past."

People kept asking me why I didn't choreograph something, too. Actually, I was considering it. I'd started to put together a tape of Dixieland Jazz selections by the musician Doc Evans with the idea of setting abstract mood pieces to each selection. Though I knew I had something individual to give to my dancing, also my teaching, even my writing, I somehow felt it escaped me in choreography. I'd probably end up with another "me too" ballet, so why do it?

Leon thought I was afraid to try.

When Lew asked me why I didn't try, I told him, "If I have anything to say, I'd rather say it with words."

I already knew the ideas I liked best translated into words better than dance movements. I can still hear Lew admonishing, "Keep your ideas simple. If you try to say too much, it just gets muddled. Complex ideas in ballets don't work."

One other thing that bothered me about this season; some of the kids were choreographing themselves into their own ballets—usually in the lead roles. This was something we had discouraged from the beginning. We didn't want dancers using these ballets as ego tools. If nothing else, they wouldn't see their work from any distance, with any objectivity. It was a sound rule, I thought, but one proving hard to enforce.

One of our older dancers decided to mount a production of *Princess Aurora*, doing everything himself, including sewing the costumes and dancing the role of *Prince Désiré*. Originally he asked me to alternate the role of *Aurora* with Jocelyn. I was to dance it the second weekend with his friend. But then he didn't have enough money to make me a costume of my own and he didn't want me to share Joce's. Then he got some extra money, but started fighting with his friend over his own costume. It went on and on. I trusted Lew wouldn't let it get completely out of hand. I felt Lew was laughing while giving them the rope they needed to hang themselves. Harold looked on and said, "Sally, you don't want to be involved in that, do you?"

I didn't. I thought it would be canceled for sure after the first weekend. It looked terrible, it got panned, and the Ludwigs were horrified. They wanted it taken out immediately. They also wondered where the money for the costumes came from. Harold agreed that Lew must really boss things more, that he couldn't admit it looked all right. Even Joce and Bobby felt it was out of place.

However, Lew made no move to drop it, and neither did anyone else. I guess no one wanted to crush the poor fellow. Maybe Lew felt he'd make his point more strongly by leaving it in; no one would try doing something like this again. At any rate, it stayed in. I ended up dancing it the second weekend—with him, not his friend. I tried to be philosophical about it; dance the role as best I could and use it as a study in the old style.

I remember years later coming across some photos taken during those performances of *Aurora*. I was in the archives of the Performing Arts Library and Museum (PALM) in San

Francisco. I'd offered to identify dancers in photos from the '60's for them. I recognized myself in one of them. That same feeling of embarrassment came flooding back that I'd experienced when, during one of those rehearsals, Harold Zellerbach—one of our long-time Board members—came over and sat down beside me to ask, "Sally, is this supposed to be good?"

I didn't include my name on the back of that photo.

While all of this was going on, I was reading Moss Hart's book, *Act One*. One thing he said that struck me; "There exists in the theater, perhaps to a greater degree than in any other art form, a rough justice. Its practitioners receive, if they stay in it long enough, just about exactly what they deserve. No more and no less."

Another thing he said; "The morale of a company is one of a play's hidden assets and sometimes its most valuable one." Our recent N.Y. reviews were a good example of what happens when it is missing.

By mid-July the season was in such a mess that I thought I'd better rejoin the fray and make some decisions I felt needed making. Lew wouldn't step in. He led me to believe that he wanted us to make fair decisions by ourselves. I told him what I planned to do and why. I thought he was in agreement. In fact, I even felt he was encouraging me. So I took matters into my own hands.

Therefore, I was completely taken aback when, during our demonstration for the visiting teachers, Lew took the opportunity to "punish" me in front of them. I refrained from getting too upset, or at least I controlled myself. I don't remember what it was that Lew actually did—I didn't write it down in my journal, but I remember thinking he probably hurt himself more than me. The teachers were not stupid. He revealed to them a petty, childish side of his nature when he was supposed to be impressing people. At Leon's cocktail party after the lecture, I sensed that many of the teachers were upset at his display. Many of them went out of their way to be complimentary to me. Neither Lew nor Gisella showed up at the party.

As to all the plotting and counter-plotting, I felt Lew really needed to keep it in check more than he had. He should make up his mind, once and for all, to take full responsibility for the Company, rule with an iron hand, and be "Father" when necessary.

I was coming awfully close to telling everyone to go to hell, and then walk off. That was my natural inclination, anyway. But then, as Moss Hart also wrote, "It is nonsense to pity oneself and consider as wasted the years one has spent doing exactly as one wanted to do. The true waste would be to let them go, throw them away."

By the end of July, however, after spending a night in Belvedere with my family, I felt much better. Dad hit it on the head when he said Lew was trying to make his point; it could be mine, but I had to take it. He was trying to force me to be strong enough to start running things for myself. I shouldn't answer to anyone but Lew, Leon and Harold.

The rest of the summer passed, and by mid September twelve of us flew to Chicago to start our Ballet '64 tour. I was in charge of everything; teaching, rehearsing, casting, organizing, the money draws. I was also dancing. It was a great deal of responsibility, yet a wonderful position to be in, as long as I could handle it all. Wilder's Caesar was right; the more responsibility one had, the greater the freedom. Resentments were present because of the power I now had, yet everyone contributed in giving it to me. No one else wanted all the responsibility that went along with it. I was amazed how swiftly my position had changed; quite a difference from the beginning of the summer. It might not be what I'd like to end up with, but it was fine for now.

Exactly how I arrived in this position, I don't quite remember. I have a program from that tour in front of me; I am not listed among the staff, only as one of the dancers. Joce and Bobby are still listed as the Company Coordinators, but neither of them came along on tour. One thing I do remember is that by the end of the summer I spent a good deal of time going over motel accommodations and theater specifications with Pat TeRoller, a dancer who was now working as Leon's assistant.

All of our arrangements were made well in advance. We were part of a concert package sold by Columbia Artists to local Community Concert Associations. The package usually included several single artists, a small chamber group of three or four performers, and a larger attraction. We, numbering twelve dancers, were considered a larger attraction. Bookings began a year in advance so that our itinerary and performance dates were set in ample time to make travel arrangements.

Questionnaires were sent to each town, requesting information about its theater, and then returned to us so we'd know what to expect. Our stage manager carried these questionnaires in his briefcase. Some stage facilities were pretty primitive; small stages, makeshift dressing rooms, cramped backstage area, little lighting equipment—that's why we brought our own—and not much source of power to plug into. I remember our stage manager, Rich Tidwell, rolling his eyes and saying, "Sally, we've got another one that's 'off' and 'on.'" The lights went off and they went on, and that was about it.

My job was to make sure everything pulled together enough to get the show on, and then collect the money afterwards, unless it had already been sent to Leon. We charged a flat fee, the raising of which was the responsibility of each local organization. They gave me the fee in the form of a check—I seem to remember the figure $1400—which I sent on to Leon. Once a week Leon would send me a check for $1,000 or so from which we would all draw on our salaries.

I remember Leon warning me, "Don't have money calls in view of other people. Have them on the bus or in your hotel room, but never in the lobby, never in a public place. Don't show that you are the money man."

Rich, who was tall and burly, came each week with me to the local bank while I cashed the check. I then put the cash in a plain brown envelope and stuck it in my purse, which I hung on my shoulder on a short strap and tucked firmly under my arm. The purse stayed there at all times until we arrived at the theater. Then I gave it to Rich to lock up in one of the equipment cases. I never had any trouble with the money.

I had some trouble because of the money, though. Our bus driver, Nick, thought he should have some of it, as well. When I had money draws for the kids he would ask, "Don't I get some, too?"

My understanding was that his bus company, whom we were contracting out of New York, paid him. This was our money for our salaries. I said, "No."

One afternoon, about an hour before bus call for the theater, I had a money draw in my room. Nick came along and was still there after the last of the kids left. My bed was unmade because I had taken a nap earlier. He was sort of lounging on it.

On telling this story to my husband, he exclaimed, "My God, how did you get him out of your room?"

I don't remember having a problem, really. I just gave no recognition at all to what he was suggesting. I said I had more things to do before bus call and—I think in a pleasant manner—asked him to leave. And he did.

This wasn't the end of it, though. I don't remember exactly when this next occurred—it was probably a couple of days later—but both Nick and the kids, who from the beginning had been continually testing me, decided to strike at one of our lunch stops. We were out in the middle of Wisconsin, about 150 miles from our next engagement. The kids were now particularly rebellious because we were in the middle of a sixteen-day stretch without a break. This was against union rules. They weren't going a mile farther.

I had called Leon after the show the night before because Nick had been getting more insistent about the money thing. I wanted to know exactly how our contract with him read. Was I responsible in any way for any of his expenses?

Poor Leon; luckily the hour wasn't as late in California as it was where we were. I remember I was pretty mad, and we talked for a while. Besides telling him about my problem with Nick, I also asked him what to do about the kids and the sixteen performances in a row.

Leon was great. He told me to stand firm, don't pay Nick anything, and if he gave me any more trouble to call his company in New York, information on which I had in my files. They wanted our contract next spring for two buses. As far as the kids were concerned, tell them they would be paid overtime, with the promise of no more sixteen-day stretches.

We were at a Howard Johnson's, I remember. There was a phone booth inside the restaurant into which I and my files promptly went. I was so mad my hands were shaking. All the kids were watching me, wondering what was going to happen next. Luckily, I got one of the bus company owners on the phone. He didn't like what I was telling him and asked to speak to Nick. I then came out of the phone booth and Nick went in. He stayed in for several minutes while the kids watched and silently ate their lunch. I was so mad I couldn't eat.

I remember Rich looking at me with some concern— this was our main meal of the day—and saying, "Sally, you'd better eat your lunch." I think I burned off about five pounds that day.

Eventually Nick came out of the phone booth with a stormy look on his face. After lunch we all climbed back on the bus and proceeded to our next engagement. Nick remained silent for about three days and would look away whenever I happened to catch his eye in the rearview mirror of the bus; I now sat in the front, right, "office" seat and could easily see his face in the mirror. I told the kids they would be paid extra, and there was no more trouble. I decided to act as if nothing had happened and gradually good dispositions returned.

About a week later we were in Washington D.C. with our first free day in sixteen ahead of us. Our performance wasn't until the following evening. We were staying in a hotel in downtown Washington, and Nick planned—all on his own time—a wonderful tour of the area for us, including a trip out to Mt. Vernon.

I'd already made plans ahead of time for this free day, though. Mary Jasperson had arranged with her mother that we meet for lunch; we were going to the exclusive Sulgrave Club. I was looking forward to this. I remember waiting for Mary's mother on the curb outside our hotel and waving goodbye to the kids and Nick as they drove off in the bus. I was so glad to be free of everyone.

I was also in touch with a friend I'd made on my European study trip. She now worked in Washington D.C., and her family lived in Alexandria. She invited me to come out to her family's home for dinner, and then spend the night. She brought me back into town the following morning and left me off at the National Gallery. This 24-hour break was like a breath of fresh air.

When I returned to the hotel, I found my box stuffed with messages crying, "Where are you? I need money. Please call as soon as you get in."

I had the purse.

I hadn't even thought of it.

Here they were, with a free evening in Washington D.C. and no money. The kids could have drawn money on the bus on our way into town, but it hadn't occurred to them, or me. I think poor Nick lent them what money he could.

I know it wasn't nice of me, but I laughed and laughed to myself. I couldn't help but find it terribly funny. They had all been so awful.

The rest of the tour went like clockwork. Everyone was in good form, relaxed and happy. Morale was terrific.

While in Cranford, N.J., Columbia Concerts came in full force—including Junior—to see our show. They seemed to like it. One of their agents had unexpectedly dropped in on us in Ashtabula, Ohio, and was enthusiastic about it then, too.

I also received a wonderful letter from Leon, congratulating me on the conditioning and obvious good spirits of the personnel of Ballet '64. He wrote, "I know you have had your moments." He said the revues had been excellent. They spoke of the dynamics, vitality and enthusiasm of the dancers; all important qualities. He told me to keep up the good work. He signed his letter formally as Managing Director of the San Francisco Ballet, then scrawled in ink under his signature, "Love & Kisses", as he always did in memos to us.

Soon after this, we heard that Brooklyn Academy of Music wanted us to appear with them before returning home. Unfortunately, we didn't have time. Our tour was scheduled through to the last week in November, and we had to get home to prepare for *Nutcracker.*

Near the end of our trip, representatives from the bus company met us in Buffalo, New York. Nick had taken us out to Niagara Falls for an excursion; they were waiting for us at the motel when we returned.

Nick introduced me to them and they immediately asked, "How is everything going? Is everything all right?"

All was just fine, and I told them so. I knew they wanted me to give Leon a glowing report on them. I did, and they got the contract for next spring.

Of our arrival at the San Francisco Airport at the end of tour, I remember my Dad telling me, "You kids looked like a bunch of Marines as you got off the plane. You all looked proud of yourselves and proud of each other."

CHAPTER NINE

The U.S. Cross-Country Tours

7: The Jig's Up

LEON WAS LIKE A PROUD FATHER UPON OUR RETURN. OUR performances had gone well, and we came back in better dancing condition than when we left. He spared me no amount of praise. Everyone admitted I handled the tour well. Even Lew came right out and said I did a good job. Harold started teasing me.

And shortly after this the squelching began, again. My casting for **Nutcracker** was good enough—I was scheduled to dance the opening with Bobby—but a TV special of **Nutcracker** came up and Cynthia Gregory and David Anderson were cast in the *Grand Pas de Deux*. They had performed it only once before. I was upset. This time I complained to both Lew and Leon. Lew gave me some lame excuse Leon knew I wouldn't swallow. Leon didn't even try to give me a reason. All he said was, "Sally, I wish you'd stop fighting things." Harold offered me a job.

While still on tour I read an article in *TIME Magazine* (10/30/64) on Balanchine's new baby ballerinas. They were performing almost to the exclusion of the older principal dancers. The article spoke of Balanchine's displeasure at dancers who used his choreography to show off their personal virtuosity. I knew both Jacques and Melissa Hayden had developed quite a following dancing his ballets. The article quoted one dancer as saying, "You have to watch out. If you get too good in a part you'll lose it." It mentioned Maria Tallchief stating she definitely was not dancing enough, of wistfully remembering that some of Balanchine's greatest roles were created for her.

Balanchine now had the power to continue like this, but I wondered how long the audiences would buy it. Lew was obviously following Balanchine's pattern, but would he have to shift a little in order to gain more success? I felt sure the audiences would demand a change, but would it come before I stopped dancing?

I recognized that Balanchine was doing a lot to organize good ballet in the U.S., but I could see why others were worried. His ego was having free rein; his ballets were what mattered, not the dancers who danced them. He wanted fine dancers, but as tools to show off his choreography; not the other way around. The article mentioned Balanchine's pride at having the cream-of-the-crop of dancers, of having the sieve become finer and finer. That's what he was really using the Ford Foundation for.

By the year's end, I was still at odds with Lew, though this time not with anyone else. It was Lew's and my problem that Lew was seeing me as a threat, and each time I did something well, I was more so.

Now, as I look back on this, I see some questions. Who was whose tool, now? Was I still Lew's tool, or was he becoming mine? Was he afraid I might cancel him out, so he'd better cancel me out first? That was ridiculous. I didn't want to cancel him out.

Was Balanchine asking himself these same questions when Lew was helping him keep his young company together, when Lew was choreographing ballets the audience loved, but he wasn't?

Maybe this is what Balanchine was feeling when, with some bitterness, he'd remarked to Gisella, "They always like what Lew is doing big, but not my work."

Perhaps Balanchine was still thinking this when Nancy and I premiered Lew's **Con Amore** with his company and the three of us got such good reviews. And all this time, what Lew wanted more than anything else, was to work with and learn from this man he respected so much.

Over the years I've pondered this need to squelch people who do good work. Why should anyone want to do that? I've always thought the more good people you have around, the better the end product. For a long time I thought it was like some familial, fatal flaw that was passed down from one generation to the next. However, Lew wasn't the only one Balanchine squelched, and I wasn't the only one Lew squelched.

It wasn't until I read for the second time Serge Grigoriev's book, *The Diaghilev Ballet, 1909-1929* that it hit me. Grigoriev was Diaghilev's *Régisseur* throughout the life of that company. He told how Diaghilev got rid of each of his choreographers—Fokine, Nijinsky, Massine, and Nijinska—when they no longer served his purpose. While Diaghilev was developing the young Lifar as his *premier danseur*, he brought in Balanchine, fresh from Russia and obviously gifted, as his new choreographer. Balanchine greatly admired Diaghilev, and would have been happy working with him forever. However, Gregoriev felt Balanchine's days were numbered from the start. He wrote, "Balanchine's ideas were already, so to speak, crystallized, and he would consequently prove too independent to act as a mere instrument for the realization of Diaghilev's own conceptions." The only reason Balanchine wasn't replaced was because Diaghilev suddenly died.

What struck me was Gregoriev's phrase, "too independent to act as a mere instrument". There was that concept of being a tool. The dancer was the choreographer's tool and the choreographer was the Artistic Director's tool. Though the Artistic Director often was a choreographer, he didn't need to be. Diaghilev wasn't. The crux of the problem was the "artistic vision". There was room for only one. Should there be more than one—which independence could well introduce—one would ultimately cancel out the other.

This year, 1965, was shaping up to be the best yet for the Company. Our Spring Tour was ending with a week's engagement at Lincoln Center in New York City, in the New York State Theater—Balanchine's theater. The theater was designed and built exactly to Balanchine's specifications and was now the home of his New York City Ballet. Bookings for this theater were hard to come by. We felt lucky to get in at all.

Before tour, we had a February Season at the Opera House for which Lew choreographed two new works—sensations we hoped. The first ballet was, as Lew described it, "a do-it-yourself disaster". He called it *Life—A Pop Art Ballet.* It was his commentary on today's four stages of man; incipiency, virility, maturity, and resignation—all four full of violence, whether underlying or overt, and ultimately meaningless. The other ballet, we called it *Lucifer* though it was listed on the program as *Concert Music for Strings and Brass Instruments,* was quite different. It was based loosely on the fall of Lucifer, from Milton's *Paradise Lost,* but was more about movement than ideas. Everything about it was grand; grand music, grand movements, grand scenery, and a grand price for our costumes. Though they were mainly leotards and tights, we all wore helmets, neckpieces, and belts made of gold kid that cost over $300 a set.

A European tour would probably follow our New York appearance—every so often Leon let me know that Junior was still working on that—and there would be another concert tour in the fall, this year Ballet '65.

The Guild, using the Ford Foundation school expansion money for a down payment, was able to buy the school property and expand the building. We definitely needed additional space. And besides this, the Guild was guaranteeing fifteen of us—for the first time ever—a year-round salary of $100 per week when we weren't performing. Though small, it was never-the-less steady.

Everything seemed to be coming together; bookings, recognition, and money.

As for the tension between Lew and me, by the time our February Season began, all seemed to have smoothed out. I thought the casting was really quite fair. Lew didn't use me in *Life*, but he used me in *Lucifer*.

A lot of other tensions were floating around, though. Everything was now so "important". Among the girls there was additional jockeying for soloist roles because, with the recent rash of marriages within the Company, there was now a rash of pregnancies. Three of our soloists were out for the spring; Zola Dishong and David Anderson's baby was born in January, Nancy Robinson and Bobby Gladstein's baby was due soon, and Sue Loyd and Henry Berg, who married just before Christmas, were now expecting.

Marcelle Gregory quit as wardrobe mistress over some blow-up, which was probably just as well for Cynthia without her mother in that position. Pat Bibbins took over for Marcelle as wardrobe mistress and would be going on tour with us. I was delighted to have my old friend Pat to pal around with, again.

Harold's nose was out of joint, too. Leon said he was always like this before a tour. As I saw it, the only time Harold didn't feel "out of it" was when Ford Foundation Scholarship time came around for the School—his school. He was convinced the Company was trying to take over his school. He couldn't bring himself to admit that the School needed the Company just as much as the Company needed the School. Instead of feeling he was contributing to something growing and exciting, he felt he was constantly being taken advantage of.

On top of all this, there was a big upheaval in the Arts of San Francisco in general. The directors of the Actor's Workshop, Herbert Blau and Jules Irving, were going to Lincoln Center in New York. The director of the Museum of Art, George Cullers—who had been unpopular with certain factions ever since he'd taken over—was leaving for Philadelphia.

In the midst of all of this uproar, I went to a cocktail party given by Stanley Eichelbaum, movie and drama critic for the *Examiner.* I met Stanley through Jeff Hobart the summer of Rocky's illness, and we became friends. I sometimes accompanied him to various events. Much of the press was at his party, some of whom had been writing about us in uncomplimentary tones. The culture crisis, naturally, was in the fore; so much so that no one wanted to discuss it. The papers the day before had dropped a bomb concerning Lew and Lincoln Center, saying he might leave, too. I figured, if Lew got too frustrated, he could go back to Balanchine— in the same capacity he'd always had—but I doubted he wanted to. He was probably using this announcement as a lever to get something under way about a theater. He admitted as much.

My friends the Lathrops, whom I'd met through Stanley, were also at this party. Welland Lathrop was a well-known modern dancer and his wife, Nina, was a psychoanalyst who practiced out of her home. They asked me several times to phone any free evening and come for supper. Why not come before tour? So I did. I later realized how truly thoughtful and supportive they were.

Now that I look back on it, others were supportive, too. In mid-February Tilly asked me to join her for dinner with a doctor friend of her family's. The doctor was concerned about young people wasting their potential. Our conversation was mainly about why some women—like Tilly and me—were inclined to settle for second best in men. Tilly was now raising a young daughter by herself after an unfortunate first marriage, teaching for Harold at the School, having a hard time meeting eligible men, and currently involved with one of the male ballet teachers. Tilly knew it would be foolish to let her attachment grow into marriage. Her situation, plus all the recent Company marriages and pregnancies, convinced me that I had recovered from all such inclinations. The doctor and I agreed that these men pick a strong woman to support them emotionally as well as often economically.

By the end of February we were off on tour once more. We were traveling so often, now, that I could keep in touch with friends all over the country, saying, "Oh, I'll see you, again, in March." I looked forward to seeing these friends. They were so easy to talk to, even about personal things. They asked direct questions and gave direct answers, so unlike the kids in the Company who were always so circuitous, who had this great need for ambiguity.

As to the morale of the Company, it seemed to vacillate. Sometimes it was up, sometimes it was down. In Port Arthur Lew finally clamped down on the permissive attitude that seemed to seep in so quickly. The kids responded well to his discipline. Father cared, after all.

While in Daytona Beach, Florida we got the news from home that we had been allotted $13,000,000 for a new theater in the Opera House Complex, right across from the Opera House and the Veterans Auditorium on Franklin Street. It was to be on the corner where the old Standard Station stood, right where Lew wanted it. Of course, it had to be voted through, but they hoped to have it completed in three years.

Within two weeks Leon received an article stating the amount was $29,000,000 and that the Symphony was to move into the new theater. The Opera and the Ballet would remain in the Opera House. I wondered how much of a fight there would be for us to keep our share. I knew Lew wouldn't compromise.

By the time we got to Baton Rouge, the article on Lew and *Lucifer*—with photos of Clinton Rothwell as *Lucifer,* and Cynthia and me as *Angels*—came out in *TIME.* There was nothing about the **Pop Art Ballet**, yet, but Lew said something might come out in *NEWSWEEK* before we hit New York.

We were in New Orleans two days after *Mardi Gras.* When we arrived at the Auditorium for class and rehearsal, we couldn't have class because the surface of the stage was like glass; it had been highly polished for the *Mardi Gras* ceremonies. We brought along a barrel of stripping solution for just such occasions—sometimes to the horror of the local management—but Rich hadn't used it on the floor and didn't seem inclined to. I got after him, which he didn't like. He retorted, "That's just tough, Sally. I don't have to take anything from you this trip, only Lew."

I agreed with him, and then told Lew he'd better speak to Rich if he wanted the stage fixed. Lew chewed him out, the stage got mopped, we didn't get class but at least had rehearsal, and I wasn't at all popular. But—as I decided a while ago—I didn't care as long as the job got done.

I guess it was about this time that Nick, who had asked to drive our bus rather than the musicians' bus this spring, noticed I had a lot of nights free from dancing and I wasn't doing much else, either. He finally came up to me one day and asked, "Sally, what's going on? How come you're not doing anything?" I just sort of looked at him and shrugged. He walked off shaking his head.

Soon after this, we were in St. Petersburg, Florida, inaugurating their brand new theater complex; a lovely, modern structure right on the water. The town made quite an event of the opening. The audience was dressy and sold out. They even had gold programs. This was about the third, new, large, well-equipped theater we'd danced in; they were popping up all over—encouraging for the Performing Arts. Lew was in a marvelous mood, full of energy and enthusiasm. Now, if he'd just stay this way.

Several days later, the Rockefeller Brothers' report on U.S. Culture came out in both *U.S. NEWS AND WORLD REPORT* and *THE SATURDAY REVIEW*. It mentioned strong possibilities of Government subsidy. Both articles seemed to feel the Arts were next in line for the vision of the Greater Society.

Then one day I overheard Lew, Leon and Larry discussing the **Pop Art Ballet**, which hadn't been going over too well. Leon quoted one woman in Florida as saying, "I think I've been in Panama City too long." Lew and Larry agreed that people weren't getting the message. Lew said he cared. He wanted them to feel stupid and dirty, to go home despising themselves after seeing it.

We arrived in Saginaw, Michigan two days before our scheduled performance. We were given the use of the theater both days from 10:00 AM to 4:00 PM. We got a lot of work done. Besides putting Cynthia, David and me into the ending of **Lucifer**, strengthening our roles a bit, Lew worked on the pas de deux from **Beauty and the Beast** with Cynthia and David. Joce had gone to Pittsburgh while we were in Saginaw to do some publicity and teach a few master classes. I wished she would get more pleasure out of doing such things. She wanted to just still dance, though. Bobby, who danced the *Beast* to Joce's *Beauty*, was upset. I could see fireworks in the offing.

Lew and Joce continued being chummy; more than just singing the "Good Morning Song" together first thing on the bus each morning regardless of our loud groaning. But I didn't go along with the general gossip that they were having an affair. It didn't quite look like it to me. For one thing, there was no snappishness between the two of them; something that tends to happen when people are intimate. It occurred to me that Lew might be encouraging this image, not so much to hurt Gisella, but as a way to control Joce, maybe get her to stop dancing.

Upon our arrival in New York, we discovered the city had been flooded with ballet all spring. We were sandwiched into the New York State Theater between Ballet Theater and the New York City Ballet. The only reason we got the dates at all was because no one else wanted them. They were during Easter Week, which also contained Passover this year, a combination known to kill anyone. No one in New York City came to the theater during this combination of holidays. But for us, it was now or not at all.

Things started out well enough. We got a spot on Ed Sullivan's TV show, which was a nice break for both the Company and me, personally. Bobby and I danced the leads in the waltz from *Caprice*.

The following day—it was probably still a couple of days before our opening—I went back to the hotel with Pat to rest during one of our breaks. Pat finally had the cast lists for our Lincoln Center performances. Lew, as usual, was waiting until the last moment to post them, but she had to get the costumes ready. She showed the lists to me.

I was stunned. I was given almost nothing to do. I was scheduled to dance every night, but not in anything special, certainly not anything that could be considered a showcase. This was our big chance and I was being passed over. For me, I could see everything going down the drain.

I think I must have sat there in disbelief for some time. Pat, not knowing what else to say, finally said, "Sally, I'm sorry."

I remember that day just wandering around the streets of New York in a daze, saying to myself over and over again, "The jig's up. What am I going to do, now?"

I'd always had this feeling of timing being in my favor. Now, suddenly, it was not. This year I would turn thirty-three, coincidentally the same age as Lew when his dancing career was cut short by World War II. Now, this was it for me. I wasn't going any further with this company and I was too old to start over with a different one.

I was too numb to notice, but no one else was coming off too well, either. These performances were about Lew's ballets, not his dancers. They were to be presented without his strongest casts. I guess he didn't want his older dancers' personalities to detract. And, like Balanchine, the dancers he did capitalize on were his young ones.

The night of our opening I was definitely "on automatic". I don't know that anyone else noticed this—I still danced my assigned roles as best I could—but as far as I remember, I was pretty much just going through the motions. The program shows that we opened with **Concert Music for Strings and Brass Instruments, Life—A Pop Art Ballet**, and **Divertissement d'Auber**, Lew's extended version of his **Pas de Trois**.

I remember a big, fancy reception at the theater afterwards. Carrie and Jacques were there—I would be spending a week with them after our season was over—and so were many of our other New York friends. Even some of our Guild Board members were there. They'd flown in from San Francisco for the occasion. I particularly remember the Ludwigs and the Uptons being there. I also remember that I wore the peridot earrings I'd bought in Burma and my dress of peridot-colored brocade with sunbursts of gold thread woven into it. And I remember that Junior was there. I think he said hello, but he still didn't come over to talk.

Suddenly, out of the blue, Dr. Upton came up to me and said, "Sally, don't marry someone you don't know."

His remark amazed me, but instinctively I answered, "Why, of course not."

He looked me in the eye and said, "Good," then wandered off into the crowd, leaving me standing there wondering, "Now, what was that about?"

Then I remembered Junior standing on the other side of the room and I started thinking, "Oh, my. Something is indeed going on, and a lot of people know more about it than I do."

Under such circumstances, my gut reaction is to sit tight until I also know what is going on.

There was still time to change the casting.

So . . .

What was I supposed to do, anyway? How could I do anything? Junior and I were still strangers. He'd always kept his distance. He'd never come close enough for me to see what he was like. All I knew was that he tended to be suspicious and controlling, two traits I was learning to like less and less.

And he didn't know me any better than I knew him. He knew what others thought of me, but that was about it. He might be in for a surprise. I had a sneaking feeling that the person the poor fellow was looking at from afar was *Eve*. I was quite sure it wasn't me.

He never did come closer, and I never found out exactly what was going on. Mostly, it just didn't matter anymore. I no longer cared. However, I remember one time when we all cared a lot. This incident took place just before one of our earlier U.S. tours. Leon had called a Company meeting; I distinctly remember him saying, "Give me one year of your lives, just one year, and I'll put this Company on the map." We were all sitting there, nodding, "Yes, yes." At that time we all felt part of something growing, something exciting, something bigger than ourselves—and we all were willing to do whatever it took to make it happen.

I wasn't that willing any longer.

As to our New York engagement; we proceeded through our week of scheduled performances, expecting the critics to be hard on us, and they were. They had been feuding with Balanchine over his insistence on presenting only his ballets and using his "baby ballerinas" to the exclusion of his older stars. But what angered them even more was the huge Ford Foundation grant he received when groups they considered equally worthy—but non-Balanchine oriented— didn't receive anything. He was now controlling ballet in America, which they didn't like one bit. We were considered a satellite of Balanchine's and easier to attack than he, so they attacked us.

Actually, by the end of the season, I thought the consensus of the critics was quite fair; the dancers looked pretty good but weren't given enough to do to show themselves off; Lew's ballets came across as weak, with fancy, expensive costumes covering up a lack of choreography. As Jacques commented, after attending almost all of our performances, "Lew doesn't lack choreographic ideas—he has many of those—but he doesn't carry them through."

With reviews like this, our houses—destined to be small because of Easter Week—got even smaller. Too much was against us now. It was obvious we were not going to have a success. Balanchine was absolutely gleeful. He came around the theater every day with a big, magnanimous smile on his face. He even spoke to me. Lincoln, on the other hand, looked genuinely concerned for us all.

Without a success, our hopes for a European Tour— or any other tour, for that matter—vanished. No one would be interested in booking us, now. We were going to need some time to recover from this one. I figured it would take at least four years; longer than I had, at any rate.

Sally Bailey in a jazzy pose for Ballet 1960, S.F.

Roderick Drew and Sally Bailey as *Adam and Eve* in *Original Sin*, S.F. 1961. Photo by Henri McDowell.

Roderick Drew and Sally Bailey with Michael Smuin as
Temptation in **Original Sin**, S.F. 1961. Photo by Dale Smith.

Sally Bailey and Robert Gladstein in **Danses
Concertantes**, S.F. 1963. Photo by Henri McDowell.

Jest of Cards, S.F. 1963. Back row left, Royalty on stilts, Patricia Norman, Michael Rubino. Front row left, Michael Smuin as *the Joker* with *Clubs* David Anderson, Sally Bailey and Lee Fuller.

The San Francisco Opera House audience from the stage; I used to like to say, "Where the magic of live theater takes place."

The three Christensen Brothers, from left; Harold, Lew, and Willam. Backstage during the 50th Anniversary Gala Celebration, February 1983.

CHAPTER TEN

Gradual Exit

NOT ALL THE DANCERS RETURNED TO SAN FRANCISCO AFTER OUR New York appearance; most noticeably Cynthia Gregory and Terry Orr. Lew kept moaning, "Give me back my dancers." Or else he'd moan, "I haven't any money. I can't do anything without money."

Leon kept trying to maneuver me into talking with him, but wouldn't come right out and say, "Sally, let's have a talk." Therefore, I avoided him.

Classes and rehearsals started soon enough because we had engagements at two theaters-in-the-round, a new experience for us; the conductor was "front", but we had to play to people in every direction. One theater was in Anaheim, right next to Disneyland. The other was in San Carlos, on the Peninsula just south of San Francisco. They were under joint management. I was wryly amused. Now that it didn't matter anymore, my casting couldn't be better.

I worked hard, but became more and more detached. I wasn't ever going to allow myself to become so absorbed in just one thing, again. Perhaps because of this changed attitude, I relaxed and danced better for it. From here on I don't remember worrying about particular steps. Doing one seemed really quite like doing another; you just moved your body this way instead of that. The control seemed to be there, regardless. Before, I had always picked out the hardest part of whatever I was dancing to worry about, and then be relieved when it was over.

For the school's summer session this year, Harold gave me a full load of classes to teach. I was busy and happy with my new schedule. I danced in only one of the Summer Ballet '65 programs, which was fine with me, and spent the rest of rehearsal time working with the younger dancers in Lew's ballets, giving them "polish". I was still to manage the concert tour in the fall, which was shorter this year—only five weeks and only in the west—and probably booked by Junior before New York.

With my present schedule, I had weekends free; I hadn't had free weekends in years. I made more "outside" friends. I didn't even take class—a first for me, ever—until five weeks before we were to take off on tour. I remember at the time being surprised how easily I got back into condition. I also remember thinking I was probably lucky this time and shouldn't make a practice of it.

About half way through the summer, gossip grew rampant about Lew and Joce. They were having an affair. Everyone was having a fit. Gisella went by herself to their country place near Ben Lomond for the summer while Lew remained in San Francisco. I think I mostly ignored the hullabaloo and went on about my business. However, I do recall one evening in the school's basement dressing room after a performance—it must have been during the one program in which I danced—noticing that Lew was pushing Joce to go somewhere with him afterwards. Joce was clearly agitated and finally snapped at him. This is the only time I ever remember her speaking harshly to him.

The Ballet '65 Tour came and went without my making any entries in my journal, but I kept a copy of *Bravo*, the music magazine in which Columbia Artists Management inserted our program, so I have a general idea of the dates, the dancers, and our repertoire. This year, I notice, I was listed as Ballet Mistress.

I also have the map on which I marked our route and some snapshots taken on tour. I remember we had wonderful fall weather wherever we went. I also remember this as a happy time; everything going smoothly and everyone getting along. I had mostly younger dancers with me this year. The babies were arriving and keeping some of my "regulars" at home. Carlos Carvajal was the only other person my age to come along—we were using his **Siempre Bach** in our program—and this may be one of the reasons everything went so smoothly; I was becoming mother hen.

A wonderful *Peanuts* comic strip appeared in the funnies around this time. It showed *Snoopy* ecstatically dancing across the strip, feet flapping off the ground, arms waving in the air, with this blissful smile on his face. The caption read, "To live is to dance. To dance is to live." This little strip began showing up in many places; on dressing room mirrors, taped inside makeup kits, on our makeshift bulletin boards.

I enjoyed the kids; I enjoyed working with them and I enjoyed discussions with them when we weren't working. I remember one discussion in particular. We were on a longer-than-usual bus trip after a performance. The hour was late, and we had stopped at an all-night liquor store for some snacks which we were now sharing. I was sitting next to one of the younger male dancers. We got onto the subject of loneliness; meeting people, making friends, getting along, being *homo* or *hetero.*

I remember my young friend finally pausing, and then asking in a rather plaintive voice, "Sally, why do you have to *be* anything?"

I responded, "Well, why do you?"

And he answered, "If I weren't, I wouldn't have *any* friends."

I also remember a comment made by one of the younger girls. We were in a town where some local ballet dancers came to the theater early to watch our class and rehearsal, and then stayed on to visit with us backstage until show time.

Earlier in the day I had received an invitation from the local Community Concerts Board asking us all to come to a party afterwards. When I made the announcement to the group, this girl piped up and asked, "Is it for dancers, or will people be there, too?"

Her remark caused me to stop and reflect; dancers *or* people? Touring was so normal for us dancers—get on the bus by 8:00 AM, jiggle along for four hours to the next town, check in at the motel, adjust to a new theater, perform that night, eat lunch at midnight after having had dinner at noon. Even toe shoes seemed normal. Had we, indeed, become different than people?

I started asking myself, "Is it maybe time for me to get off the bus?"

One performance I clearly remember, too. It took place in Gallup, New Mexico, a town known mainly for the Indian powwows that took place there each August. Three days before we were to arrive, Rich discovered a big problem with the theater we were to use. He, as usual, had been going through the questionnaires on the bus, looking at theater specifications in order to anticipate problems. By doing this, he often saved himself time, which was always crucial. I remember him coming over to my seat this day and saying, "Sally, there's something strange here. If this isn't a mistake, we're in big trouble. It says the stage is seventy feet wide and eight feet deep. It looks as if they expect us to dance in front of their movie screen."

It was an old movie theater. Old movie theaters often had nice-sized stages behind their screens. Why didn't they just remove the screen? At any rate, I thought I'd better phone ahead and see what the story was.

Well, the story was that they did, indeed, expect us to dance in front of the movie screen. It was a huge, permanent structure. There was no way they could move it. I said it was impossible to dance on something seventy feet wide and only eight feet deep. A single person turning in *arabesque* took up almost eight feet. The patterns of ballets were choreographed for square or rectangular spaces, not strips. Our show was flexible and could be set it up almost anywhere, as long as there was space. Wasn't there a school gym we could use? Our contact in Gallup, who happened to be the local Community Concerts Association President, as well as the high school principal, said he'd see what he could do.

When we arrived three days later, he was waiting for us at the hotel with a long face. He hadn't been able to do anything about a space for us. A basketball game was scheduled for the high school gym that evening. It couldn't be changed. There was nowhere else for us to perform. Could we, please, at least take a look at the theater? He hated to cancel the performance.

The poor man looked so tired and discouraged. He had probably spent a lot of time and effort getting the Community Concerts to even "go" in Gallup. I think he was President because no one else wanted to be. Now, if we canceled on him, this could be it for Community Concerts.

Rich, the kids, and the man all looked at me. What were we going to do? If we tried to put the show on, it would mean restaging every single step of every ballet to fit this ridiculous stage. Nothing would look the way it was choreographed to look, but at least we'd give them a show. It would take time, though. Bus call for the theater was usually 5:30 PM. If we left at 4:00, we might just make it by show time.

I finally said, "O.K. Let's see what we can do, but that means being back on the bus in forty-five minutes."

Everyone was back on the bus in time. No one complained. I've never seen such cooperation, and I've never seen such a look of relief on a man's face.

When we got to the theater, I gave a short warm-up, and then we went to work. Carlos restaged his ballet, and all of us came up with solutions for the others. If sections were set in a square, we did them in a staggered line. Steps that moved backwards or forwards we did from side to side. For traveling in a circle, we went straight down to one end of the stage, turned around, and then came back. We were all having a hilarious good time.

Half way through all this, we noticed an Indian woman sitting in the front row. She must have wandered into the theater, I guess to watch us. She was just sitting there, smiling.

We got the show ready on time. Everything went amazingly well. I could hardly believe it. The kids remembered all the changes and danced beautifully. They had big smiles on their faces the whole time. During the *finale* of our closing ballet—where six dancers were to execute leaping turns in a circle—we judged our leaps and turns carefully, jumping just straight ahead, and turning only when our arms and legs were together. Otherwise we would crash into each other. Every time we passed on this long, narrow strip, when our eyes met, we flashed big grins.

During the performance, I also remember looking down into the semi-darkness of the audience and seeing the Indian woman, still in her front row seat, still smiling. Everyone around her was smiling, too.

I'm sure this show looked like no other. I'm also sure our audience loved it. They weren't a ballet audience, but they certainly responded to what we were doing. The Principal was so relieved that he took us all out to dinner afterwards.

After we were all packed up and ready to leave the theater, we noticed the same Indian woman, still sitting there in her seat, still smiling, almost as if in a trance.

Finally the Principal had to go over to her and ask her to leave; we were all leaving, we were locking up. I can still see her walking up the isle and out the door into the night, still smiling.

Wasn't this what performing was all about?

The tour ended as it had begun, with all going like clockwork. Once again we came back home a success, with high morale and improvement in our dancing. Our surprise was to learn that Lew had been in the hospital practically the whole time we were gone. A malignant tumor was found in one of his testicles. It was removed, but the cancer had already spread; the doctors weren't sure how far. Lew was having cobalt treatments—20,000 volts worth—but whether or not the treatments would do the trick, time would have to tell. Evidently this tumor had been coming on for about five years. Now it was obvious there had been a physical reason for Lew's lacking the energy to push. This had been undermining him all that time.

I went to see Lew in the hospital as soon as I got home. We both felt we should patch up our differences and forget the resentments as best we could. However, the fact remained; he was my teacher. I had learned to do well what he taught me, and in one area I'd learned to do better. I just wished he would be satisfied with the knowledge that in the creative, choreographic area I was not even suited. There was no competition.

I remember Lew lying there in the hospital bed, looking ash-gray. He said he was feeling better, and would like to go home to San Bruno, but he still needed more cobalt treatments. He had gotten so he dreaded them. This big black thing would come down on him, then ZAP, and afterwards he'd feel awful. He just wanted to get out of the hospital.

Shortly after this, I went to see Gisella. Evidently Lew had come home by the end of the summer and patched things up with her. I noticed Joce seemed to be friends with both of them. Gisella had needed a cataract operation—a much lengthier process than now, involving a whole month of keeping one's head still—before Lew discovered he had cancer. He was supposed to take care of her. She certainly couldn't take care of him. All she could do was sit there with these big thick glasses on. Luckily, Clelia was there to help out, but Clelia didn't drive.

The doctors said Lew could come home, as long as he returned for his cobalt treatments. Lew didn't want to ask, so Gisella asked; could I please take turns with Joce driving Lew back and forth to the hospital?

Of course I said, "Yes."

I don't remember how long the two of us did this. I don't think it was for too long. I remember picking Lew up at his house with him looking quite perky, and then bringing him back home looking gray and sniffing from his bottle of smelling salts; probably the same smelling salts he'd held for me in the wings that night I was sick in Guayaquil.

None of us knew if Lew was going to live or not, or what was going to happen to the Company. I remember feeling some comfort in the fact that Lew's color was gray and not waxy yellow—the color of a friend of mine before she died of cancer. I somehow felt he wasn't dying now, that he would live at least another year or so. I thought that if he should get well, his work would again have the strength it was lacking this whole time.

Carlos took over as the Company's Ballet Master as soon as we returned from tour. This didn't bother me at all. Carlos got along well with the kids, he drilled them well, and he could continue developing his choreography. My only concern was that he might not be tough enough to get the most out of everyone.

Béné Arnold came down from Salt Lake City to help put *Nutcracker* on; she knew the ballet and Carlos didn't. I noticed her rehearsals got more results than Carlos's did, and felt this was perhaps where I could come in. I'd pretty well proven that I could get excellent results from the kids. I could train them well, keep them performing at a high level, and keep up morale. If I took on this capacity, I need not be in conflict with Carlos. He might resent me a little, but if we could work together, he'd leave me free to dance a little longer. I at least wanted to dance through the Spring Season. My dancing was just now becoming fun for me, and I could tell people responded to it.

This year I was cast to dance **Nutcracker** with Clinton Rothwell. We enjoyed working together. However, I was not able to finish my scheduled performances with him; I tore some ligaments across the top of my foot during our next-to-last performance. For stage maintenance, hot wax had been applied to the edges of the risers; some of it splattering onto the stage surface. We "rosined" the spots well, but they were still slick. I was slightly off balance in the *coda* as I began my fast diagonal turns. If I'd been right on balance, even though the wax was there, I probably would not have slipped, but now, in that I was "off", I didn't have the needed traction to get back "on". I turned my ankle—all the way over, I was told. I finished fine, but by evening I looked as if I had a club foot.

This is the only time in my whole dancing career that I injured myself. It took me four days to admit I might be out for a while. I went to the theater each day, trying to rehearse, trying to see if I could do enough of the *pas de deux* to get by for my last scheduled performance. I remember Clint patiently going through the steps with me each day, both of us finally shaking our heads and saying, "Well, not today, maybe tomorrow."

Eventually tomorrow—the day of our last scheduled performance—came, and it was still no good. I knew I would not be able to give a good performance. It was only then that I went to see the doctor, who, naturally, was furious with me for taking so long. He threatened to put me in a cast if I didn't stay off my foot. From then on, until it was healed, I stayed off my foot.

My ligament tear turned out to be nastier than I had at first thought. I ended up being off my foot for two months.

I missed the first half of our Spring Season. Interestingly, I found I didn't mind; I loved having the unexpected free time.

My only obligation was to go to Dr. Fuerstner's office each day for my diathermy treatments. In that I had to stay off my foot as much as possible, there was no point in going to the studio. I started filling my days with things I'd never had time to do before; taking a correspondence course through U.C. Extension in creative writing, joining a World Affairs Council study group for young adults, throwing a big cocktail party, auditing a college seminar at S.F. College for Women that Harry Isbell, husband of my old Salt Lake City friend, Lyn Cosgriff, was teaching on Eastern European literature. This course affected me for good. To read all those powerful writers from early Pushkin to the modern poet Yvetushenko is certainly to broaden one's outlook on almost everything. I'd never read so much in my life. It nearly killed me, but it was wonderful. As the quote of Sir Isaac Newton states, "By standing on the shoulders of giants, one can see farther."

Our first Ballet '66 performance for the year was at Cabrillo College, just south of San Francisco, near Santa Cruz. I was still in charge, using my fall tour cast. I wasn't dancing yet, so was functioning only in my directional capacity. Leon was pressuring me to get back on my foot; our Spring Season was opening in just two weeks. He even had the insurance company phone Dr. Fuerstner to find out if I was faking. I finally told him, "Look. I'll be back on my foot as soon as it's working properly—not sooner."

I remember feeling strongly about giving my ankle time to heel properly, then once I started training again, to train slowly and correctly. I had seen too many dancers rush to get back into shape after an injury, favor their injury, then consequently injure something else. Some ended up with chronic injuries. This wasn't going to be me.

Leon pressured me more; I was no longer being paid. I was getting workman's compensation instead, but would be going off that in a week.

Finally I started to train—slowly—when I felt my foot was ready. I was encouraged. It did seem to be mending properly. When I told Lew this, he said he would wait until the second half of the season to put me on—in *Original Sin* with David. This was now a little longer than necessary for me to be off, but I supposed they had to call the shots. At least I was being paid, again.

Our 1966 Season opened at the Opera House in the middle of February. The upper balcony was closed off, but the rest of the house was surprisingly full. The audience was warm and friendly, the kids were pulled together, and the show went well. Carlos's new ballet, *Alpenfest,* was cute and fun and Balanchine helped out by giving us *Scotch Symphony*—along with his costumes and scenery—to add to our repertoire. For the opening, Leon and Wana went out of their way to make sure I had a seat, a definite place to light. Wana and I sat together. We were all quite dressy, which was fun. I did appreciate their thoughtfulness.

I felt kind of funny during intermission, talking over and over about nothing but my ankle, or the new surface for the stage; a roll-up linoleum surface, non-slip, which would go with us everywhere. I don't know that I was entirely responsible for our getting it, but I called it "my floor", anyway. The Guild paid for it, and Jim Ludwig, after inquiring about my ankle, smiled and nodded "Yes" when I asked him if I was the case-in-point for needing the new surface.

The second half of the season opened with me again dancing full out. Lew, who was slowly regaining his strength, was raving about Carlos. He said he didn't know how he would have gotten along without him. I, too, felt Carlos was doing an excellent job, though I still thought he lacked that final decisiveness. I mentioned this to the Bodreros, who had kindly phoned to say they'd missed me in the first half of the season. I also mentioned that Lew was probably fond of Carlos because Lew never considered Carlos a real threat. All they said was, "Yes, but he needs a threat, as does Balanchine."

About this same time, we received a grant from the Federal Government Title III Program to give lecture/demonstrations to public schools, K through 12, in "culturally deprived" areas. Lew went back to New York for several weeks to work with Balanchine on developing these. Balanchine would also be giving them in New York State. By the end of our spring season we were ready to launch our program in Merced County, a farming area located in the heart of California's fertile Central Valley

I remember all of us moving into the Motel 6 in Merced for a couple of weeks, then driving from there each day to a different school in the County. We danced in their auditoriums or cafeterias.

In this program I started out as just one of the dancers, with either Lew or Leon giving the lectures, but soon into our stint, they asked me if I'd like to try a lecture, too. I had already done some public speaking and rather enjoyed it, so I said, "Sure." One day I just jumped in; it was a sort of test by fire. Kids are great audiences, but they're not easy. They let you know exactly how they feel.

Next came Summer Ballet '66, and this year I participated in it, again. It's funny, but I don't remember teaching for Harold this summer. I remember Carlos set a ballet to Shostakovitch music called *Three Diversions.* He set a lovely, romantic adagio for Sue, Henry, himself, and me. He also choreographed another ballet, *Voyage Interdit,* which explored an LSD "trip". The psychedelic scene, with its mind-expanding drugs, was now upon us. Free spirits, the joy of movement, bright colors, the beauty of nature, the quest to look at things anew, to love rather than hate; these concepts were popping up all over and had a definite appeal. Carlos captured the essence of all this in his ballet. I was not in this one, but remember watching many of its rehearsals. I was enthusiastic about it. The critics were, too.

Around this time I began hearing comments about Carlos moaning, "She doesn't like my kind of man." I was surprised. It had never occurred to me to be interested in Carlos. I'd known him forever; we'd always been friends, but his personal life had always been his own. I wasn't even sure he liked girls. However, we were spending a lot of time together—both working and otherwise—and enjoying each other's company. But when I showed the least bit of interest in return, the games immediately started up—those same old games I'd learned to hate. Always the little tests, always the ambiguity, and always including a third party, always other people knowing more about what was going on than I. Why couldn't people just be direct? I'd had enough of go-rounds to last me the rest of my life. I was wary. At any rate, I thought it wisest to just continue playing it cool.

By now, the Company had become quite domesticated. All the babies had arrived and sat in their bouncers at the front of the studio during class and rehearsal each day. We all enjoyed them and played with them when we weren't dancing.

About this time, Carlos bought a house just a few blocks from Haight and Ashbury Streets, an area burgeoning with psychedelic shops that was fast becoming a hub for the hippie scene. I called it his "Hippie House". He painted it all up with colors and designs—a big old house with many rooms—and had lots of friends live in it with him, like a commune. I think Carlos considered himself a sort of guru. He was gaining quite a following among the younger dancers.

During this time I started reading Maurice Goudeket's book, *The Delights of Growing Old*. Goudeket spoke of refraining from saying, "In my day, my dear sir." I thought this a marvelous thought to keep in mind as one grew older. "My day" should always be the present. The one who can always keep up with the present will not feel old.

I was beginning to feel old in ballet.

Our activities for the fall included a return to Merced County for more lecture/demonstrations and some scattered Ballet '66 performances. In November Lew announced in the newspapers that, as of **Nutcracker**, I was appointed Assistant Ballet Mistress. We all considered this a prestigious move. Shortly after this, I received an application from *Who's Who of American Women in the West.*

I didn't notice at the time, but now, as I look at the program from our fall Ballet '66 performance at Stanford University, Carlos is listed as Ballet Master.

I ended the year by gluing portions of a newspaper review of Gina Berriault's book, *The Son (An Oedipal Tragedy)* into my journal. It was from the *Chronicle,* dated 11/13/66. One portion was a quote from an unpublished letter of Miss Berriault's. "Women harbor a myth of men, a myth that men have perpetuated and that women also perpetuate because, in spite of all its resultant disillusion and the emotions of disillusion, it is easier for women to accept the myth than to strike out for themselves."

I didn't make another journal entry for six-and-a-half years. I started a new journal when my husband Bob and I went on a study/trip into the Amazon jungle with a group of scientists through U.C. Berkeley Extension. This journal was part of an assignment for which I got an "A" and three college credits in Biology.

I still danced after I was appointed Assistant Ballet

Mistress. In the spring of 1967 Carlos choreographed a contemporary ballet, **Kromatika,** for Bobby and me, but I was no longer enjoying dancing the way I used to—with one exception.

This spring I danced Lew's **Shadows,** his ballet about a woman in search of her shadow. I loved doing this ballet. It was taking on a whole new meaning for me. In the ballet everyone has a shadow except this one woman. No matter how hard she searches, she can't find one for herself. In desperation, she tries to take the shadows of everyone else, but none of them stay with her. She ends up on stage by herself, still testing to see if her hands can't cast some little shadow. Finally a shadow appears on a screen at the back of the stage. In order to join him, she goes behind the screen and becomes a shadow, too. What Lew was saying, I don't know. He would never tell us. We were to read what we wanted into such things. He'd tease us if we got too cerebral. What I saw in it was a correlation between shadows and images. We were spending our lives pursuing images to project to audiences. If you did that long enough, that is what you'd become; an image, not substance.

I took on more and more of the rehearsing, which I found I did well. The only trouble; I felt myself becoming a martinet, a side of my nature I didn't particularly want to develop. I was also becoming everyone's mother, always making them do their best, always making them do what they knew they should be doing, anyway. I sometimes felt like yelling, "Either do it, or don't. It's up to you." If I was going to mother someone, I'd rather it be my own child than a bunch of nineteen-year-olds.

Also, in that I wasn't interested in choreographing, I was now mostly cleaning up everyone else's work. These days I was the first one in the theater and the last one out. I had even less time to myself than before. I saw my life narrowing down to a point, like a wedge; becoming arid and bleak. An image that came to mind was a once-vibrant fall leaf gradually losing its color and drying up. I didn't want that to be me.

I remember returning to Merced for yet another stint of lecture/demonstrations in late spring. By now, with Lew's encouragement, I was spending a lot of my time writing up the lectures. We both hoped someone would published my efforts as a little informational booklet.

We also filmed *Beauty and the Beast* for TV. Lynda Meyer was *Beauty* and David Anderson was the *Beast*. I was in this film, too. I did the *Roses Waltz Adagio* with Clint.

With summer came Ballet '67. I think Lew mostly left the running of the Company to Carlos and me while he and Gisella stayed down in the country. The two of us continued to work well together.

I know I also taught for Harold, because I remember one particular morning during Teachers' Week; I was teaching a class and some of the visiting teachers—many of whom were at least forty—were standing in the doorway intently watching. There was such earnestness on their faces. Suddenly it struck me; there wasn't a woman over forty in ballet that I wanted to be like, from Fonteyn on down.

I realized what I loved most about ballet was the dancing and I knew I wouldn't be doing that much longer. In August I would be thirty-five, the age I had always claimed dancers should stop dancing, the age an athlete could expect to start going downhill.

About this time, I had an unfortunate confrontation with Harold for which I think he never forgave me; not so much for the incident as for seeing something that was supposed to remain hidden—a crack in the facade of family loyalty. The incident, itself, was actually sort of dumb. Harold wanted to use *Beauty's* Act II tutu for one of his students in the School Demonstration. Lew wasn't around, so I told him he couldn't.

He knew that Company costumes were used for Company productions only. That was one of Lew's rules.

At this point Harold, practically in tears, burst out at me, "Lew's rules, always Lew's rules. Who is Lew, anyway, but my baby brother?"

All those years of resentment simmering below the surface came bursting out in that statement. He had spent his life staying home, running the school, paying the bills, so that his brothers could run off and do glamorous things. Now, his baby brother Lew was God of the San Francisco Ballet. Harold probably felt he'd bought that costume three times over.

I remember Ruby coming up to me later and saying, "Sally, you shouldn't have done that."

I thought I was just doing my job.

A couple of years later, when Gisella and I were working on her Cecchetti letters (published by Dance Perspectives, N.Y. 1971, as *Letters from the Maestro: Enrico Cecchetti to Gisella Caccialanza*), I told Lew of this incident. I can still see the three of us sitting out on the deck of their summer place in Ben Lomond sipping highballs under the redwood trees. Lew's face lit up—like the corny, proverbial light bulb suddenly switching on—as the implications of what I was saying gradually sank in. It was a revelation to him. I honestly don't think he'd ever thought of it before. And I think this new understanding helped him in his relationship with Harold the last few years of their lives. At least I hope it did.

The great hippie summer of love was at its height this summer of 1967. Its influence was now being felt far beyond the current pop scene; it could be found in all the arts, in fashion, certainly in advertising. We, of course, felt right in the middle of it, what with Carlos living at its center. I attended many of the parties Carlos gave after performances that year. Though I considered myself more an observer than a participant, I did try marijuana several times. I can still hear Carlos saying, "You're turned on, Sally. Oh, you're on." and me thinking, "What's so different about this? I feel like this—the heightened awareness—every night I perform."

Carlos used to get exasperated with me, saying, "Sally, why do you keep saying 'no' to life. You're so stubborn."

I remember one day walking into a rehearsal of Carlos's— I forget what he was working on, something new at any rate— and everyone was high. I could see they were all having an intense experience communicating with each other, thinking they were creating something wonderful together. To my cold, sober eye it looked terrible; I said as much. I told them, "You can't expect people to pay good money to come see this."

I began to realize that, though some of these drugs might expand the mind, they also affected one's judgment, which was not so good.

Before the summer was over, I found myself seriously contemplating just getting out. At first this idea surprised even me. I had no idea what I'd do instead. I could still teach, but I'd still be in this confined world. I knew that, with my body, I could probably dance another five years or so, but why push it? Why not bow out gracefully now? Why not quit while I was ahead? Besides, if I was going to change my life-style, it would be much easier at thirty-five than forty.

The more I thought about it, the more it made sense. Yet, for the first time in my life, I didn't quite trust my gut feelings. Were they constructive or destructive? Was I gracefully letting go or throwing everything away? Up until now I had always been so sure of my decisions.

At first I didn't talk to anyone about what I was thinking. I didn't want to tell my family until I made up my mind. I was pretty sure they'd think I was throwing everything away. However, I was still seeing Tilly frequently, so I told her. She thought maybe I should talk to her family's doctor friend, again, the friend who took us to dinner two years before, the one who was so concerned about us wasting our potential.

A couple of evenings later, Tilly and I went over to the doctor friend's apartment for a drink. He asked me to tell him what I had on my mind, so I told him. I also mentioned that I wasn't sure if my thinking was healthy or unhealthy.

I remember him saying, "I'm not going to tell you what to do, but I will tell you that your thinking is healthy."

That was all I needed to know.

Then he asked, "How much guts do you have?"

I remember Tilly laughing and saying "Don't worry about that."

He then suggested that I make two lists; one of all the good things about leaving ballet, the other of all the bad things. Then see which one was longer.

I went home and did this. The list of good reasons was longer.

There was now no question in my mind. I was going to leave.

He also suggested that I keep the two lists in a drawer for times when I got discouraged. At such times I should pull them out and read them, again.

I never read them, again. I came across the lists while packing up my things before marrying Bob. I thought, "Well, I won't be needing these, anymore," so I tossed them in the fire along with my "Rocky" journals.

While I was going through all this major decision-making, Lew was setting a new ballet for the workshop, *Il Distratto*, to music of Haydn. I was in this one; one of two couples in the *adagio* part doing slightly zany things while this beautiful music played on. The four of us were dressed all in black, except for the other girl's upper body and my lower body, both of which were white. At a certain point in the *adagio*, the lights were turned off and replaced with black light, leaving only the white now-florescent parts of our bodies visible. The two of us became one body disconnected at the waist. The "arms" went off in one direction while the "legs" went off in another.

This is the last ballet I danced; a quirky pair of legs in a workshop ballet. I remember my last performance; at the end I took my bow—like any other night—then went downstairs, took off my make-up, quietly packed up my things, and walked out the door.

I waited until after our last Ballet '67 performance to announce that I was retiring. I told Carlos earlier—I felt I needed to do that—but I hadn't told either Lew or Leon. I told everyone at a Company meeting that was called to discuss what was coming up next. For the first time in years, not much was coming up except our delayed new production of **Nutcracker**. This was the perfect time for me to bow out along with the old production and before there were definite commitments for the future.

I remember everyone being shocked. I don't think anyone believed me. I'm sure both Lew and Leon thought I'd be back before **Nutcracker**, but I knew I wouldn't. I was sure of my decision.

I remember feeling sort of giddy with anticipation, as if I was jumping out into an unknown ocean with no idea of where I'd come up. But it didn't matter. I would eventually find out, and along the way I'd have all sorts of new adventures.

I suddenly felt young, again. In fact, to this day, I have not felt as old as I did that last year I danced.

EPILOGUE

THE SAN FRANCISCO BALLET MANAGED TO SURVIVE THIS BLEAK period and did, indeed, regain its footing; today it holds a position of high, international prestige. However, it went through a lot of ups and downs along the way. For a while I thought the Company would just collapse.

Through it all, the Ballet Guild Board remained determined and supportive. It remained supportive of me, too. When I stopped dancing, they gave me my first job. I'd gone to several employment agencies, but no one would hire me. When they asked me what I'd done until now, I said, "Dancing and teaching." Then they asked, "Well, why aren't you still?" and I answered, "Because I don't want to any more." Until this time, the Guild office had been run by volunteers. The Guild took me on as their first paid employee. While I learned some office skills, my knowledge of the Company helped them.

I stayed with the Guild for two years. During this time I didn't go around the Company much. I preferred to do things I hadn't done before. However, I kept loosely in touch and went to most of the performances. I remember going to the opening of the new *Nutcracker*. It was a big Gala affair. The Ludwigs gave a fancy supper party beforehand and asked me to come, then kept me with them the whole evening. I realized how thoughtful this was of them. I spent much of that evening fielding people's questions about why I wasn't dancing.

Shortly after *Nutcracker*, because Company plans were so uncertain, many of the dancers left. Robert Gladstein and several others joined Ballet Theater. Bobby's wife, Nancy

Robinson, along with Sue Loyd and Henry Berg, joined the Joeffrey Ballet. That summer both companies appeared in the Bay Area at the same time and Bobby gave a party for the whole SFB gang at his uncle's home in the City.

Bobby phoned me and asked if I would please come. Royes would be there. I hadn't seen Royes since that odd dinner with John in New York. Royes left New York City Ballet as soon as Ballet Theater started up, again. Over the years his career had gone well. He was usually the Prince in whatever he danced. I don't think his knee bothered him, again, after that one long time. I remember Bobby meeting me at the door at the bottom of the stairs of his uncle's flat, and Royes rushing half way down to greet me on the landing; the same old Royes, the same passionate kiss for a greeting.

After he finished kissing me, he held me at arms' length, studying me for a few moments, then said, "I hate you. You look so alive."

Then he added, "The only time I feel alive anymore is when I'm on stage."

There it was; Lew's ballet ***Shadows***.

In order to feel alive, Royes had to go on stage—become his image. His image was his life, now.

Royes and I had a wonderful time catching up, enjoying each other's company once more. We talked and talked.

That was the last time I saw Royes. He stopped dancing a few years later and started teaching, I think at SUNY Purchase in New York. He died of lung cancer not too long afterwards. When I heard that, I thought of him on our Middle East tour, often laughing and saying, "Live fast, die young, and have a beautiful corpse."

My thoughts were now a bit rueful. He may have lived fast—though I think he actually took quite good care of himself—and he did die fairly young, but unfortunately, if he died of cancer, he didn't have a beautiful corpse.

Shortly after this, I remember talking to my old friends Connie and Chris about him; we were driving home from some performance together. I commented, "After all that's happened, I might as well have had an affair with him," then thinking to myself, "Too bad I didn't." Yet I still wonder; which one of us was controlling the situation, him or me? And if neither of us had controlled it, would our lovely friendship have lasted so long?

It may have been this same summer that Leon had an odd accident. I don't know how many people knew about it. I think he tried to keep it quiet. I know that years later, when I mentioned it to a friend who was on the Board at the time, she had no idea such a thing had happened. As I remember, Leon got out of the car to open the garage door. When he bent down to turn the door handle, the car lurched forward, crunching his head between the bumper and the door. The resulting injury was serious; the damage done was probably permanent. At any rate, after this, he started making misjudgments he never would have made before.

Two of Leon's misjudgments were grave; I feel they were what did him in as far as the Company was concerned. The first one I didn't think was an error until it was done and over with. Leon booked a tour for the Company the way it used to be, not the way it was now. He was operating on the assumption that if you had work, you could buy dancers. At the time I agreed with him—until I saw it not work. The new dancers didn't know the repertoire, they weren't used to working together, they hadn't been trained alike, and therefore they didn't dance alike. There was no unity of style. The upshot; the dancers couldn't pull off some of the ballets and several bookings had to be cancelled. The Company was really bad news, now. No one in their right mind would take them on.

The second error Leon made I saw coming. I tried my best to stop him, but he went ahead, anyway. He just got mad at me. There was a bookkeeping discrepancy in a financial report he presented to the Board. He allocated the same cost in two different places and wouldn't give a satisfactory explanation why. A special Executive Committee meeting was called to discuss the report further. As Guild Secretary I was at both meetings, taking the minutes. Leon refused to make any corrections to the report and wouldn't give a logical reason for not doing so. He just sat there, saying nothing to their repeated questions. I could see that he was in for big trouble if he didn't come up with a good reason.

After the meeting, which had been held at Jim Ludwig's office in Saks Fifth Avenue—Ludwig was manager of the store—I followed Leon outside. I remember standing on the corner of Stockton and Post Street, in the heart of downtown San Francisco, arguing with Leon for over an hour. I kept trying to get him to change his tactics, to clear up the discrepancy. But Leon only got angrier and angrier with me. Finally he spouted, "Sally, don't you think you should get at least a little dry behind the ears before you start telling me how to run my business?"

I didn't give up easily. I kept on arguing with him. Finally—I don't know how much later—Jim Ludwig walked by on his way to the parking garage. When he saw the two of us standing there on the street corner, arguing, this quizzical expression came across his face. He nodded to us both, and then walked on.

A few days later Leon's resignation was announced in the newspapers. I felt terribly.

During the summer of 1969, when many of my old dancing buddies returned to San Francisco, I hardly even noticed. I was still working for the Ballet Guild, but my interests had moved on. I was working with Gisella on her Cecchetti letters, going to a writers' workshop once a week, socializing in several groups of "young adults", going through one of a series of "relationships", and not attending many performances. However, according to some newspaper clippings for Ballet '69 that I later read, Bobby Gladstein came back for the season, Nancy Johnson and Dick Carter brought their San Diego Ballet to S.F. as an addition to one of the programs, and Rocky Drew returned. I knew that because I'd seen Rocky's picture in the newspaper with Joce. I also knew that Carlos built a rather sensational ballet around him called *The Way*. But that was about it.

Sometime during the fall, when I was walking through Saks Fifth Avenue on my way to a Guild meeting in Jim Ludwig's office, I suddenly saw Rocky standing behind one of the counters. I was astonished. I went over to him and asked, "What on earth are you doing here?"

To me he looked ridiculous standing there. I noticed he had aged some. His hairline was starting to recede. He had this funny half-smile on his face. He answered, "I've quit dancing. I have a job here."

Maybe he thought I looked ridiculous, too, walking in with my secretary things. I don't know. We talked for a few minutes. I remember him saying that he had injured himself once more while dancing with the Harkness Ballet. He returned to San Francisco to recuperate and then he rejoined our Company. Why he was quitting now, he didn't say. His latest injury was fine. He said something about not having any friends left. He said the same thing about Leon Danielian—that Leon didn't have any friends left, either, except for his long-time fiancée. But then I had to get on to my meeting.

I didn't see Rocky when I left the store after the meeting, or again after that, but not long afterwards I heard that he was dancing the *Cavalier* to Lynda Meyer's *Sugar Plum Fairy* for this year's opening of **Nutcracker**. I thought, "Oh, well."

But in early December I got a phone call from Carlos at the Guild office. He blurted out, "Sally, Rocky has injured himself. He was scheduled to do *Cavalier* opening night, but he's not going to be able to dance, now."

He paused a little, and then asked, "Will you talk to him?"

I was immediately on guard; that same old pattern repeating itself. Rocky knew I would recognize it. The injury, the spiral downwards, then . . . me to pull him back up again? I felt that nothing I could say or do, now, would help. He hadn't done much to change what he hated about himself. In fact, he'd flaunted it and frittered away most of his talent in the process. No one else could do it for him. The best thing for Rocky would be to just accept himself as he was. But he couldn't do that, either.

Finally I said, "Carlos, it wouldn't do any good. It wouldn't make a bit of difference. No."

I felt that sooner or later Rocky would succeed in killing himself. And he did, in little more than a month. He committed suicide in New York on January 30, 1970, just before he turned thirty.

I didn't know about it at the time. I had somehow missed the announcement in the newspaper, and though I was working with Gisella on her Cecchetti letters and going to their house every week, neither she nor Lew said a word about it. I later heard that Lew was terribly upset. It wasn't until about six months later, after I'd moved on to a new job at Crown Zellerbach, that I received a phone call from Renée Renouf, the San Francisco correspondent for *Dance News*. She asked me if I knew that Rocky had killed himself. I answered, "No, I didn't know. I'm not surprised, though. Thank you for telling me."

I've always appreciated her telling me. To this day no dancer has mentioned him to me; not Carlos, not Joce, not Lynda, not Bobby before he died. I finally looked up Rocky's obituary in the dance archives and read it.

For quite a while after this, in that I no longer worked for the Ballet Guild, my only contact with the Company was through Gisella, and that ended when our monograph was published in 1971. I did take my new husband, Bob Jasperson, to meet Lew and Gisella after we were married in 1972, though. I remember going to their house after dinner for dessert one evening. Clelia was there, too. I remember Clelia several times looking at Bob, then leaning over to Gisella and exclaiming, "*Que bello, que bello*," then smiling at me.

I don't think I saw Lew again until 1979, at his 70th Birthday Party given at the home of Mrs. Fred Kohlenberg, a Board member who owned a spacious, ornate, Mediterranean-style villa in Pacific Heights. Bob and I were invited along with many others. We hired a baby sitter for the evening; our son, Teddy, was then two. I remember wearing a long dress. It was a big night out for us.

By this time Lew's health had started to deteriorate again, this time from degenerative heart disease, not a recurrence of cancer. I heard that someone on the Ballet Board wanted him to step down, and when he found out, he was furious. People went to great lengths to keep the two of them from being in the same room. I was also aware that Lew allowed Mike Smuin—who returned to the Company while it was fighting bankruptcy—to take on more and more of the load. Mike was even listed as Co-Director. I remember being amazed at that.

At one point in the evening, a group of us were having drinks in a penthouse room on the roof. I remember sitting next to Lew on a small couch. We were reminiscing about ballets, *Original Sin* in particular. He thought it might be fun to restage the ballet.

I remember telling him, "I don't know, Lew. It was wonderful and sensational in its time, but now it might seem dated—and certainly tame. Today people appear on stage in the nude. Some things may be better left to memory."

Suddenly he turned to face me and said, "Sal, you must hate my guts."

This time he didn't say why he thought I should hate him, and I didn't ask. I simply said, "No, Lew, I don't hate you."

And I didn't. What had happened could have been a blessing in disguise. It gave me the push to get out. I now had a full and happy life. I might not have, had things gone differently for me those last few years.

I knew Lew felt badly about what happened. I remember one time shortly after I'd stopped dancing; he told me, "Sal, you did it well." I think that was the one time he ever complimented me.

I also remember answering, "I know."

I'm not sure Lew believed me, now, when I told him I didn't hate him, but each time I ran into him after this, his face would light up with a big, warm smile and he'd say, "Sal, come back and see us, anytime."

I made a point to go to the ballet at least once a year after this.

In 1983, the year of the San Francisco Ballet's 50th Anniversary, the Company threw a huge, lavish, week-long Gala at the Opera House. Lew gave Mike free rein to put it on. Mike involved everyone who had ever been part of the Ballet's history. Cobbett Steinberg wrote *San Francisco Ballet; the First Fifty* Years for the occasion. Besides the dancing on stage—some of which had been reconstructed from early films—Mike used film clips, projections, balloons, fireworks, and even let pigeons loose at the end. He managed to engage Hollywood Star Gene Kelly as Master of Ceremonies. He called all of us old ballerinas back to appear on stage with our directors; Bill's ballerinas with Bill, and Lew's ballerinas with Lew. We came out one at a time when our names were called, curtsied to the audience, and then walked over to stand by our directors.

The amount of preparation for this appearance was the

same as if I'd been dancing. We had two tech rehearsals, then the week of performances. We had to arrive at the theater early each night, just like always. The rest of my life went on hold until the Gala was over. My mother came to take care of Teddy, who was now five. I remember bringing him to one of the matinees and having a great time showing him off backstage.

The night of the opening, which included a sit-down dinner in the rotunda of City Hall after the show, and dancing on stage after that, Bob came backstage with me to my dressing room. He said it was weird. As soon as I sat down at the dressing table to touch up my makeup, I started disappearing back into the theater right before his eyes. He decided to head back out front to the bar.

I must admit, being back in the theater for that whole week seemed so "usual". Everything was so familiar; the backstage smell, the doormen, the musicians, the electricians and stagehands—many of whom were still the same as when I danced. My old friend Pat Bibbins was still there, now heading a much larger costume department. Those of us who returned for this celebration had so much fun being together, again. It was a grand reunion. The only people I didn't know were the current dancers.

Bill, Harold and Lew were there every day, too, standing around in their tuxedos, waiting with the rest of us. Bill and Harold seemed in good health, but Lew had weakened even more. I remember he and Gisella again moved into the New Alden Hotel next door so that he could save his energy. Then a funny thing happened. Lew got noticeably stronger each day. Gisella laughed and said it wasn't the lack of commuting; it was his not being at home. He was used to being sick at home. He automatically dragged around there. In the theater nobody is allowed to be sick, and consequently, each day he felt better.

Lew and Gisella still teased each other, always with great affection. I felt their marriage had mellowed into a warm and delightful two-way relationship. I remember Lew telling me during one of our long waits, "You know, Sal, I don't know what I would have done without Gisella. She's always kept me headed in the right direction."

I knew that Gisella always loved Lew, that sometimes he had been hard on her, that she rarely complained openly, but she never let him get by with anything, either. I remember once, while she and I were still working on her book, we started talking about the time all the scandal was swirling around Lew and Joce. Gisella said she felt she had no choice but to go to the country by herself that summer, but somehow she never quite believed all the rumors. When I told her I didn't believe them, either, she laughed and told me the following story.

This incident occurred shortly after Lew's bout with cancer. He was pretty well recovered from that, but was now home for several days with a bad back. He could hardly move. He was spending most of his time on the bedroom floor; it hurt to sit in a chair or lie in bed. Joce came down one afternoon to see him. Gisella showed her into the bedroom and brought both of them a cup of coffee, then went back into the kitchen.

Lew called after her, "Gisella, why don't you bring in some coffee for yourself and join us?"

She could tell he was uncomfortable, so she made some excuse and stayed in the kitchen.

Lew grew more and more insistent, "Gisella, please come in and join us." But she just stood there in the kitchen and laughed and laughed.

I remember her saying, "Sally, that wasn't very nice of me, but it did my heart good."

Before the spring was out, the San Francisco Ballet moved into their huge, impressive new Ballet Building; a fundraising marvel accomplished by Richard LeBlond, the

Ballet Association's current President and CEO. [In order to avoid bankruptcy, the Ballet reorganized in 1975 and became the San Francisco Ballet Association.] I was also invited to the opening celebration for this. I attended it with Pat. She gave me a private tour of the facility afterwards. I'd never seen such a place. It contained everything anyone could possibly want, even a therapy room with a sauna. I couldn't help but remember Lew's comment about dancers becoming lazy and losing their creativity when they got too comfortable. I reminded Pat of this and told her I thought I'd remind Lew. She shook her head and warned, "Oh, Sally, don't. There are so many things he's unhappy about."

Not long after this, I saw Lew at a party that Tilly gave. I couldn't resist asking him, "Hey, Lew, do you remember what you used to say about dancers getting too comfortable?"

He sighed, then looked at me sadly and said, "Sal, nobody has any guts anymore."

Then he pursed his lips and began to mince, "They hurt here. They hurt there. They need this. They can't do that." I could see there was plenty he was unhappy about.

More recognition came to Bill, Harold and Lew in the spring of 1984 when they received the Capezio Annual Award for being "western pioneers who grew out of American vernacular dance and who have made ballet prosper wherever they settled." The three brothers were flown back to New York with their wives for the ceremony. The dance world took this occasion seriously; everyone of any stature was there.

By the time Lew got back to San Francisco, his health had deteriorated to the point where he rarely came into the City anymore. He left most of the running of the Company to Mike. Rumblings began to be heard; Mike had too much freedom, he was changing the integrity of the

Company, it was becoming too film-oriented. Everyone was picking up on the catch-phrase, "too show biz". Some complained that the quality of the dancing was going downhill.

That spring I happened to go to more performances than usual and liked what I saw. I thought the Company looked good. I thought they were dancing well, and I liked Mike's ballets—especially the ones that were being deplored the loudest. The motorcycle on stage in **Ode to the Beatles** didn't offend me. I thought it was appropriate for what the ballet was about. In any case, I didn't agree with the complaints.

I suspected that this was Lew again, squelching his competition. He didn't have the strength to come in and do the work, himself, and he couldn't keep Mike from going off in directions of his own. Lew probably felt Mike was lifting the Company right out of his hands.

I also felt that Richard LeBlond didn't like Mike. I heard rumors that LeBlond wanted Mike out and someone—anyone—else in.

That summer the Company danced at the Olympics in Los Angeles and received bad reviews. I didn't see any of those programs, so I don't know whether they were good or bad, but according to LeBlond in his book, *FROM CHAOS TO FRAGILITY; My Years at the San Francisco Ballet Association,* "people in the dance field were beginning to voice their concerns." He knew many of them. He had served on panels and boards across the country. Were all these people now influencing him? Or was he influencing them?

At any rate, some on the Board were pushing to get rid of Mike, whose contract was up for renewal in the fall. When one has enemies in camp, it is prudent not to give them a handle to use to toss you out. Evidently Mike was not wise about his budget; I was later given several examples of his disregard for costs. This, along with the perceived lowering of artistic standards, was all they needed. Mike's contract was not renewed.

I didn't know about any of this until I read in the newspaper one morning that Mike had been fired. I immediately telephoned Mike, LeBlond, and Lew to find out what was going on.

I phoned Mike first. He was absolutely crushed. He looked upon Lew as a father. He never thought this would happen to him. He told me, "I'd go to Lew's house and talk with him. We'd even discuss plans for the new *Nutcracker*. I'd come away thinking everything was all right, then I'd go to the school the next day and be told I was out." Mike felt LeBlond worked on Lew when he wasn't around and Lew didn't have the strength to oppose LeBlond.

Next I phoned LeBlond. He was cordial to me, saying, "Oh, Sally, it's terrible, but over half the Board will just not have him any more. They feel he has not only allowed the artistic quality of the company to go down, he is also irresponsible with money."

I liked Jim Ludwig's response to that; "Isn't it part of the Board's job to keep him in line?"

Or, perhaps, to give him enough rope to hang himself.

Then I phoned Lew and asked him what had happened. All he said was, "Mike blew it, Sal. He blew it. He thought he was God's gift to choreographers, and he blew it."

That was that, the same old story. But this time it was slightly different; Mike decided to fight back. I was upset for Mike, and when Mike's lawyer asked if they could use my name in support of Mike, I said, "Yes."

My name appeared in the newspapers as one of Mike's defenders, and then my phone began ringing.

Bill Christensen was the first to call. "Sally, what are you doing?" So I told him.

Then Nancy Johnson called and asked the same thing. In turn I asked her, "Well, what is Lew doing?" She answered, rather dryly, "The usual."

I heard that same reply from many of my old friends that day. All of us who had experienced Lew's "squelch treatment" at one time or another recognized this. However, those still connected with the Company were afraid to speak out; they didn't want to lose their jobs. Evelyn Cisneros, the Company's rising young ballerina, was the only dancer to get up in front of the Board and protest.

I received other calls, too. "Sally, you're mistaken. You don't know what's going on. Think of the family." I found myself in the thick of the fray. It was a mess. The Board was polarizing; the whole organization might split apart. In the middle of all this, Lew died.

At the time of Lew's death, I was mad at him for what had happened to the Company. I was mad at him for not keeping Mike in line, for not having the strength to stand up against LeBlond and those on the Board who wanted Mike out. Now I wonder; if Lew had not been suffering from a degenerative heart condition, would things have worked out differently? A question I have always been interested in—I look for it in every biography I read; how much of success is due to sheer energy?

A Memorial was given for Lew at the Opera House. I did not attend. I'd been teaching ballet for Walnut Creek Civic Arts Education ever since Teddy was born, and this evening I had reserved the theater in Walnut Creek for my ballet demonstration. The date would be hard to change, but I didn't even try. I was glad to have an excuse not to go. In a way, though, I felt this little demonstration was my own tribute to Lew. It was, after all, built on the principals he taught me. I think he would have liked it.

Another ten years passed before I finally began to understand what Lew's feelings were about. It was funny how it happened. Mike had recently returned to San Francisco after successfully taking on Broadway, TV, films, and regional theater; things he might not have been able to try had he been running a ballet company. But now he was ready to run a ballet company, again—his own company, "where I don't have to answer to anyone else," as one newspaper quoted him.

I was looking forward to the opening of his Smuin Ballets/ San Francisco—SB/SF for short. Bob and I went to the dress rehearsal. I was enthusiastic about what I saw. His works made for a well-balanced program. I was looking forward to seeing them on stage. The program for Opening Night listed what we had seen at rehearsal. However, just before the second half started, Mike came out on stage and announced that he was giving us a "surprise". He was inserting two of his favorite pieces into this evening's program; the *pas de deux* from his ***Romeo and Juliet*** and an excerpt from his theater production, ***Fred Astaire in Rehearsal***.

Mike's full-length ***Romeo and Juliet*** was one of his biggest successes at San Francisco Ballet—as well as one of his award-winning TV productions—and the following evening the SF Ballet was premiering Helgi Tomasson's new version of that ballet. Helgi was the new Director of the SFB. I'm sure this galled Mike no end. He probably inserted his ***Romeo and Juliet*** *pas de deux* in tonight's program as a defiant "in your face".

I'm not sure why he inserted the ***Fred Astaire*** piece, except that Fred Astaire was one of his all-time heroes. At any rate, neither piece fit in with the rest of the program. I thought they were both artistic mistakes. I realized that if my name had been on the program in any directional capacity, I would have argued long and hard with him against inserting either one.

I felt completely deflated. By the end of the evening I didn't know what to say. I did not go backstage afterwards to congratulate Mike on his opening.

I still felt let down the following day. Some of the critics blasted Mike for exactly what I'd thought. I was sorry they did, yet felt he had it coming. Then it began to dawn on me; this must be how Lew felt when Mike made decisions he didn't like. As long as Lew's name was on the program as Artistic Director, anything that went on stage reflected his artistic integrity. Towards the end, he didn't have the strength to out-argue Mike. This is why he let him go.

At last I understood. Others could share an Artistic Director's vision, even give guidance, but when disagreements arose, the artistic director had to have the final say—in order to maintain his vision—even when it was a mistake.

Helgi Tomasson continues to have his artistic vision guide the San Francisco Ballet, and his vision has brought the Company to new heights. Michael Smuin continues to "not have to answer to anyone else", and his innovations and his company continue to flourish. If and when a given Board doesn't like the vision at hand, they can always buy another, but it is still one vision at a time.

That's how it works.

Printed in the United States
80099LV00003B/17